Forever Settled

A Survey of the Documents and History of the Bible

"Forever O, LORD thy word is settled in heaven."
(Psalm 119:89)

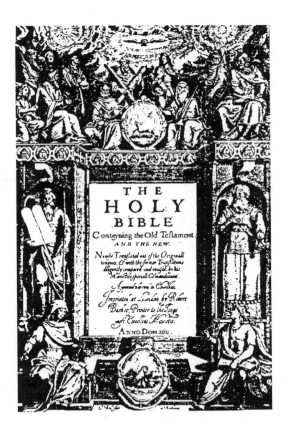

Compiled by
Dr. Jack Moorman

Published by

The Dean Burgon Society Press
Box 354
Collingswood, New Jersey 08108
U.S.A.

Phone: 609-854-4452

First Printing, July, 1999

Copyright, 1999
All Rights Reserved

ISBN #1-888328-06-1

DBS1428

Author's Foreword

Many believers have studied World History and know something about the history of their country. Not so many have studied Church History and traced the silver thread of those who maintained the Pure Faith down through the centuries. Fewer still have studied the history of the Bible--from the time that it was breathed out by God, through its various stages of transmission, down to its present form in our day. This book attempts to do this.

Three kinds of books have been written on this subject. The first is from a totally naturalistic viewpoint, with the author denying that there was anything supernatural about the Bible's production and transmission. The second affirms the Bible's inspiration but takes a basically naturalistic position regarding its transmission. The third recognizes that the promises within the Scriptures declare just as forcibly its preservation as it does its inspiration--that both are supernatural. It is here that this book stands. It is trusted that it will meet the need for a fuller treatment from this viewpoint.

I believe that God laid a hot coal on my heart concerning this subject some sixteen years ago, and the present survey is a systematizing of material gathered during that time. I have also relied heavily upon *Believing Bible Study* by Edward F. Hills; *The Identity of the New Testament Text* by Wilbur N. Pickering; *Which Bible* by David Otis Fuller and many others. On the other side, I have frequently referred to *The Text of the Greek Bible* and *The Bible and the Ancient Manuscripts* by Frederick Kenyon; *The Books and the Parchments* by F. F. Bruce, etc. Many other authorities have been drawn upon with recognition being given in the text. This book is presently being used in Gethsemane Bible College here in Johannesburg, South Africa.

Forever Settled is dedicated to all who love and defend the Word of God.

Jack Moorman
Johannesburg, South Africa
October, 1985.

Publisher's Foreword

The Publisher. This book, *Forever Settled*, is published by the Dean Burgon Society, Incorporated (DBS). The Society takes its name from Dean John William Burgon (1813-1888), a conservative clergyman from the Church of England. The DBS is recognized by the I.R.S. as a non-profit, tax exempt organization. All contributions are tax deductible. The Society's main purpose is stated in its slogan, **"IN DEFENSE OF TRADITIONAL BIBLE TEXTS."** The DBS was founded in 1978, and, since then, has held its annual two-day conference in the United States and Canada. During this time, many excellent messages defending the King James Bible and its underlying Hebrew and Greek texts are presented. The messages are available in three forms: (1) video cassettes, (2) audio cassettes, and (3) the printed message books. For information on receiving any of the above, plus a copy of the *"THE ARTICLES OF FAITH, AND ORGANIZATION"* of the Dean Burgon Society, please write or phone the office at **609-854-4452**. You may use your CREDIT CARD if you wish, or send your order by **FAX** at **609-854-2464** or by **E-Mail** at **DBSN@Juno.Com**.

Our Name. The Dean Burgon News says this about our name: *"The DEAN BURGON SOCIETY, INCORPORATED proudly takes its name in honor of John William Burgon (1813-1888), the Dean of Chichester in England, whose tireless and accurate scholarship and contribution in the area of New Testament Textual Criticism; whose defense of the Traditional Greek Text against its many enemies; and whose firm belief in the verbal inspiration and inerrancy of the Bible, we believe, have all been unsurpassed either before or since his time!"*

The Present Reprint. The DEAN BURGON SOCIETY, INCORPORATED commends Dr. Jack Moorman for his careful work in *Forever Settled*. He is a valuable member of our DBS Executive Committee. This present hardback book assists our purposes **"IN DEFENSE OF TRADITIONAL BIBLE TEXTS."**

Acknowledgments. We thank Mr. D. A. Waite, Jr., our DBS Treasurer, for his many hours in preparing this book for printing and Mr. Daniel S. Waite, a member of our DBS Advisory Council, for his assistance in securing the printer and guiding the project on to completion.

Sincerely for God's Written Words,

D. A. Waite

Pastor D. A. Waite, Th.D., Ph.D.
President, THE DEAN BURGON SOCIETY

Table of Contents

Photographs and drawings have been taken from:

The New Bible Dictionary, Intervarsity Press
Our Bible and the Ancient Manuscripts, Eyre and Spottiswoode
Believing Bible Study, The Christian Research Press

PART ONE:

A SURVEY OF THE OLD TESTAMENT DOCUMENTS

I. The Hebrew Scriptures

1. Christ and the Old Testament

During His earthly life, the Lord Jesus Christ appealed unreservedly to the very words of the Old Testament text (Matt. 22:42-45; John 10:34-36), thus indicating His confidence that this text had been accurately transmitted. Not only so but He also expressed this conviction in the strongest possible manner:

> Matt. 5:18--*For verily I say unto you, till heaven and earth pass, one jot or one tittle shall in no wise pass from the law till all be fulfilled.*
> Luke 16:17--*And it is easier for heaven and earth to pass than one tittle of the law to fail.*

Here our Lord assures us that the Old Testament text in common use among the Jews during His earthly ministry was an absolutely trustworthy reproduction of the original text written by Moses and the other inspired authors. Nothing had been lost from the text. It would have been easier for heaven and earth to pass than for such a loss to have taken place.

Moreover, our Savior's statements are also promises that the providential preservation of the Old Testament text shall never cease or fail. That same Old Testament text which was preserved in its purity during the Old Testament dispensation shall continue to be faithfully preserved during the New Testament dispensation until this present age is brought to an end and all the events foretold by Daniel (Dan. 9:27; Matt. 24:15) and the other ancient Prophets come to pass. So our Lord has promised, and today the Holy Spirit gives to all true believers the assurance that their Savior has kept and will keep his promise.

Christ's promises of the preservation of the text are in addition to those already given by inspiration in the O.T.

> Psa. 12:6, 7--*The words of the Lord are pure words; as silver tried in a furnace of earth, purified seven times. Thou shalt keep them, O Lord, Thou shalt preserve them from this generation forever.*
> Psa. 119:89--*For ever, O Lord, thy word is settled in heaven.*
> Isa. 40:8--*The grass withereth, the flower fadeth; but the word of our God shall stand forever.*

The O.T. text has been preserved. Christ has kept His promise. The following will help us to better understand some of the details of this preservation.

2.   The Hebrew Scriptures Written by Moses and the Prophets

The O.T. books as they appear in the Hebrew Bible are divided into three main groups, namely, the Law, the Prophets, and the Writings. The principle on which they were so classified was mainly that of authorship rather than of date or subject matter.

The first five books constitute the Law. They were grouped together because they were all written by one man, Moses. The Law or Torah is an undivided unit. Briefly we know that it was written by Moses for three reasons:

(1)   The testimony of Christ, "Did not Moses give you the Law?" (Jn. 7:19)

(2)   Mosaic authorship is the traditional belief of the Jews from time immemorial.

(3)   The evidence of archaeology in Palestine strongly supports this traditional view.

Next in the Hebrew Bible comes the Prophets. This second division is subdivided into the Former Prophets and Latter Prophets. The books of the Former Prophets are Joshua, Judges, 1 and 2 Samuel, and 1 and 2 Kings. The books of the Latter Prophets are Isaiah, Jeremiah, Ezekiel, Hosea, Joel, Amos, Obadiah, Jonah, Micah, Nahum, Habakkuk, Zephaniah, Haggai, Zechariah and Malachi. There is good evidence also that originally Ruth and Lamentations were included among the books of the Prophets. All the books of the Former and Latter Prophets were written by men who held the prophetic office, men who were definitely called by God to serve Him in this way. Christ and the other N.T. writers quote from this portion as inspired scripture.

The third division is called the Writings. The books placed in this category are Psalms, Proverbs, Job, Song of Solomon, Ruth, Lamentations, Ecclesiastes, Esther, Daniel, Ezra, Nehemiah and Chronicles. With the exception of Ruth and Lamentations, these books were written by men who were inspired of God but were not prophets in the official sense. They were not specifically called by God to labor as prophets among His people. David and Solomon, for example, were inspired, but they were kings, not prophets. Job, though inspired, was not a prophet. Neither was Daniel a prophet in the official sense, for he did not labor among the people. Ezra was a priest, and, according to ancient opinion, Chronicles also was written by him. Again Christ and the N.T. writers quote frequently from this third division.

3. The Hebrew Scriptures Preserved by the Priests

The duty of preserving this written revelation was assigned not to the prophets, but to the priests. The priests were the divinely appointed guardians and teachers of the Law.

Deut. 31:24-26--*And it came to pass, when Moses had made an end of writing the words of this law in a book, until they were finished, that Moses commanded the Levites . . . Take this book of the law, and put it in the side of the ark of the covenant of the Lord your God, that it may be there for a witness against thee.*

Thus the law was placed in the charge of the priests to be kept by them alongside of the most Sacred Vessel of the sanctuary, and in its innermost and holiest apartment. Also the priests were commanded to read the law every seven years.

Deut. 31:12--*Gather the people together, men, and women, and children, and the stranger that is within thy gates, that they may hear, and that they may learn, and fear the Lord your God, and observe to do all the words of this law.*

The priests were also given the task of making correct copies of the law for the use of kings and rulers, or at least of supervising the scribes to whom the king would delegate this work.

Deut. 17:18--*And it shall be, when he [the king] sitteth upon the throne of his kingdom, that he shall write him a copy of this law in a book out of that which is before the priests and Levites.*

Apparently a goodly number of such copies were made. The numerous allusions to the law in all the subsequent books of the O.T. indicate familiarity with it. Psa. 1:2 describes the pious by saying:

His delight is in the law of the Lord, and in His law doth he meditate day and night.

The admiration and affection for the law expressed in such passages as Psa. 19:7-11, Isa. 40:7, 8, and the exhortations and rebukes of the prophets based upon the requirements of the law imply an acquaintance with it such as could only be produced by its diffusion among the people.

Not only the Law of Moses, but also the Psalms were preserved in the Temple by the priests, and it was probably the priests who divided the Hebrew Psalter into five books corresponding to the five books of Moses. It was David who taught the priests to sing Psalms as part of their public worship service. We are told when David brought the ark to Jerusalem:

I Chron. 15:16, 17--*He spake to the chief of the Levites, to appoint their brethren to be singers with instruments of music . . . So the Levites appointed Heman . . . Asaph . . . Ethan.*

Like David, Heman, Asaph, and Ethan were not only singers but also inspired authors, and some of the Psalms were written by them.

It is likely that the books of Solomon were collected together and carefully kept at Jerusalem. Some of Solomon's proverbs, we are told were copied out by *"the men of Hezekiah King of Judah"* (Prov. 25:1). During the period of the kings also private and partial collections of the books of the Prophets had already been formed and were in possession of individuals. This is apparent from the frequent references made by the prophets, such as Jeremiah and Ezekiel to the language of their predecessors or to the former history of the nation, from the explicit mention of a prediction of Micah, delivered a century before, by the elders in addressing the people (Jer. 26:17-19), and from *"the books"* of which Daniel (9:2) speaks at the close of the captivity, and in which the prophecies of Jeremiah must have been included.

Except for periodic revivals under Godly rulers, such as Asa, Jehoshaphat, Hezekiah and Josiah, the days of the kings were times of spiritual darkness in which the priests neglected their God-given task of guarding and teaching God's holy Law. Note for example the years which preceded the reign of good king Asa.

II Chron. 15:3--*Now for a long season Israel hath been without the true God, and without a teaching priest, and without law.*

During the reign of Manasseh, the original copy of the Law had been mislaid and was not found again until Josiah's time (II Kings 22:8). Because the priests were thus unfaithful in their office, Jerusalem was finally destroyed and the Jews were carried away captive to Babylon (Mic. 3:11, 12). But in spite of everything, God was still watching over His holy Word and preserving it by His special providence. Thus when Daniel and Ezekiel and other true believers were led away to Babylon, they took with them copies of all the Old Testament Scriptures which had been written up to that time.

After the Jews returned from the Babylonian exile, there was a great revival among the priesthood through the power of the Holy Spirit.

Zech. 4:6--*Not by might, nor by power, but by My Spirit, saith the Lord of hosts.*

The Law was again taught in Jerusalem by Ezra the priest, who:

Ezra 7:10--*Prepared his heart to seek the law of the Lord, and to do it, and to teach in Israel statutes and judgements.*

By Ezra and his successors, under the guidance of the Holy Spirit, all the Old Testament books were gathered together into one Old Testament canon and preserved until the days of our Lord's earthly ministry. By that time, the Old Testament text was so firmly established that even the Jews' rejection of Christ could not disturb it. Unbelieving Jewish scribes transmitted this traditional Hebrew O.T. text, blindly but faithfully, until the dawn of the Protestant Reformation, at which time it again passed into the possession of the Christian Church.

4. The Difference Between the Preservation of the Old and New Testament Texts

Old Testament Israel was under the care of the divinely appointed, Aaronic priesthood, and for this reason the Holy Spirit preserved the O.T. through this priesthood and the scholars that grouped themselves around it. The Holy Spirit guided these priests and scholars to gather the separate parts of the O.T. into one canon and to maintain the purity of the text. In the New Testament Church, on the other hand, this Aaronic priesthood has been abolished through the sacrifice of Christ. Every believer is a priest before God, and for this reason, the Holy Spirit has preserved the N.T. text not through any special priesthood but through the universal priesthood of believers, that is, through the usage of God's people, the rank and file of all those that truly trust in Christ.

Jesus Christ, when He was on earth, acknowledged the authority which the priests, the sons of Aaron, had received from God to guard and to teach the O.T. Scriptures. Due to their frightful sin and worldliness, the priests had largely abandoned these functions, leaving them mainly in the hands of scribes and Pharisees who were not of the priestly race. Probably only a minority of the scribes were priests in the days of Christ's earthly ministry. But, even so, the order of scribes had developed out of the priesthood and was fulfilling the teaching office which God, through Moses, had assigned to the priests. Hence these scribes and Pharisees, in spite of their hypocritical lives, possessed a certain divine authority. It was this fact that Jesus called to the attention of His disciples.

> Matt. 23:2-3--*The scribes and the Pharisees sit in Moses' seat. All therefore whatsoever they bid you observe, that observe and do; but do ye not after their works, for they say and do not.*

5. The Traditional (Masoretic) Hebrew Text of the Old Testament

From the end of the first century until the Protestant Reformation the Hebrew Old Testament was preserved not by Christians but by non-Christian Jews.

Rom. 3:2--*Unto them were committed the Oracles of God.*

During this period, Christ was faithful to his own promise that the O.T. Scriptures would not perish or suffer loss. By His special providence He raised up among the Jews generations of scribes, who faithfully transmitted those treasures from which, in their unbelief, they refused to benefit. As Augustine said, those Jewish scribes were the librarians of the Christian Church.

Hebrew MS. -- tenth century
British Museum Or. 4445
(Actual size 16¼ in. × 13 in.)

Hebrew MS--tenth century. British Museum Or. 4445

According to G. F. Moore (1927), the earliest of these scribes were called Tannaim (teachers). These not only copied the text of the O.T. with great accuracy, but also committed to writing their oral tradition, called Mishna (a work of six main sections, dealing with agricultural laws, feasts, laws regarding women, fines sacrifices, purifications). The Tannaim were followed by a group of scribes called Amoraim (Expositors). These were the scholars who in addition to their work as copyists of the O.T. also produced the Talmud, which is a commentary on the Mishna.

The Amoraim were followed in the sixth century by the Masoretic (Traditionalists) to whom the Masoretic (meaning Traditional) Old Testament text is due. These Masoretes took extraordinary pains to transmit without error the O.T. text. Many complicated safeguards against scribal slips were devised. W. J. Martin states the number of letters in a book was counted and its middle letter was given. Similarly with the words, and again the middle word of the book was noted. They collected any peculiarities in spelling. They recorded, the number of times a particular word or phrase occurred. It is generally believed that vowel points and other written signs to aid in pronunciation were introduced into the text by the Masoretes. God working in Jewish scribes to preserve the purity of the text can be summed up in the words of Rabbi Akiba (died about A.D. 135), *"The accurate transmission is a fence for the Torah."* He also stressed the importance of preserving even the smallest letter. Thus the promise of Christ in Matt. 5:18 was fulfilled.

It was this traditional (Masoretic) text which was printed at the end of the medieval period. The Psalms were printed in 1477. And in 1488 the entire Hebrew Bible was printed for the first time. A second edition was printed in 1491 and a third in 1494. This third edition was used by Luther in translating the O.T. into German. F. F. Bruce says, *"For centuries, printed editions, of the Hebrew Bible followed the text of an edition printed in 1524, under a Hebrew Christian named Jacob Ben Chayyim."* Before this in 1514-17, Cardinal Ximenes of Acala Spain produced the Complutum Polyglot Bible (Complutum is Latin for Acala). In this edition, the Hebrew, Greek and Latin Vulgate texts were printed side by side, together with the Aramaic Targum of Onkelos for the Pentateuch.

All too often much of the research in the transmission of the Text of Scripture has been done by men who do not hold God honoring views regarding the inspiration and preservation of the Bible. Much sifting has had to be done and it is trusted that fact has been separated from fiction.

6.   The Main Surviving Manuscripts

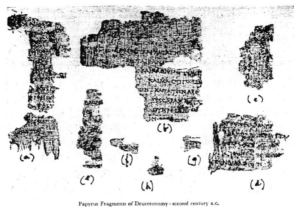

Papyrus Fragments of Deuteronomy - second century B.C.
John Rylands Library, Manchester

Papyrus Fragments of Deut--2nd century B.C. John Rylands Library, Manchester

The total number of Hebrew manuscripts is about two thousand, but the greater part contains only fragments or portions of the Old Testament. Any account of the principal Hebrew manuscripts must begin with Moses ben Asher and his son Aaron. These two were the last in the line of a family of Tiberian Masoretes which can be traced back to the second half of the eighth century A.D. This was the period of the rise of the Karaites, a kind of *"back to the Bible"* movement which, setting itself against the prevailing Rabbinical exegesis, helped greatly to stimulate the study of the actual text of the Old Testament. In the words of the founder, *"Search ye well the Torah and do not rely on my opinion."* The Karaites thus played their part in the movement towards fixing the Tiberian text, which in turn has been transmitted to us in manuscripts actually prepared by Moses ben Asher and his son. The ben Asher manuscripts are:

1)   A codex (book) of the Former and Latter Prophets written in A.D. 895. It is presently in a Karaite Synagogue in Cairo. A photographic reproduction is in Berlin.
2)   The Aleppo Codex of the complete O.T.--about 903. It made its way to a synagogue in Aleppo Syria in the fifteenth century. It was seen by Maimonides the great Jewish authority, at the end of the twelfth century and approved by him. Synagogue

authorities this century would not allow it to be copied or photographed, and it is now reported to be destroyed.

3) British Museum Codex of the Pentateuch (No. Or. 4445) containing Gen. 39:20-Deut. 1:33. It is not dated, but is thought to belong to the 9th or 10th century.

4) The Leningrad complete Old Testament, 1008. Ginsburg assumed that it had been copied from the Aleppo Codex, but Kahle shows that it was copied from another ben Asher Codex, now lost. This has been selected as the basic text of the fourth edition of Kittel's Hebrew Bible. It is designated by the sign "L."

Among other manuscripts of the ben Asher group listed by Kahle are a Pentateuch scroll of A.D. 930 and others of 943 and 946; Prophets dated 946 and 989 and a Hagiographa (Holy Writings) of 994--all at Leningrad.

Mention should also be made of:

5) The famous Leningrad Codex of the Prophets, written with Babylonian punctuation and dated 916.

6) Reuchlin Codex of the Prophets, dated 1105, now at Karlsruhe, West Germany. Kenyon says: *"It contains a text in the recension of ben Naphtali, another Tiberian Masorete. The differences between ben Naphtali and ben Asher were studied and described by Mishael ben Uzziel in the tenth century, who cites more than 800 of them. Although the ben Asher text came to be universally adopted, that of ben Naphtali was not without its effect."* Kenyon claims that both types were used as a basis of the early printed Hebrew Bibles. It should be remembered that those differences are mainly in areas of pronunciation.

Unger's Bible Dictionary lists several others MSS:

7) Codex Laudianus, 11th century, Bodleian Library at Oxford. It is said to agree quite closely with the Samaritan Pentateuch.

8) Codex Caesenoe, end of 11th century, Malatesta Library in Bologna. It contains the Pentateuch, sections of the Prophets, and portions of the Writings.

9) Codex Parisiensis, 12th century, National Library in Paris. It contains the entire O.T.

10) Codex 634 of De Rossi, 8th century. Contains Lev. 21:19 and Num. 1:50.

11) Codex Norinbergensis, 12th century, Nuremberg. Contains the Prophets and Hagiographa.

Chester Beatty Codex of Numbers Deuteronomy - second century

Chester Beatty Codex of Numbers- Deuteronomy--Second Century

One other source of information regarding the Hebrew text is that of readings quoted in the Middle Ages from Manuscripts since lost. The chief of these is a MSS known as Codex Hillelis, which was at one time supposed to date back to the famous Jewish teacher Hillel, before the time of Christ. It is, however, probable that it was really written after the 6th century. It was used by a Jewish scholar in Spain, and a considerable number of its readings have been preserved by references to it in various writings. Other lost manuscripts are sometimes quoted, but less often, and their testimony is less important (Kenyon).

7. The Burial of Hebrew Manuscripts

The fact that, in comparison to Greek MSS of the N. T., these Hebrew MSS are of a relatively late date is not far to seek. It is largely bound up with the veneration which the Rabbi's regarded the copies of Holy Scriptures. When these were too old and worn to be of any further use, they

were reverently interred. It was better to give them an honorable burial than
to allow the risk of them to be improperly used or profaned. Before they
were taken to consecrated ground for burial, they were stored for a shorter
or longer time in what is called a genizah--a room attached to the
Synagogue where documents no longer in use were stowed away or hidden.
"Genizah" literally means a *"hiding place"* (F. F. Bruce in *The Books and
the Parchments*).

8. The Divisions of the Hebrew Text into Verses and Chapters

The division into verses is quite early and can be traced back to the
early centuries of the Christian era. There were fluctuations of practice as
to verse division but these were standardized and fixed by the Masoretic
family of ben Asher about A.D. 900. This system divides the thirty-nine
books of the Old Testament (as we reckon them in our English Bible) into
23,100 verses. The Hebrew text is also divided into paragraphs. The
division into chapters on the other hand, is much later, and probably was
first done by Cardinal Hugh of St. Cher in 1244 (Bruce).

II. THE GREEK *SEPTUAGINT*

Commonly denoted the *"LXX,"* the *Septuagint* is a Greek translation
of the Hebrew Old Testament.

1. The Origins of The *Septuagint*

Its precise origins are still debated. A letter, purporting to be written
by a certain Aristeas to his brother Philocrates during the reign of Ptolomy
Philadelphus (285-246 B.C.), relates how Philadelphus, persuaded by his
librarian to get a translation of the Hebrew Scriptures for his royal library,
appealed to the high priest at Jerusalem, who sent seventy-two elders (six
from each of the twelve tribes) to Alexandria with an official copy of the
Law. There in seventy-two days they made a translation which was read
before the Jewish community amid great applause, and then presented it to
the king. From the number of the translators it became known (somewhat
inaccurately) as the *Septuagint*. The same story is told with variations by
Josephus, but later writers embellish it with miraculous details.

Aristeas' letter belongs in fact to the 2nd century B.C. (*The
International Standard Bible Encyclopedia* suggests a date about 100-80
B.C.). Many of its details are exaggerated and even legendary, but it seems

fairly certain that a translation of the Law only was made in Egypt (in the time of Ptolomy Philadelphus), primarily for the benefit of the Greek-speaking Jews there. This was the original *Septuagint*. The remaining books were translated piecemeal later, with the canonical books done some time before 117 B.C. Reference is made to them by the grandson of Sirach (a man after whom one of the Apocryphal books is named) in the prologue to that Apocryphal book. Subsequently the name *Septuagint* was extended to cover all these translations. The Apocryphal books are interspersed among the canonical books. Bruce believes evidence suggests that prior to the translation of the *Septuagint*, a number of individual and partial attempts were made at translating the O.T. into Greek.

2.   The Quality of the Translation

The Greek of the *LXX* is not straightforward Koine Greek. At its most idiomatic, it abounds with Hebraisms; at its worst it is little more than Hebrew in disguise. But with these reservations the Pentateuch can be classified as fairly idiomatic and consistent, though there are traces of its being the work of more than one translator. Outside the Pentateuch some books, it seems, were divided between two translators working simultaneously, while others were translated piecemeal at different times by different men using widely different methods and vocabulary. Consequently the style varies from fairly good Koine Greek (as in part of Joshua) to indifferent Greek (as in Chronicles, Psalms, the Minor Prophets, Jeremiah, Ezekiel, and parts of Kings) to literal and sometimes unintelligible translation (as in Judges, Ruth, Song of Solomon, Lamentations, and other parts of Kings).

Thus the Pentateuch is generally well done, though it occasionally paraphrases anthropomorphisms offensive to Alexandrian Jews, disregards consistency in religious technical terms, and shows its impatience with the repetitive technical descriptions in Exodus by mistakes, abbreviations, and wholesale omissions. Comparatively few books attain to the standard of the Pentateuch; most are of medium quality, some are very poor. Isaiah as a translation is bad; Esther, Job, and Proverbs are free paraphrases. The original *LXX* version of Job was much shorter than the Hebrew; it was subsequently filled in with interpretations from Theodotian. Proverbs contains things not in the Hebrew text at all, and Hebrew sentiments are freely altered to suit the Greek outlook. The rendering of Daniel was so much of a paraphrase that it was replaced, perhaps in the 1st century A.D. by a later translation (generally attributed to Theodotian, but differing from his principles and antedating him), and the original *LXX* rendering is nowadays to be found in only two MSS and the Syriac. One of the translators of Jeremiah sometimes rendered Hebrew words by Greek words that conveyed similar sound but utterly dissimilar meaning.

Dr. D. A. Waite states, *"It can be clearly seen . . . that the Septuagint is inaccurate and inadequate and deficient as a translation. To try to reconstruct the Hebrew Text (as many connected with the modern versions are attempting to do) from such a loose and unacceptable translation would be like trying to reconstruct the Greek New Testament Text from the Living Bible of Ken Taylor."* Dr. Waite has written a booklet dealing with A.S.V., N.A.S.V., and N.I.V. departures from the Masoretic Text.

3. The *Septuagint* and Messianic Prophecy

Aquila's Version of the Old Testament: Palimpsest MS. from the Cairo Geniza
Cambridge University Library

Aquila's Version of the O.T.: Palimpsest MS. from the Cairo Geniza
Cambridge University Library

In an earlier paper, I indicated that the *LXX* weakened Messianic prophecy. At this writing I cannot find what I thought to be the source of that information. In contrast to this, Terence Brown, a strong defender of the Masoretic Text has written, *"Before the incarnation of the Savior the Jews held the Septuagint in high esteem, but after his birth and earthly ministry they turned against that version because it was used so effectively by Christians to demonstrate that the Messianic prophecies of the Old Testament were fulfilled in the Person and Work of the Redeemer."*

A little before the middle of the second century of the Christian era, Aquila--who had been a professing Christian, but was cast out of the Church for some misdemeanor (some say astrology)--became a Jewish proselyte. Having then learned the Hebrew language, he made a new translation of the Old Testament into Greek, in opposition to the *Septuagint*, translating many passages concerning the Messiah otherwise than they had been rendered by the *LXX*, so as to make it impossible to apply these passages to the Lord Jesus Christ. Not long afterwards, Symmachus, a Samaritan by birth, who became a Jew, then professed the Christian faith, then attached himself to the Ebionites (Judaizers who denied the deity of Christ), made another translation from the Hebrew into Greek. About the same time, Theodotian, who had once professed faith in Christ and afterwards became a Jew, produced yet another Greek version.

Jerome of Bethlehem, who saw these Greek translations of Aquila, Symachus, and Theodotian, makes it quite plain that these men were Judaizing heretics, and that their versions were made out of hatred to Christianity.

Before the birth of Messiah the Jews used to observe a feast in memory of the translation of the *Septuagint*. Philo the Jew, who lived in the time of Caligula the Roman Emperor, while the Apostles were fruitfully engaged in the preaching of the Gospel, tells us in his *Life of Moses* that to that time they kept a yearly feast in memory of the Scriptures having been translated into Greek by the seventy-two interpreters. After Philo's days, the Jews turned that feast into a fast, lamenting that such a translation had been made. As the version became more popular with Christians, it fell from favor with the Jews, who preferred to use a version which the Christians could not so easily apply to the Messiah.

As an example of their tampering with Messianic prophecy, in Isaiah 7:14 Aquila, Symmachus and Theodotian departed from the rendering of the *Septuagint PARTHENOS* (Virgin) and substituted *NEANIS*, a term which may be applied to *"a young married woman."*

Gooding in commenting upon the revisions of the *Septuagint* says, *"Now, laborious as is the work of eliminating revisers' readings, it is of practical importance. The expositor who appeals to some LXX word or phrase must be sure that it was not introduced by a reviser after New Testament times. Thus the original Septuagint may have been faithful in translating verses of Messianic prophecy, but this becomes marred by later revision."*

4.   Other Revisions of the *Septuagint*

After discussing Aquila, *Unger's Bible Dictionary* says the following:
*"Possibly somewhat earlier than Aquila, Theodotian revised the Septuagint.
His version won wide popularity among Christians.* [This contradicts what
was said above.] *Theodotian's rendering of Daniel prevails in all extant
Greek Manuscripts except one.* [Gooding says two.] *Probably toward the
end of the second century Symmachus revised Aquila.   By the time of
Origen, A.D. 185-254, the text of the Septuagint had become woefully
corrupt.   Origen's Hexapla was a colossal undertaking to revise the LXX
text. It contained five columns in Greek. The first column consisted of the
Hebrew. The second comprised the Hebrew Text rendered in Greek letters,
the third Aquila's version, the fourth Symmachus' version, the fifth the
Septuagint revised by Origen, and the sixth Theodotian's version."*
Lucian, a scholar of Antioch (martyred 311) also is said to have made
a revision of the *Septuagint.*   Jerome mentions another revision by a certain
Hesychius of Alexandria (also probably martyred in 311).   Gooding says:
*"Well-intentioned as all this revisory work was, it has introduced
multitudinous readings which have laboriously to be eliminated to
reconstruct the earlier stages of the LXX Text."*

5.   The Question as to Whether There Was Actually
   a Pre-Christian Era *Septuagint*

Paul Kahle (a famous O.T. scholar) who has done extensive work in
the *Septuagint* does not believe that there was one original old Greek
version and that consequently the manuscripts of the *Septuagint* (so-called)
cannot be traced back to one archetype.   The theory, proposed and
developed largely by him, is that the *LXX* had its origin in numerous oral,
and subsequently written translations for use in the services after the
reading of the Hebrew original. Later an official, standardized version of
the Law was made, but did not entirely replace the older versions; while, for
the rest of the books, there never was a standard Jewish translation, but only
a variety of versions (Gooding).
Peter Ruckman (in the *Christian's Handbook of Manuscript
Evidences*) has taken a similar position.   His argument can be summarized
as follows :
   1)   The letter of Aristeas is mere fabrication (Kahle calls it
        propaganda), and there is no historical evidence that a
        group of scholars translated the O.T. into Greek between
        250-150 B.C.

2)   The research of Paul Kahle shows that there was no pre-Christian *LXX*.

3)   No one has produced a Greek copy of the Old Testament written before 300 A.D.

4)   In fact, the *Septuagint* "quotes" from the New Testament and not vice versa, i.e. in the matter of N.T.-O.T. quotation, the later formulators of the Greek O.T. made it conform with the New Testament Text.

He then states further, *"The nearest thing to an Old Testament Greek Bible anyone has found was the Ryland Papyrus (No. 458), which had a few portions of Deuteronomy 23-28 on it. And even this piece of papyrus was dated 150 B.C. [He later says this date is questioned.], fifty to one hundred years later than the writing of the so-called Septuagint."* What scholars refer to as "*Septuagint* papyri" are 24 pieces of paper, written 200 years after the death of Christ. These fragments are as follows :

1)   Berlin Genesis (200-400 A.D.) contains pieces of Genesis.

2)   Amherst (200-400 A.D.) contains pieces of Genesis.

3)   British Museum (200-400 A.D.) contains pieces of Genesis.

4)   Oxyrhyncus (200-400 A.D.) contains pieces of Genesis.

5)   A Bodleian papyrus leaf (600-750 A.D.) contains part of Song of Solomon.

6)   An Amherst papyrus (600-700 A.D.) contains part of Job 1 and 2.

7)   An Amherst papyrus (400-550 A.D.) contains parts of Psalm 5.

8)   Fragmenta Londinensia (600-750 A.D.), in British Museum, contains parts of Psalm 10, 18, 20- 34.

9)   British Museum "230" (220-300 A.D.) contains Psalm 12:7-15:4.

10)   A Berlin papyrus (250-400 A.D.) contains Psalm 40:26-41:4.

11)   Oxyrhyncus papyrus "845" (300-500 A.D.) contains parts of Psalm 68, 70.

12)   Amherst papyrus (600-700 A.D.) contains parts of Psalm 108, 118, 135, 138, 139, 140.

13)   Leipzig papyrus (800 A.D.) contains part of the Psalms.

14)   Heidelberg Codex (600-700 A.D.) contains Zech. 4:6-Malachi 4:5.

15)   Oxyrhyncus "'846" (500-600 A.D.) contains part of Amos 2.

16)   A Rainer papyrus (200-300 A.D.) contains part of Isa. 38.

17) A Bodleian papyrus (200-300 A.D.) contains part of Ezek. 5, 6.
18) Rylands Papyrus (1300-1400 A.D.) contains Deut. 2, 3.
19) Rylands Papyrus (500-700 A.D.) contains Job 1, 5, 6.
20) Rylands Papyrus (400-600 A.D.) contains Psa. 90.
21) Oxyrhyncus volume (200-300 A.D.) contains parts of Exodus 21, 22 , 40.
22) Oxyrhyncus volume (200-300 A.D.) contains parts of Exodus 21, 22 , 40.
23) Oxyrhyncus volume (200-300 A.D.) contains parts of Genesis 16.
24) Oxyrhyncus volume (300-400 A.D.) contains parts of Genesis 31.

Thus Ruckman believes that manuscript evidence for a pre-Christian *LXX* is totally lacking.

Other important manuscripts containing large portions of the Greek O.T. are as follows:

1) Codex Vaticanus (B), 350 A.D., Vatican Library.
2) Codex Alexandrinus (A), 450 A.D., British Museum. (Unger says it follows Origen's *Hexapla*.)
3) Codex Sinaiticus (Aleph), 350 A.D., British Museum.

Regarding these three famous manuscripts (which will be looked at more thoroughly when we come to the N.T. text), Gooding summarizes, *"Even the great uncials B, A, and Aleph are not immune from pre-Origen revision. Vaticanus follows the Hexapla in Isaiah while in Judges it represents a 4th century A.D. revision. Generally, however, it is a copy (a poor one, as its numerous omissions show) of a text critically revised according to the best evidence available early in the Christian era. Hence it sometimes presents a text purer than that of still earlier papyri . . . Alexandrinus has suffered far more from revision. Sinaiticus, generally speaking, holds a position mid-way between B and A."*

4) Codex Ephraemi Rescriptus (C) 5th century, Bibliotheque Nationale Paris. The text on sixty-four O.T. leaves has been erased to make room for a treatise for St. Ephraim of Syria in the 12th century. It is thus a palimpsest and the underlying Biblical text can be deciphered only with great difficulty.

Septuagint manuscripts are quite numerous in the world's libraries. The earliest are called uncial (large lettered) and the later, cursives (small flowing script). There are about 240 uncial manuscripts now in existence (containing mainly small portions of the O.T.) (Unger).

With this basic manuscript evidence before him, the student is better able to consider whether there was a pre-Christian era Greek O.T. The majority feel there was, though Kenyon says, *"It must be admitted that Kahle makes out a very strong case."*

As shown above, scholars state that the fifth column of Origen's *Hexapla* is the *Septuagint* revised by Origen. Ruckman, however, says that the so-called *LXX* in fact originates with Origen's fifth column. I assume by this he means that the 5th column is based on and constructed from the versions in the other columns. Thus, according to Ruckman, the *"LXX"* does not appear until the *Hexapla* is completed in 245 A.D. Further, as the Apocrypha has always been *"part and parcel"* of the *Septuagint*, it is remarkable that it is in the fifth column that it appears. Thus, we believe, this fifth column has been a leading source of O.T. corruption and had a huge influence on Jerome's *Latin Vulgate* and its inclusion of the Apocrypha (380 A.D.).

Regarding the Apocrypha, Kenyon says, *"The Greek Old Testament includes a number of books which apparently circulated in the Greek-speaking world (led by Alexandria) and obtained equal acceptance with the canonical books. These never obtained entrance to the Hebrew Canon."* Thus Alexandria and its "greatest" teacher Origen are the impetus for bringing the Apocrypha into the Bible. At this writing, I cannot find any clear information to show that the Apocrypha was part of any Bible prior to the *Hexapla*. It does survive in some Old Latin Version manuscripts, but see the discussion on that version.

Ruckman says further, *"Origen's fifth column is a translation of the O.T. into classical Greek not Koine, and Origen (as Vaticanus) uses the orthography of 400-200 B.C. (Plato, Euripides, and Aristophanes). To conceal this obviously 'non-neutral' text, Eberhard Nestle has informed his readers that the orthography of Vaticanus and Sinaiticus has been altered to the Koine of the first century, so you will think that these manuscripts were written in the language of the New Testament. This is why Nestle had to alter it in publishing his critical text; see remarks on p. 63, on English Introduction, Nestle, Novum Testamentum, 1956."* [I do not fully understand this statement, but have included it believing it to be pertinent.]

6.   The Question as to Whether the New Testament Quotes from the *Septuagint*

From a Bible-honoring point of view and taking the position that there was a pre-Christian era Septuagint, Terence Brown says, *"At the time of our Lord's earthly ministry, it was the universal practice of Greek-speaking Jews throughout the whole of the Middle East to read in their synagogues and to quote in their discussions the Old Testament Scriptures in this Greek*

Version.

It is agreed that the Septuagint was far from perfect, and no claim can be advanced for the divine inspiration of the translators. However, if we observe the manner in which the Apostles refer to the Old Testament Scriptures, we see a striking indication of the inspiration under which they themselves wrote. When they refer to the Septuagint, they do so under the supernatural guidance of the Holy Spirit, the Divine Author of the original revelation. Their authority is therefore higher than that of a translator.

This higher authority is shown in three ways. Firstly, where the LXX translators were correct, the Apostles quote verbally and literally from the Septuagint, and thus remind their readers of the Scriptures with which they were already familiar in that particular form. Secondly, where the LXX is incorrect, the Apostles amend it, and make their quotations according to the Hebrew, translating it anew into Greek, and improving upon the defective rendering.

Thirdly, when it was the purpose of the Holy Spirit to point out more clearly in what sense the quotations from the Old Testament Scriptures were to be understood, the Apostles were guided to restate the revealed truth more fully or explicitly. By the hands of the Apostles, the Holy Spirit thus delivers again His own inspired message, in order to make more clear to later generations what had been formerly declared through the prophets in an earlier age. By giving again the old truth in new words, the Holy Ghost infallibly imparted teaching which lay hidden in the old, but which could only be fully understood by a later generation if given in a different form.

There are about 263 direct quotations from the Old Testament in the New, and of these only 88 correspond closely to the Septuagint. A further 64 are used with some variations, 37 have the same meaning expressed in different words, 16 agree more closely with the Hebrew, and 20 differ both from the Hebrew and the Septuagint. [Note, this tabulation adds up to only 225.] From this it is evident that the Holy Spirit exercises independence of all human versions when He guides His Apostles to quote in the New Testament that which He had caused to be written in the Old. The Lord Jesus Christ, being One in Divine power and glory with the Eternal Father and Eternal Spirit, demonstrated the same independence, and exercised the same authority."

Dr. D. A. Waite (also from a Bible-honoring point of view) is prepared to question whether there was a pre-Christian era *Septuagint* and says, *"There are various references in the New Testament which would show that the Lord Jesus referred to the Hebrew O.T. rather than to the Greek Septuagint or other versions.*

    1)   Matt. 5:17, 18--*Think not that I am come to destroy the law or the Prophets: I am not come to destroy, but to fulfill.*

> *For verily I say unto you, Till heaven and earth pass one jot or one tittle shall in no wise pass from the law, till all be fulfilled.*

The reference to the 'Law or the Prophets' is a reference to the two major portions of the three-division Hebrew Canon, including the Writings! And of course our Lord's reference to 'jot' and 'tittle' could only refer to the Hebrew and not the Greek Old Testament.

2)   Matt. 7:12--*Law and the Prophets*
3)   Matt. 11:13--*all the Prophets and the Law*
4)   Matt. 22:40--*all the Law and the Prophets*
5)   Luke 24:27, 44--*And beginning at Moses and all the prophets, He expounded unto them in all the Scriptures the things concerning Himself . . . These are the words which I spake unto you, while I was yet with you, that all things must be fulfilled, which were written in the Law of Moses, and in the Prophets, and in the Psalms, concerning me.*

Here is a very clear indication of the threefold division of the Hebrew Canon into Law, Prophets and Psalms (or the Writings in which they are found). The Septuagint interspersed with the Apocrypha does not have this threefold division, thus Christ was not using it.

6)   Luke 4:1 6-21--*He went into the Synagogue on the Sabbath day, and stood up for to read. And there was delivered unto Him the book of the prophet Esaias.*

Since the language of the Jews in their synagogues was Hebrew, we can be certain that it was the scroll in Hebrew which was delivered to Him. Even today the Jews read and use Hebrew in their Synagogues since it is their one and only holy language in which their Scriptures were originally written. The Lord showed great respect for God's O.T. Word and upheld it completely.

7)   Matt. 23:35--*That upon you may come all the righteous blood of righteous Abel unto the blood of Zacharias son of Barachias, whom ye slew between the temple and the altar.*

By this reference, the Lord intended to charge the scribes and Pharisees with all the blood of righteous people shed in the entire O.T. Abel is found in Genesis, but Zacharias is found in II Chronicles 24:20-22. If you look at your Hebrew Bible, you will find that II Chronicles is the very last book (i.e. it is the last book in the third section, the Writings). If, on the other hand, you look at your Septuagint edition, such as that published by the American Bible Society, 1949, Third Edition, edited by Alfred Rahlfs, you would find that it ends with Daniel followed by "Bel and the Dragon"!! This is a clear proof that our Savior referred to and used the Hebrew and not the Greek Old Testament."

Regarding the origin of the *Septuagint*, Waite says, *"The first real evidence of a Greek O.T. is in a group of new translations in the second century A.D."* By this he means those of Aquila, Symmachus and Theodotian, beside scanty remnants of further anonymous versions.

Coming now to the matter of quotation, he says, *"Quite often I hear the objection being voiced that we cannot take the Masoretic Text as the proper basis of the Old Testament translation process because the N.T. allegedly quotes from the LXX thus sanctioning that translation as a whole!"* Let's analyze this objection as follows:

1) Does the N.T. actually quote from the *LXX*? How do we know that the present text of the *Septuagint* was not that found in those Greek O.T. translations of the second century A.D. by Aquila, Symmachus and Theodotian, or even that of Origen and his Hexapla. If this were the case, this text would follow that of the N.T. and you might have these translators quoting the O.T. quotes found in the N.T. rather than vice versa!

2) Suppose you reject this hypothesis. Does a mere similarity in wording of the N.T. to that of the Greek O.T. necessarily mean that those were direct quotations? Is not God the Holy Spirit, who inspired the very words of the O.T. and the N.T., able to pick and choose what set of words He wishes to employ to reveal His truth in the N.T.? Is He bound to His own words exactly on every occasion in the O.T. Hebrew text, or does He not have liberty to alter, reinterpret, add to, or subtract from that text as He presents truth in the New Testament?

3) But suppose you reject this thought. Does it necessarily mean, just because there appears to be a similarity in wording, and in some instances perhaps following the Greek O.T. more closely than the Hebrew that this is some sort of proof that the Greek O.T. is somehow superior to the Masoretic Text? Most assuredly not! This does not hold true for the particular passage quoted, nor does it hold true for the entire Greek O.T. God did not inspire the Greek words of the O.T. only the Hebrew words! This is a very important distinction and caution which must be borne in mind in this matter of O.T. translation.

The debate about the *Septuagint* will continue to go on but the student now has before him the main points at issue. However, when in doubt, or until the facts prove otherwise, always take the view that is most God-honoring.

III. THE OLD LATIN VERSION

The earliest Latin version of the Old Testament was a translation not from the Hebrew, but the Greek O.T. Scholars think that this translating was probably done at Carthage in North Africa during the later part of the second century A.D. The importance to us today of the Old Latin Version or *Vetus Itala* as it is called to distinguish it from the later version of Jerome, is much greater in the New Testament than the Old. In the former, it is one of the earliest translations of the Original Greek which we possess, and is an important witness for the kind of text used in the second century. In the later it is a translation of a translation. Thus we refer to it as a *"secondary translation,"* a *"primary translation"* comes from the original Hebrew.

The Old Latin exists today only in fragments. No entire manuscript survives of the O.T. And what does remain is often from the Apocrypha (no doubt because of lack of use and see below). For the rest, we are indebted for most of our knowledge of this version to the quotations of the early Latin Fathers. P. Sabatier made a collection of these in the 18th century. Since then, further evidence has accumulated which has helped to establish its text.

As has been said, the Old Latin version is first known in North Africa and is quoted by Tertullian (died 221) who certainly had a partial if not complete Latin Bible. Our best authority is Cyprian, bishop of Carthage (died 258), who quotes copiously and accurately from all parts of both Old and New Testaments.

As with the *Septuagint*, some have questioned (probably wrongly) as to whether the *Old Latin* was one standardized version or in fact a plurality of versions. Augustine said at about the time that Jerome was preparing the *Vulgate* (380 A.D.) that there was *"an infinite variety of Latin translations,"* and Jerome himself said, *"there were as many texts of this version as there were manuscripts."* In both cases, though, this is seen as propaganda designed to promote the new version of Jerome. (Much of the above is based on Kenyon.)

Regarding surviving MSS:

1)　Codex Vindobonesis 17, a palimpsest MS now at Naples, contains fragments of Genesis, Exodus, Leviticus and portions of Samuel and Kings.

2)　A 5th century MS at Lyons, contains portions of Genesis, Exodus, Leviticus, the whole of Numbers, and the first two chapters of Deuteronomy. At the Bibliotheque Nationale in Paris is the rest of Deuteronomy, the whole of Joshua and Judges 1:1- 11:21.

3)   At Madrid there is a MS containing Ruth and Esther (Kenyon).

History shows that this version spread from North Africa throughout Europe. Regarding the matter of the Latin language, Unger says, *"During the first two centuries the Church of Rome was essentially Greek speaking. The same holds true of Gaul; but the Church of North Africa seems to have been Latin speaking from the first. As the Latin language spread through Europe so the need for the Latin Bible."* Benjamin Wilkinson says, *"Since Italy, France, and Great Britain were once provinces of the Roman Empire, the first translations of the Bible by the early Christians in these parts were made into Latin. The early Latin translations were very dear to the hearts of those primitive churches, and as Rome did not send any missionaries toward the West before 250 A.D., the early Latin Bibles were well-established before those churches came into conflict with Rome. Not only were such translations in existence and well-established long before the Vulgate was adopted by the Papacy, but the people for centuries refused to supplant their Old Latin Bibles by the Vulgate. God in His wisdom invested these Latin versions by His Providence with a charm that outweighed the learned artificiality of Jerome's Vulgate. For nine hundred years, we are told, the Old Latin held its own after the Vulgate appeared. The critical version of Jerome never displaced it, and only replaced it when the Latin ceased to be a living language."*

Concerning the inclusion of the Apocrypha in the Old Latin version, Peter Ruckman quoting the International Bible Encyclopedia says, *"The Old Latin manuscripts used by the Waldensians (1170- 1600) do not contain the Apocrypha. The Apocrypha was added to many Old Latin manuscripts by the admirers of Origen and Augustine."*

Wilkinson declares that the very word "Vulgate" was falsely used by Jerome. *"The word Vulgate means 'commonly used,' or 'current.' This word has been appropriated from the Bible to which it rightfully belongs and given to the Latin Bible of Jerome. It took hundreds of years before the common people would call Jerome's Latin Bible the Vulgate."*

As to revisions of the Old Latin O.T., Ruckman states that in 540, Cassiodorus had it revised to bring it into line with the *"LXX"* of Origen.

IV. The *Vulgate* of Jerome

1.   The Historical Impetus

As stated earlier, in order to gather and sift through as many facts as possible, it has been necessary to draw from the research of men like Kenyon, Bruce, and others who hold to a basically naturalistic transmission of the text. What a breath of fresh air it is to read behind men who believe in the promises of God to providentially preserve His Word through the centuries. Unfortunately though, for too long, the bulk of textual research has been left in the hands of the former group, who treat the text as they would any other piece of literature. It is trusted though when out of necessity I have had to draw from these sources, that the facts have really been the facts and have been properly interpreted.

The naturalistic scholars unite in telling us (Kenyon is typical), *"By the end of the fourth century, the imperfections of the Old Latin Version had become evident to the leaders of the Roman Church. Not only was the O.T. translation taken from the Greek [a valid point], but the current copies of it were grossly disfigured by corruptions."* Unfortunately, we do not have enough pre-3rd century manuscript evidence to fully test this claim, but we do have the promises of God that He would preserve His Word. The hue and cry of two Roman Fathers Augustine and Jerome (quoted above) against the Old Latin should probably be taken in about the same light as the outcry of modern Bible revisors against the *"many errors'"* of the King James Version. Remember that the first textual critic was the one who said in the Garden of Eden, *"Yea hath God said"*!! But the historical fact is, it was not the errors of the Old Latin Version that gave impetus for a new version but rather the desire of the Roman Church to bring out a version which would be more in line with the rapidly developing Papal system. For Benjamin Wilkinson's excellent summary of this, see *"The Latin Vulgate of Jerome"* in *A Survey of the New Testament Manuscripts and Versions."*

2.   The Steps in the Revision

Regarding his O.T. revision. He began first with the Psalms and produced three versions all of which are still extant. The first was a very slight revision of the Old Latin version, with references to the *Septuagint*, and is known as the *Roman Psalter*. It was officially adopted by Pope Damasus, and still remains in use in the Cathedral of St. Peter at Rome. The second, was made between 387 and 390 in Bethlehem, still with reference to the *Septuagint*; but Jerome attempted to bring it into closer conformity with the Hebrew by using Origen's Hexaplar text (first column).

This version was first adopted in Gaul, whence it is known as the *Gallican Psalter*, and it has held its place as the Psalter in general use in the Roman Church and the Roman Bible from that day to this, and this in spite of the superior accuracy of the third version which Jerome subsequently published. This is known as the *Hebrew Psalter*, being an entirely fresh translation from the original Hebrew. It is found in a fair number of MSS of the *Vulgate*, often in parallel columns with the Gallican version, but it never attained to general usage or popularity.

About the time when Jerome produced his *Gallican Psalter*, he also revised some of the other books of the Old Testament (such as Job) with reference to the *Hexapla* text. (Job still survives in this form.)

But it would appear that this undertaking was not carried to completion. It is probable that Jerome, as his knowledge of Hebrew increased, grew dissatisfied with the task of merely revising the Old Latin translation. He then resolved to take in hand an altogether new translation from the Hebrew. He appears to have been convinced as to the superiority of the Hebrew text over the Greek (i.e. the *Septuagint*), and in all cases of divergence regarded the Hebrew as alone correct. This great work occupied him from about the year 390 to 404. The first to appear were the books of Samuel and Kings, next the Prophets, then Ezra, Nehemiah and Genesis, then after an interval the books of Solomon and the remainder of the Old Testament (Kenyon).

Jerome did not want to include the Apocrypha but consented reluctantly. He made a hurried translation of Judith and Tobit, but left the remainder untouched as it presently appeared in the Old Latin. (This last statement is the view of our naturalistic textual scholars. As stated above, those who followed Origen added the Apocrypha to their Old Latin Bibles, but those used by the Waldensians do not contain the Apocrypha. Certainly the presence of the Apocrypha in the fifth column of Origen's *Hexapla* was the primary influence for its inclusion in the *Vulgate*.)

3.   The Reception of the New Version

In addition to what was said above, Kenyon adds, *"In the prefatory letters prefixed to these books, Jerome tells us much of his work and its reception. In spite of much individual support which he received, the general attitude towards it was one of great hostility. The sweeping nature of the changes introduced . . . alienated those who had been brought up to know and love the old version. . . . Jerome felt this opposition keenly, and raged against what he regarded as its unreasonableness. This finds vigorous expression in his prefaces."* Which Bible states that in 400 A.D. Augustine himself expressed preference for the Old Latin Version.

4.   Revisions of the *Vulgate*

Merril Unger refers to the textual corruption that befell the *Vulgate*. *"Meanwhile the text of the different parts of the Latin Bible (the Vulgate) was rapidly deteriorating."* He states that the simultaneous use of both versions was a principle cause. *"The growing corruption which could not be checked by private labor, attracted the attention of Charlemagne, who entrusted to Alcuin (about 802) the task of revising the Latin text for public use. This Alcuin appears to have done simply by the use of manuscripts of the Vulgate, and not by reference to the original texts. His revision probably contributed much toward preserving the Vulgate text. But the new revision was gradually deformed, though later attempts at correction were made by Lanfrome of Canterbury (1089), Cardinal Nicolaus (1150), and again by the Cistercian Abbot Stephanus."*

The above, revisions apply to the New Testament also. We will look at these and the MSS when we come to the New Testament of the *Vulgate*.

Alcuin's Vulgate–ninth century
British Museum
(Actual size of complete page 20 in. × 14½ in.)

Alcuin's Vulgate--ninth century, British Museum (Actual size of complete page is 20 in. x 14.5 in.)

V. The Samaritan Pentateuch

The Samaritan Pentateuch is not really a translation into a different language, but a direct descendant of the original Hebrew Scriptures in the same language and written in the same characters, though as Kenyon says, *"in a somewhat degenerate form."* Thus more accurately it is the Hebrew Pentateuch of the Samaritans.

1. Its Origin

In 732, the far northern areas of Israel were overrun by the Assyrian king Tiglath-Pileser III, and many of its inhabitants were deported to other parts of the Assyrian Empire. Eleven years later, a similar fate befell the remainder of the Kingdom of Israel at the beginning of the reign of Sargon II. Sargon tells how he removed 27,290 people from Samaria. In II Kings 17:24-41 we are told of the colonists whom the Assyrian Kings sent to take the place of the deportees, and how they intermarried with the people left in the land, which was now organized as the Assyrian province of Samaria. Although these colonists at first worshiped their own gods, they ultimately gave up their idolatry and worshiped Jehovah, as did the native Samaritans. In the closing centuries B.C. the Samaritans were as free from idol worship as the Jews.

After the return of the Jews from the Babylonian captivity in 530 B.C., the Samaritans offered their aid in rebuilding the Jewish Temple. The books of Ezra and Nehemiah show that this was rightly refused. They then became the inveterate enemies of the Jews and did all in their power to hinder the work. Under Nehemiah's governorship, the grandson of the high priest Eliashib was discovered to have married the daughter of Sanballat, the governor of Samaria and a bitter foe of the Jews. This incident, which took place around 432 B.C., has been widely regarded as furnishing the historical background of the Samaritan split with the Jews.

Josephus, the historian of the first century A.D. displaces this account by putting it a century later. He names the expelled priest as Manasseh and says that he took with him a copy of the Law when he fled to Samaria. Though reasonable, some have questioned Josephus' account. Yet all agree that the copies of the Samaritan Pentateuch have descended from an archetype not later than the 5th century B.C.

About 400 B.C., the Samaritans built their own temple on Mount Gerizim near the ancient sanctuary of Shechem. To this place the woman of Sychar referred when she said to Christ: *"Our fathers worshiped in this mountain."*

Until the Romans came, the Samaritans were under Jewish domination. They survived as an Israelite group (though repudiated by orthodox Jewry) for many centuries in a variety of centers. To this day, a small remnant has survived in Palestine. They have preserved their ancient traditions and worship at Nablus near to ancient Shechem.

The Samaritans regard the Pentateuch alone as canonical and they have preserved a text of these five books in Hebrew which has been transmitted independently of the Masoretic text. (The above is drawn from Bruce and Unger.)

2. An Evaluation of the Samaritan Pentateuch Based on Surviving Manuscripts

The Samaritan Pentateuch was known to some of the Church Fathers such as Eusebius (265-340) and Jerome (340-420), but down to within the last 250 years no copy had reached Europe, and it began to be pronounced as fiction. W. J. Martin, writing in the *New Bible Dictionary*, says *"The first copy of this version reached Europe in 1616 through Pietro della Valle, and in 1628 an evaluation of it was published by J. Morinus, who claimed it to be far superior to the Masoretic text. This seems to be the case with every new discovery of documents, prompted either by a preference for the LXX or an innate hostility to the traditional Jewish text. There was in this instance another motive at work: the desire on the part of certain scholars to weaken the position of the Reformers in their stand for the authority of the Bible. Gesenius, probably Germany's greatest Hebrew scholar, brought this barren controversy to an end and demonstrated the superiority of the Masoretic text; We are witnessing in our day an attempt to reinstate the Samaritan Pentateuch."*

It departs from the Masoretic text in about 6,000 cases; of these about 1,900 agree with the *LXX* (Unger). It is not easy to account for the agreements; one possibility is that when corrections had to be made in the Samaritan Pentateuch, an Aramaic targum was used. (The Samaritan dialect and Aramaic are practically identical, and the Samaritan version in places agrees verbatim with the Targrum of Onkelos.) There are numerous traces of the influence of the Aramaic targums in the *LXX*. (Martin) See The Aramaic Targums.

Dt. xxvii. 4 from the Samaritan Pentateuch. Mount Gerizim is substituted for Mount Ebal at the beginning of line 4.

Deuteronomy 27:4 from the Samaritan Pentateuch. Mount Gerizim is substituted for Mount Ebal at the beginning of line 4.

The most important Samaritan Variants are the ones which reveal the fundamental points at issue between the Samaritans and Jews. The Samaritans emphasized the importance of Shechem and Mount Gerizim and declared that God had chosen them to be the center of the nation. Thus, where Moses in Deuteronomy 12:5 and other places, speaks *of "the place which the Lord your God shall choose"* (later identified as Jerusalem), the Samaritan edition translates it *"the place which the Lord your God has chosen"*--meaning Mount Gerizim, which has already been specified in Deuteronomy 27:4-8 where Moses commands that the stones bearing the words of the Law and an altar of unknown stones are to be set up on Mount Ebal. The Samaritan text has Gerizim for Ebal. After the Ten Commandments in Ex. 20 and Deut. 5, the Samaritan Pentateuch inserts Deut. 27:2-7 with Mount Ebal replaced by Mount Gerizim and Deut. 11:30 with Gilgal changed to Shechem. It reads thusly:

> *And it shall be that when Jehovah thy God brings thee into the land of the Canaanite . . . thou shalt erect for thyself great stones and shall plaster them . . . upon **Mount Gerizim** . . . thou shalt sacrifice . . . and eat there and rejoice before Jehovah . . . that mountain is across Jordan in the direction of the going down of the sun . . . over **against Shechem**.*

They made sure that there would be no mistake about the identification of the mountain! This addition is reckoned by the Samaritans to be the Tenth Commandment. What we call the First Commandment is said by them to be a preamble (Bruce).

The extant manuscripts of the Samaritan Pentateuch are of a late date. No manuscript is (as far as known) older than the tenth century. There is a Samaritan MS dated A.D. 1211 in the John Rylands Library at Manchester, where older fragments are also to be found. What is probably the oldest Samaritan MS in codex form is in the university library at Cambridge which contains a note that it was sold in A.D. 1149, and in the opinion of Paul Kahle may have been written some centuries earlier (Kenyon).

The most interesting, if not the most important MS is a parchment roll in the possession of the Samaritans at Nablus. It has a colophon or scribal tailpiece, which makes the remarkable claim, *"I Abishua, son of Phinehas, son of Eleazar, son of Aaron . . . have written this holy scroll at the gate of the tent of assembly on Mount Gerizim the House of God, in the thirteenth year of the settlement of the children of Israel in the land of Canaan."* In fact the first half of it (to Numbers 34) is dated from the 13th century A.D., the latter part from possibly the 11th century A.D. (Bruce).

The most recent printed edition (as of 1958) was that of A. von Gall in 1918. It was based on eighty MSS and fragments of varying dates.

(Kenyon).

As to translations of the Samaritan Pentateuch into other languages, Paul Kahle's research has shown that several Arabic versions were made from the 11th to 13th centuries. From about fifty quotations preserved in the notes of Origen's *Hexapla*, it is believed that there was a Greek translation known as the *Samariticon* (Unger).

In reading about this version, how thankful we can be that God has preserved a pure stream of transmission through the Masoretic text of the Hebrew scriptures, the text underlying the King James Version. When naturalistic critics say, *"The text of i.e. Exodus has many corruptions"* what they are in fact saying, is that the Hebrew disagrees with the *LXX* or Samaritan Pentateuch, as if they were the standard to follow. By now we trust the student can see how foolish such an assertion is.

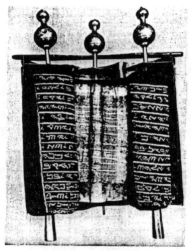

Samaritan MS. from Nablus
(Original height, excluding rollers, about 19 in.)

Samaritan MS from Nablus; Original height, excluding rollers, about 19 in.

VI. The Aramaic Targums

Aramaic, traditionally the language of Syria, became in Old Testament times the chief language of most of the peoples from Mesopotamia to the Mediterranean Coast and indeed continued to be so until the Arab conquests in the seventh and eighth centuries A.D. (Kenyon). It is a close cognate, though not a derivative of Hebrew. The letters are the same in the two languages. It was formerly inaccurately called "Chaldee," but since the Chaldeans are known to have generally spoken Akkadian, the term Chaldee has been abandoned.

In the closing centuries B.C. when Hebrew was becoming less and less familiar to the ordinary people as a spoken language, it became the practice in the synagogues to accompany the public reading of the Scriptures by an oral paraphrase in Aramaic. This paraphrase was called a targum. The word means *"to translate from one word to another"* or *"to interpret"* (Bruce, Unger).

This was probably more than a strict translation, embodying a certain amount of interpretative comment. The methurgeman (the translator), we are told was not allowed to read his interpretation out of a roll, as the congregation might mistakenly think he was reading the original Scriptures. With a view to accuracy it was further laid down that not more than one verse of the Pentateuch and not more than three verses of the Prophets could be translated at one time (Bruce).

At first these paraphrases were simply given by word of mouth, extemporaneously. They were unofficial, and varied from place to place. Subsequently they were written down. It is to those written paraphrases that the word Targum most directly applies. The first mention of such a written Targum is that of Job in the first century A.D. (Kenyon). Otherwise the earliest Targum we possess seems to have been committed to writing by the 5th century A.D. (D. F. Payne in the *New Bible Dictionary*).

Targums are extant covering all the Old Testament between them, except for Daniel, Ezra, and Nehemiah. We have several of the Pentateuch notably Targum Onkelos and two Jerusalem or Palestinian Targums. On the Prophets (both Former and Latter) we have Targum Jonathan ben Uzziel.

וְעֵינֵי עַמֵּעֶם דִלְמִין יֶחֱזוּן
בְּעִינֵי חוּן וּבְאֻדְנִיחוּן
יִשְׁמְעוּן וּבְלִבְּחוּן יִסְתַּכְלוּ
וִיתוּבוּן וְיִשְׁתְּבֵק לְחוּן

Targum Jonathan (Is. vi, 10) ending
. . . and they turn and it should be forgiven
them', as in Mk. iv. 12, whereas *MT* has '. . . and
be healed'.

Targum Jonathan (Isaiah. 6:10) ending "and they turn and it should be forgiven them" as in Mk. 4:12, whereas *MT* has "and be healed."

Onkelos is claimed by some to be the Aquila who translated the Scriptures into Greek (250 A.D.), see *Septuagint*. His Targum is very literal and adheres closely to the original. Jonathan ben Uzziel lived in the 1st century B.C. and his is much more interpretative (Payne).

One marked feature of the Targums is their avoidance of the anthropomorphisms which often characterize references to God in the Old Testament. One frequent device is the use of the phrase *"the Word of God"* instead of simply "God." Thus in Gen. 3:8, instead of *"they heard the voice of the Lord God walking in the garden,"* the Targums of Onkelos have *"they heard the voice of the word of the Lord God walking in the garden."* Where the Hebrew O.T. says *"God was with the lad"* (Gen. 21:20), the Targumic equivalent is: *"the Word of God was with the lad."* Edersheim counted 179 occurrences of this in Onkelos (Bruce). See *The Books and the Parchments* by F. F. Bruce for many examples of the liberties that the Targums take with the Hebrew text.

Perhaps the most serious perversion can be seen from the Targum of Jonathan in his rendering of Isaiah 53. Here the servant is clearly identified as the Messiah, but all the ascriptions of suffering to Him are transferred either to the Jewish people suffering at the hand of their Gentile oppressors or to the Gentiles receiving retribution at the hand of the Messiah (Bruce). Thus the truth of Christ's substitutionary work on the cross is obliterated.

VII. The Syriac Version

The Syriac language is virtually the same as what we have seen above. It was the language of Syria and Mesopotamia, and is called East or Christian Aramaic to distinguish it from the closely related West Aramaic which was spoken in Palestine in the time of our Lord's life on earth. In the case of the New Testament, as we shall see, several translations into Syriac were made. But of the Old Testament there was only one (apart from Paul of Tella's version of Origen's *Hexaplar* text, and some other late translations from the *Septuagint* of which only fragments remain). The Syriac was known as the Peshitta, or "simple" version. Whether this was to distinguish it from Paul of Tellas with its apparatus of signs and variant readings is uncertain (Kenyon).

1.   Its Origin

Despite scholarly research into the origin of the Peshitta O.T., we have no direct information of the authors or the date of the translations. As early as Theodore of Mopsuestia (died 428 A.D.) Details concerning its beginnings were unknown. Some of the evidence indicates that it was the work of Christians and some that of Jewish translators. Although in many cases the text agrees with the Hebrew, and, what is more remarkable, with the Palestinian Targum, there are other passages which seem to presuppose the *Septuagint* (R. Gunner in the *New Bible Dictionary* and Kenyon).

Internal evidence enables us to arrive at some probable conclusions. Linguistic affinities have been noted between the Palestinian Aramaic Targum (Western Aramaic) and the Syriac translation of the Pentateuch, whereas Syriac (the name usually given to Christian Aramaic language) is an E. Aramaic language. These linguistic traces of W. Aramaic in a version which is otherwise in E. Aramaic dialect reveal some acquaintance with a Palestinian Targum of the Pentateuch. This indicates that the Peshitta Pentateuch originated in an E. Aramaic district which had some relationship with Jerusalem.

The ruling house of Adiabene, a kingdom situated east of the Tigris, was converted to Judaism about A.D. 40. Royal children were sent to Jerusalem for their education, and some members of the royal house were buried there. Judaism spread among the people of Adiabene. They needed the Hebrew Scripture in a language they could understand--i.e. Syriac, so it is probable that parts of the Old Testament, and at first the Pentateuch were translated into Syriac in the middle of the 1rst century.

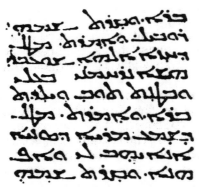

Fig. 215. Genesis xxix. 32–33 in the Syriac Peshitta version. 5th century AD vellum MS.

Genesis 29:32-33 in Syriac Peshitta version. 5th century A.D. vellum MS

Further examination of the MSS of the Peshitta Pentateuch has revealed that at an early period there existed two texts, one a more literal translation of the Hebrew and the other a rendering (as has been described above) closely related to the Palestinian Targum. Many scholars think that the literal translation is the earlier on the grounds that the Syriac Church Fathers Aphrahal and Ephraem used a text which followed the Hebrew more closely than did the text in common use in the 6th century.

There is the alternative view that the Peshitta O.T. owed its origin to the Christians of that area. Such a view is possible as the Syriac Church included a large Jewish element who would have had access to the Hebrew Scriptures and translations (R. Gunner).

As for the rest of the books of the O.T., they show considerable variety both of style and method, and are clearly the work of different hands at different times. Thus Proverbs is close to the Targum, as is Ezekiel. Isaiah and the Minor Prophets are somewhat freely translated. While Ruth is a paraphrase, Job and Song of Solomon are very literally rendered (Kenyon).

2. The Revisions and Corruption of the Peshitta

The Peshitta originally omitted the Apocrypha, but these were later added from the *Septuagint*. It is also said that it was originally without Chronicles (Kenyon). It was one of the very best early versions of the Old Testament, and was clearly God's Word for a large number of people in the world of that day. Corruptions did not enter the text until the middle of the third century, when Origen moved from Alexandria to Caesarea. Further corruptions took place during the time of Eusebius and Pamphilus (260-340) and at the time of the revisions known as the Philoxenian (508), the Harclean (616), and the Jerusalem Syriac (c 6th century). (Based on Ruckman.)

At the end of the first quarter of the 5th century, a schism broke in the Syriac Church, with the result that Nestorius and his followers withdrew eastwards. Nestorius was expelled from the bishopric of Constantinople in 431 and he took with him the Peshitta Bible. Following the destruction of their school at Edessa in 489, the Nestorians fled to Persia and established a new school at Nisibis. The two branches of the Church kept their own Bible texts. It is said that the Eastern branch of the text underwent fewer revisions, because of the more isolated location of the Church (R. Gunner).

Regarding the above-mentioned revisions. The Jerusalem Syriac was made from the *LXX*; a few fragments remain. Philoxenus of Mabbug commissioned the translation of the entire Bible from the *LXX*; again only a few fragments remain. Another Syriac version of the O.T. was made by Paul, Bishop of Tella in Mesopotamia in 617. It is based on the 5th column of Origen's *Hexapla,* with notes and readings given from the other columns of Aquila, Symmachus and Theodotian. It was known as the Syro-Hexaplaric Version (R. Gunner). There is dispute as to whether the Philoxenian Syriac Version was reissued by Thomas of Heraclea (known as the Harcleian Syriac) or whether this was an entirely new version (R. Gunner).

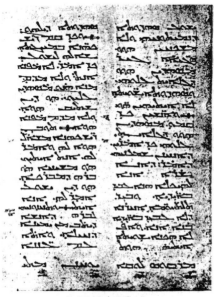

Harkleian Syriac MS.-936
British Museum
(Actual size 13½ in. x 10½ in.)

Harkleian Syriac MS--936 *British Museum* (Actual size 13.5" x 10.5")

3.   The Surviving Manuscripts

The main ones containing the Old Testament include:
1)   A MS in the British Museum, dated A.D. 464. This is the oldest MS with an actual date. It contains the Pentateuch except for the book of Leviticus.
2)   A 5th century MS of Isaiah and Psalms
3)   The West Syriac Codex Ambrosianus in Milan, 6th or 7th century. This consists of the entire Old Testament and is close to the Masoretic Text. It has been published photo lithographically (R.

Gunner)

VIII. The Egyptian Coptic Version

Coptic is the language which was used by the natives of Egypt at the time when the Bible was first translated for their use. It is indeed a modified form of the language which had been spoken in the country from time immemorial. About the end of the 1st century A.D. it began (owing to the influence of the great number of Greeks who settled in Egypt) to be written in Greek characters, with six additional letters and with a considerable admixture of Greek words. It is to this form of the language that the name Coptic was given.

There were, however, differences in the dialects spoken in different parts of the country, and consequently more than one translation of the Scriptures was required. The number of these dialects is still a matter of uncertainty, for the papyri discovered in Egypt of late years have been, and still are, adding considerably to our knowledge of them. It appears that four or five different versions of the New Testament have been identified, and four of the Old. Two of these stand out as of real importance, the others being mere fragments.

There is the Sahidic or Thebaic version of Upper or Southern Egypt, which is the oldest; and the Boharic of Lower or Northern Egypt which eventually became the Bible of the whole Coptic Church, and is the most complete. (Kenyon). Unger says the Sahidic version was completed by 350 A.D. (Kenyon 250), and that both versions were made from 4th century *Septuagint* texts. Thus we are not surprised to find that the Coptic versions contain the Apocrypha.

Gehman's textual researches on Daniel demonstrate that the Sahidic version reflects a blending of Origen's Hexaplaric text, Theodotian, and Hesychius (a reviser of the *LXX*, died 311). He found also that the Bohairic was made from the Hexaplaric text and was affected by Hesychius. Sahidic Acts shows a close connection with Codex Vaticanus (Unger).

The Sahidic exists in very considerable fragments:
1) A complete MS of Deuteronomy and Jonah (with Acts), 4th century, British Museum
2) Joshua, Judges, Ruth, (Judith), and Esther, 7th century, British Museum
3) 62 Leaves of Proverbs, Ecclesiastes, Song of Solomon, (Wisdom and Ecclesiasticus), 7th century, British Museum
4) The Psalms (complete), 7th century, British Museum
5) Psalms (incomplete), A.D. 100 (?), Berlin (Kenyon)

IX. The Ethiopic Version

With the versions of Egypt may naturally go the version of Ethiopia. The Ethiopic MSS (many of which were acquired by the British Museum at the time of the Abyssinian War in 1867) are of very late date, the oldest being of the 13th century (Kenyon). Christianity was introduced into Abyssinia by Christian missionaries in the 4th century. Between the 5th and 8th centuries the Bible was translated into Ethiopic. Gleaves' studies uphold Charles' thesis that the Ethiopic reflects Symmachus and Origen in the *Hexapla* (Unger). Naturally then, it contains the Apocrypha, with two books not usually included--Jubilees and Enoch.

Four other versions can be mentioned but being of later date they need not be considered in this survey. They are the Armenian, Arabic, Georgian Slavonic, and Gothic. Kenyon says they were all made from the *Septuagint*. Unger, however, says that the Arabic was influenced by Hebrew and Samaritan texts; that the Armenian may have come from the Syriac, and that the Armenian and Greek formed the basis of the Georgian version.

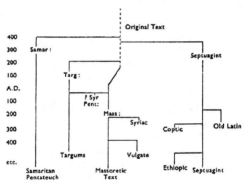

Descent from the Original Text to the MT

The main point that we would question on this diagram (from Kenyon) is the early date of the *Septuagint*.

X. The Dead Sea Scrolls

As we have seen, the Jewish rabbi's venerated their copies of the Old Testament so much that they did not allow them to be read to pieces.

As soon as they became too worn, they were stored and then reverently buried. Hence until rather recently no ancient Hebrew MSS were available to scholars, the oldest known dating no earlier than the 9th century A.D. All the available MSS, however, were found to contain the Masoretic text and to agree with one another very closely. The first to demonstrate this was Bishop Kennicott, who published at Oxford in 1776-1780 the readings of 634 Hebrew MS. He was followed in 1784-1788 by De Rossi, who published collations of 825 more MSS. No substantial variation among the MSS was detected by either of these two scholars.

The discoveries of the present century have altered this situation. The first of these new finds was a small papyrus fragment acquired in 1902 by W. L. Nash and presented by him to the Cambridge University Library. At first it was assigned to the 2nd century A.D., but W. F. Albright (1937) moved it back to the 2nd century B.C. It contains the Ten Commandments in a form closer to that found in Deuteronomy than to that in Exodus. Also it transposes the sixth and seventh Commandment, as the Greek text in Codex B (Vaticanus) does.

The Nash Papyrus, however, was but a harbinger of what was to come, namely, the Dead Sea Scrolls, which Albright hailed as *"the greatest manuscript discovery of modern times."* In the following paragraphs we will endeavor to summarize what eminent scholars say concerning this development and to state its meaning for Bible-believing Christians.

1.   The Discovery of the Dead Sea Scrolls

The Dead Sea Scrolls had been placed in earthen jars and deposited in caves near Wadi Qumran by the Dead Sea. They were first brought to light in 1947 by an Arab who was looking for a goat which had wandered away. After a few months some of the scrolls from this first cave were sold by the Arabs to the Syrian Orthodox Monastery of St. Mark in the Jordanian section of Jerusalem and others to the Hebrew University in the Israeli section of the city. In 1955 the Monastery of St. Mark sold its share of the Dead Sea Scrolls to the State of Israel. Thus these two lots of ancient writings were finally reunited under the same owners.

This collection includes the following documents:
1) Isaiah A, an almost complete copy of Isaiah in Hebrew;
2) Isaiah B, another copy of Isaiah in Hebrew, reasonably complete from chapter 41 onwards but containing only fragments of the earlier chapters;
3) a copy in Hebrew of the first two chapters of Habakkuk with a

verse-by-verse commentary also in Hebrew;
4)   the Rule of the Community, a code of rules of a community written in Hebrew;
5)   a collection of hymns in Hebrew;
6)   the Rule of War, a description in Hebrew of ancient warfare;
7)   an Aramaic paraphrase of chapters 5 to 15 of Genesis.

Of these seven manuscripts Isaiah A is regarded as the oldest. One expert sets its date at 175-150 B.C.; another expert makes it 50 years younger. The other manuscripts are thought to have been written from 50 to 150 years later than Isaiah A.

Dead Sea Scroll: Isaiah A

After these manuscripts had been discovered in the first cave, ten other caves in the same vicinity were found to contain similar treasures. Of these, Cave 4 has proved the most productive.   Thousands of fragments, once constituting about 330 separate books, have been taken from this location.   These fragments include portions of every Old-Testament book except Esther.   In 1952 also Hebrew Old Testament manuscripts said to date from the second century A.D. were discovered at Wadi Marabbal at about eleven miles south of Qumran.

2.   The Qumran Community

Near the caves in which the Dead Sea Scrolls were discovered was an old ruin called in Arabic Khirbet Qumran.   Under the stimulus provided by the Scrolls, excavations were begun at this site in 1951.

These excavations revealed that Khirbet Qumran had been the center of a Hellenistic-Roman settlement which spread nearly two miles northward along the cliffs and some two miles southward to an agricultural unit at a place called En Feskhah. The people of this Qumran settlement lived in caves, tents, and separate houses, but they possessed many things in common, such as, a common irrigation system, common stores of food and water, a common kiln for pottery, and common central buildings with rooms for gatherings and ritual meals. There was also a writing room in which they copied their scrolls.

According to F. M. Cross (1961), the members of this ancient Qumran settlement can be identified definitively with the Essenes, a Jewish sect described by Philo (died 42 A.D.) and Josephus (died 100 A.D.). Both these ancient writers mention the communistic way of life which these Essenes followed, and this fits in well with the facts disclosed by the excavations at Qumran. From the information given by Philo and Josephus and especially from his study of the Dead Sea Scrolls, Cross has reconstructed the history of the Qumran colony. He believes that this community was founded about 140 B.C. by a group of resolute Jews who steadfastly refused to recognize Simon Maccabaeus as lawful high priest. Many of these dissenters were priests themselves of the family of Zadok, to which all the high priests had belonged since the days of Solomon. Therefore, when Simon made himself high priest, these Zadokites opposed him as a usurper. For Simon was not a Zadokite, but was a member of the Hasmonaean family. Seeing that no direct resistance to Simon's power was possible, these dissenting priests retreated to the desert and established themselves at Qumran. The leader of this movement was evidently a Zadokite priest to whom the Scrolls give the title Righteous Teacher. Later the Essenes came to regard this *"Righteous Teacher"* as the forerunner of the Messiah.

3.   The Dead Sea Scrolls and the Old Testament Text

The discovery of the first Dead Sea Scroll, Isaiah A, was generally regarded by scholars as a victory for the Masoretic (Traditional) Hebrew text of the Old Testament. M. Burrows (1948) wrote as follows: *"The text of Isaiah in this manuscript is practically complete. With the exception of a few words lost where the edge of a column has been torn off and the relatively unimportant omissions to be noted below, the whole book is here, and it is substantially the book preserved in the Masoretic text. Differing notably in orthography and somewhat in morphology, it agrees with the Masoretic text to a remarkable degree in wording. Herein lies its chief importance, supporting the fidelity of the Masoretic tradition."* And according to Albright (1955), the second Isaiah scroll (Isaiah B) agrees even more closely with the Masoretic text.

But the discovery in 1952 of Cave 4 with its vast store of manuscripts has altered the picture considerably. It became apparent that the Proto-Masoretic text of the Isaiah scrolls was not the only type of Old Testament text that had been preserved at Qumran. In the manuscripts from Cave 4 many other text-types have been distinguished. In a recent article F. M. Cross (1964) presents some of the conclusions which he has drawn from his Qumran studies. He believes that three distinct ancient texts of Samuel can be identified, namely, (1) an Egyptian text represented by the *Septuagint*, (2) a Palestinian text represented by manuscript 4Q from Cave 4, and (3) a Proto-Masoretic text represented by a Greek text of Samuel also from Cave 4. And in the Pentateuch also Cross divides the text into the Egyptian, Palestinian, and Proto-Masoretic varieties.

Is. III. 16–20 from the Dead Sea Scroll (A) showing alterations to the divine Name (from *aḏōnāy* to *Yahweh* in line 3 and from *Yahweh* to *aḏōnāy* in line 4).

Dead Sea Fragments of Exodus. Phoenician Script

(1) Is 3:16-20 from the Dead Sea Scroll (A) showing alterations to the Divine Name (from *adOnOy* to *Yahweh* in line 3 and from *Yahweh* to *adOnOy* in line 4).

(2) Dead Sea Fragments of Exodus. Phoenician Script

Albright (1955) and Burrows (1958) agree with Cross in regard to his three-fold division of the Old Testament documents, a conclusion which Cross presented in an earlier article (1956). But unless these two scholars have reconsidered their positions, they differ from Cross in their estimate of the age of the Proto-Masoretic and the relationship of this text to the Egyptian and Palestinian texts.

Albright holds that the Proto-Masoretic text was developed in Babylon during the days of the captivity and was *"then brought back to*

Palestine by the returning exiles during the late sixth and fifth centuries B.C." The other two texts were derived from this Proto-Masoretic text. Burrows also believes in the superiority of the Proto-Masoretic text. *"The Proto-Masoretic text,"* he says, *"existed at Qumran and elsewhere along with the divergent texts; on the whole it is fair to say that it was the trunk and they were the branches that sprang out of it. The greatest contribution of the Dead Sea Scrolls to textual criticism is still their demonstration of this fact."* Cross, on the other hand, denies that the Proto-Masoretic text was the ancestor of the other two. He believes that it was *"the local text of Babylon which emerged in the fourth to second centuries B.C."* According to Cross, the Proto-Masoretic text did not arrive in Palestine until comparatively late.

G. R. Driver (1965) disagrees with the interpretation which Albright, Burrows, Cross and other scholars have placed upon the Dead Sea Scrolls. Denying that these documents date from pre-Christian times, he relates them instead to the Jewish Revolt against Rome in A.D. 66-73, thus making them roughly contemporary with the New Testament. He believes that the Righteous Teacher mentioned in the Scrolls was Manaemus (Menahem), a leader in the Revolt and perhaps a son of the rebel Judas mentioned in Acts 5:37. Hence, in Driver's opinion, the Dead Sea Scrolls were written in the first and early second centuries A.D., a theory which, if true, greatly alters the significance of these Scrolls both for history and for textual criticism.

Thus we see that, despite the new discoveries, our confidence in the trustworthiness of the Old Testament text must rest on some more solid foundation than the opinions of naturalistic scholars. For as the current Qumran studies demonstrate, these scholars disagree with one another. What one scholar grants another takes away. Instead of depending on such inconstant allies, Bible-believing Christians should develop their own type of Old Testament textual criticism, a textual criticism which takes its stand on the promises of Christ and views the evidence in the light of these promises.

With this summary by Edward F. Hills on the Dead Sea Scrolls, we conclude our survey of the Old Testament manuscripts and Versions. We end just where we began--that the foundation of the study on how we got our Bible is the promise of God to preserve His Word. It is tragic that so-called textual criticism has been left in the hands of those who proceed with their research totally oblivious to this promise. And worse, many who claim to be fundamentalists take the same naturalistic approach to the transmission of the Holy Scriptures.

Yes, the battle between God and Satan has raged over His Holy Word; there have been many pretenders; some streams of textual transmissions have become seriously corrupted.   But, in carefully pondering the facts and evidence as given above the student can clearly see that God has been faithful to His promise; the Old Testament has been preserved through the Masoretic Hebrew text.

"Not one jot or tittle has passed away."

PART TWO:

THE ISSUES WE FACE REGARDING THE NEW TESTAMENT TEXT

XI. The God-Honoring, Bible-Honoring Approach

As with our survey of the Old Testament Versions and Manuscripts, we begin this section with a careful study by Edward F. Hills. Dr. Hills is a graduate of Yale University and Westminster Theological Seminary. He has also received the degree of Th.M. from Columbia Seminary and the Th.D. degree from Harvard University. He is a Bible scholar of proven rank. In contrast with so many others, his is a *"scholarship on fire."* In the crucial area of the transmission of the New Testament text (i.e. how the New Testament came down to us), he begins on the basis that God has promised to preserve His Word. This is in sharp contrast to the naturalistic approach taken by so many other scholars (tragically also among fundamentalists).

An example of this latter position may be seen on page 16 of *"The Truth of the King James Version Controversy"* by Dr. Stewart Custer. Dr. Custer is a professor in one of the very finest fundamental schools-- Bob Jones University. He says on page 16, *"The believer may safely leave such problems* [i.e. the transmission of the text] *to the discussion of theological and textual experts. He should not try to become a botanist, but simply feed on the fruit of the Word.   He can let the scholars chew over dry bones; he should fill his mind and conscience with the holy Word. Then he can say with the Psalmist, 'How sweet are thy words unto my taste! yea, sweeter than honey to my mouth'* [Psalm 119:103]*."*

Now this sounds very good, and I am certain that Dr. Custer does have the experience of feeding on the Word of God. But this is typical of what we are hearing today. Just what kind of a Bible are we to feed upon? Is it the kind that has over 5,300 changes in the underlying Greek text from that which was used by Christians for over eighteen hundred years? And just who are theological and textual experts that we may safely leave these problems with? Under points three and four of his *"select Bibliography,"* Custer lists seven men--Bruce Metzger, A. T. Robertson, Kurt Aland, Eberhard Nestle, Alexander Souter, B. F. Westcott, F. J. A. Hort. With the exception of A. T. Robertson, each would be in the middle-of-the-road to liberal camp theologically. And each are firmly in the naturalistic camp textually. In the matter of textual research not one would start with the carefully stated truth in the Bible that God has promised to preserve His Word. This promise is not merely to *"truth of the Word"* but the words themselves.

♦   Psalm 12:6, 7--*The words of the Lord are pure Words; as silver*

*tried in a furnace of earth, purified seven times. Thou shalt keep
them, O LORD, thou shalt preserve them from this generation for
ever.*

♦   Psalm 119:89--*For ever, O LORD, thy word is settled in heaven.*
♦   Isa. 40:8--*The grass withereth, the flower fadeth: but the Word of
     our God shall stand forever.*
♦   Matt. 24:35--*Heaven and earth shall pass away, but my Word shall
     not pass away.*
♦   John 10:35--*The Scripture cannot be broken*
♦   I Pet. 1:23--*Being born again, not of corruptible seed, but of
     incorruptible, by the Word of God which liveth and abideth forever.*
♦   I Pet. 1:25--*But the Word of the Lord endureth forever.*
♦   Psa. 138:2--*Thou hast magnified thy Word above all thy name.*

Thus, though Stewart Custer *might*, under no circumstance will **we**
leave our Bibles in the hands of those who would chop, change, add, or
delete according to "the accepted principles of textual criticism."

A far better principle is given in Romans 14:23 *"Whatsoever is not
of faith is sin."* If I cannot by faith take the Bible in my hand and say this
is the preserved Word of God, then it is sin. If we do not approach the
study of how we got our Bible from the standpoint of faith, then it is sin.
If I cannot believe what God says about the preservation of His Word,
then I cannot believe what He says about its inspiration either--all is sin.

Now in this survey, it is often necessary to get facts from the very
textual experts (and many others) that Custer lists because Bible believers
have primarily left this field of research to the liberal naturalistic critics
who deny inspiration and preservation. But in doing so, I will be trusting
the Lord to help us to distinguish fact from fiction, and to come to the
proper and God honoring interpretation of this factual evidence.

XII. The Error of the Neutral, Naturalistic Approach to the Text of Scripture

1.   Can a Bible Believer Be Neutral?

When we regard the New Testament manuscripts from the believing
point of view, we see that they confirm the orthodox Christian faith. We
perceive that the Traditional text found in the vast majority of the Greek
manuscripts is the true text which Christ has promised always to preserve
in His Church. But there are many scholars today who claim to be

orthodox Christians and yet insist that the New Testament text ought not to be studied from the believing point of view but from a neutral point of view. The New Testament text, they maintain, ought to be treated just as the texts of other ancient books are treated. And in this they are followers of Westcott and Hort (1881) who laid down their basic principle in the following words: *"For ourselves we dare not introduce considerations which could not reasonably be applied to other ancient texts, supposing them to have documentary attestation of equal amount, variety, and antiquity."*

Why should we Christians study the New Testament text from a neutral point of view rather than from a believing point of view? The answer usually given is that we should do this for the sake of unbelievers. We must start with the neutral point of view in order that later we may convert unbelievers to the orthodox, believing point of view. Sir Frederic Kenyon (1903) expressed himself to this effect as follows: *"It is important to recognize from the first that the problem is essentially the same, whether we are dealing with sacred or secular literature, although the difficulty of solving it, and likewise the issues depending on it are very different. It is important, if for no other reason, because it is only in this way that we can meet the hostile critics of the New Testament with arguments, the force of which they admit. If we assume from the first the supernatural character of these books and maintain that this affects the manner in which their text has come down to us, we can never convince those who start with a denial of that supernatural character. We treat them at first like any other books, in order to show at last that they are above and beyond all other books."*

Although Kenyon probably advised this oblique approach with the best of intentions, still the course which he advocated is very wrong. Orthodox Christians must not stoop to conquer. We must not first adopt a neutral position toward the Bible in order that later we may persuade unbelievers to receive the Bible as God's Word. There are several reasons why we must not do this. In the first place, if we take this step, we are doing a sinful thing. We are not only allowing unbelievers to ignore the divine inspiration and providential preservation of the Bible, but we are even doing this ourselves. In other words, we are seeking to convert unbelievers by the strange method of participating in their unbelief. In the second place, when we approach unbelievers from the neutral position, we are endorsing their false method of textual criticism, a method which does not apply to the real, divinely inspired, providentially preserved Bible but to a false Bible of their own imagination, that is to say, an uninspired Bible whose history is basically the same as that of any other book. And in the third place, when we take up this neutral position,

we are not doing anything to convert unbelievers to the orthodox
Christian faith.   On the contrary, we are confirming them in their
confidence in the essential rightness of their unbelieving presuppositions.

The neutral method of Bible study, therefore, is wrong in principle;
and because it is wrong in principle, it leads to disastrous results in
practice.   In the following paragraphs, we will endeavor to list these
results in their logical order.

2.   Neutral Method Leads to Scepticism Concerning the New Testament Text

The neutral method of Bible study leads to scepticism concerning
the New Testament text. This was true long before the days of Westcott
and Hort.   As early as 1771 Griesbach wrote, *"The New Testament
abounds in more glosses, additions, and interpolations, purposely
introduced than any other book."* And Griesbach's outlook was shared
by J. L. Hug, who in 1808 advanced the theory that in the second century
the New Testament text had become deeply degenerate and corrupt and
that all extant New Testament texts were but editorial revisions of this
corrupted text.   Lachmann also in 1831 continued in the same skeptical
vein.   He believed that from the extant manuscripts it was not possible to
construct a text which would go any farther back than the fourth century.
To bridge the gap between this reconstructed fourth century text and the
original text Lachmann proposed to resort to conjectural emendation.

Westcott and Hort thought that by the judicious use of their neutral
method they had laid to rest the doubts and uncertainties which had
plagued their predecessors.   They believed that they had reduced the
margin of error in the New Testament text to very small dimensions.
*"The amount of what can in any sense be called substantial variation is
but a small fraction of the whole residuary variation, and can hardly form
more than a thousandth part of the entire text."* They were confident that
in the manuscripts B and Aleph they had discovered a New Testament
text that was almost entirely pure. *"Whatever may be the ambiguity of
the whole evidence in particular passages, the general course of future
criticism must be shaped by the happy circumstance that the fourth
century has bequeathed to us two manuscripts of which even the less
incorrupt must have been of exceptional purity among its own
contemporaries, and which rise into greater preeminence of character the
better the early history of the text becomes known."* Such were the strong
assertions which won Westcott and Hort an enthusiastic following among
conservative Christians, who mistakenly thought that Westcott and Hort
were conservative too because they said such things.

But such optimism has been unusual in the history of New Testament textual criticism. Few scholars have shared Westcott and Hort's unbounded confidence in the texts of B and Aleph. Among those that have followed Westcott and Hort pessimism has prevailed. As early as 1908 Rendel Harris declared that the New Testament text had not at all been settled but was *"more than ever, and perhaps finally, unsettled."* Two years later Conybeare gave it as his opinion that *"the ultimate [New Testament] text, if there ever was one that deserves to be so called, is for ever irrecoverable."* Later (1941) Kirsopp Lake, after a lifetime spent in the study of the New Testament text, delivered the following judgement: *"In spite of the claims of Westcott and Hort and of von Soden, we do not know the original form of the Gospels, and it is quite likely that we never shall."*

As the present century has worn on, this pessimism has continued, in spite of manuscript discoveries. *"When we speak of the original text as the object of our search,"* asks K. W. Clark (1950), *"do we mean the actual autograph of the author or the editio princeps of such units as the Four-fold Gospel and the Pauline Corpus? While the former is greatly to be desired, certainly the latter is at least a conceivable objective although even it is extremely elusive and obscure."* H. Greeven (1960) also has acknowledged the uncertainty of the neutral method of New Testament textual criticism. *"In general,"* he says, *"the whole thing is limited to probability judgements; the original text of the New Testament, according to its nature, must be and remains a hypothesis."* And R. M. Grant (1963) adopts a still more despairing attitude. *"The primary goal of New Testament textual study,"* he tells us, *"remains the recovery of what the New Testament writers wrote. We have already suggested that to achieve this goal is well nigh impossible."*

Why is it that the neutral method of Bible study has always this tendency to breed scepticism concerning the text of the Bible? The reason is plain. The reason is that it is not really possible to be neutral about the Bible. If you try to be neutral, if you ignore the divine inspiration and the providential preservation of the Bible and treat it like an ordinary human book, then you are ignoring the very factors that make the Bible what it is. If you follow such a neutral method of Bible study, you are still playing about on the surface and have failed to come to grips with the very essence of the Bible. In your textual criticism you have not yet dealt with the real, divinely inspired and providentially preserved Bible but with a false, purely human Bible of your own imagination. And since you are dealing with a false, purely human Bible, doubts as to the purity of its text must necessarily arise in your mind, doubts which you can find no means of banishing.

But if by the grace of God you drop your neutral position and take your stand on the Bible as God's infallible Word, inspired by His Holy Spirit and preserved by His special providence, then it becomes evident to you that the true New Testament text has been preserved in the God-guided usage of the Church. Hence this true text is to be found in the vast majority of the Greek New Testament manuscripts, in the Textus Receptus, and in the King Jams Version and the other classic Protestant translations.

3. The Neutral Method Leads to the Denial of the Inspiration of the Bible

The neutral method of Bible study leads not only to scepticism concerning the text of the extant Scriptures but also to modernism, that is, to naturalistic views concerning the inspiration of the Scriptures. In order to demonstrate historically that this is so let us consider the position taken by William Sanday, an outstanding English scholar of the generation immediately following that of Westcott and Hort.

Sanday was an ardent disciple of Westcott and Hort, and in his Bampton Lectures (1893) he took the further step of applying their neutral, naturalistic method not only to the text of the Bible but also to the question of its inspiration. *"We must recognize,"* he began, *"that a change has come over the current way of thinking on this subject of the authority of the Bible. The maxim that the Bible must be studied 'like any other book' has been applied."* But according to Sanday, this change was all for the better. By studying the Bible like any other book it would be possible to come to an impartial decision as to whether the Bible actually was like any other book or whether its inspiration had made it unique. *"It is better to let the Bible tell its own story, without forcing it either way. Let us by all means study it if we will like any other book, but do not let us beg the question that it must be wholly like any other book, that there is nothing in it distinctive and unique. Let us give a fair and patient hearing to the facts as they come before us, whether they be old or whether they be new."*

No believing Bible student has ever objected to Sanday's proposal to *"let the Bible tell its own story."* The only question is, how do you go about letting the Bible tell its own story? Do we let the Bible tell its own story when we study it like any other book? Not if the Bible is unique, not if the Bible is divinely and infallibly inspired. If the Bible is divinely and infallibly inspired, then the only way to let it tell its own story is to study it like a divinely and infallibly inspired Book. In other words, the essential nature of the Bible determines the method by which we ought to study it, and, conversely, the method by which we study the Bible determines the conclusions which we shall reach as to the essential nature of the Bible. If we study the Bible *"like any other book,"* then we are logically bound to reach the conclusion that the Bible is essentially like other books, and that the inspiration of the biblical writers was not such as to make the Bible fundamentally different from other religious books.

This was the conclusion toward which Sanday tended as he applied to the study of the inspiration of the Bible the same neutral, naturalistic methods which Westcott and Hort had applied to the study of the Bible text. *"When,"* he observed, *"we think of the immense part which myth and legend and vague approximations at truth have borne in the thought and literatures of early peoples, and how very partial and imperfect history of all kinds has been, and in many departments still is, there can be nothing abnormal if similar elements enter to some extent into the Bible."*

4. The Neutral Method Leads to the Denial of the Deity of Christ

F. C. Burkitt (1906) was much more thorough-going than Sanday in his modernism. Like many modernists of his day, he thought that it was possible to investigate the earthly life of Christ by that some neutral, naturalistic method which Westcott and Hort and Sanday had used in their studies. This involved ignoring all the divine factors in the life of Christ and concentrating on those features which Burkitt deemed historical. *"I have purposely abstained in these Lectures,"* Burkitt explained to his audience, *"from discussing most of those parts or features of the Gospel History which usually form the subject matter of modern controversies. The Birth of our Lord from a virgin and His Resurrection from the dead--to name the most obvious Articles of the Creed--are not matters which historical criticism can establish. As I ventured to say in the Introductory Lecture, we do not get our leading ideas of religion or philosophy from historical criticism. But the Christian religion is not only a matter of imagination and philosophy. The Crucifixion under Pontius Pilate and the Death and Burial of our Lord are as much Articles of the Christian Creed as the Resurrection itself. And in these Articles, Christianity enters the arena of ordinary history. The Interpretation of the life of Jesus Christ in Palestine is a matter of Faith; but the Tale itself, the course of events, belongs to History and is a matter for the scientific historian to determine."*

As orthodox Christians we ought to object to the false distinction which Burkitt set up in dealing with the life of Christ. His procedure, which ignored all the specifically divine features of Christ's Person and work and concentrated only on those features of our Lord's life that he thought could be explained in a purely naturalistic way, cannot be too strongly condemned. But have we earned the right to condemn Burkitt for following this method? Not if we ourselves follow Westcott and Hort's naturalistic method of New Testament textual criticism. For if we do, how can we condemn Burkitt for following in his study of the life of Christ the same method which we follow in our study of the New Testament text? If it is right for us to ignore the divine aspects of the New Testament text and treat it as we would the text of any other book, then why isn't it right for scholars such as Burkitt to ignore the divine aspects of the life of Christ and treat it as they would the life of any other great man? (We will hear more from Burkitt later.)

As R. H. Fuller (1962) and R. M. Grant (1963) point out, the efforts of Burkitt and the other modernistic scholars of his day to discover back of the Gospel narratives a purely human Jesus were unsuccessful. *"In the first half of the twentieth century,"* Grant observes, *"this kind of search practically came to a halt because of the rise of form criticism, with its emphasis on the role of oral tradition in the creation of the gospels, and the recognition that apocalyptic eschatology had been extremely important in the early Church and (probably) in the teaching of Jesus himself."* But in 1953 this search for the *"historical Jesus"* was resumed in Germany and is being carried on today. How can we orthodox Christians oppose this new modernistic effort effectively? Only by purging our own biblical study of all naturalistic elements. For if we deal in a neutral, naturalistic way with the text of the Bible, the written Word, how can we condemn these new modernistic scholars for dealing in the same way with the life of Jesus Christ, the Incarnate Word?

5. The Chain-Reaction of the Neutral Approach

It is very wrong, therefore, and dangerous to ignore the divine inspiration and special providential preservation of the Scriptures and to read and study them like ordinary, purely human books. If we study the Bible in this neutral, naturalistic way, we run the risk of setting off in our own minds a veritable chain-reaction of unbelief which will race forward with lightning speed from point to point until our whole Christian faith is (or seems to be) destroyed.

In the first place, doubt and distrust will begin to possess our minds concerning the extant text of the Bible. For if we ignore the special providential preservation of the Bible, how can we be sure that the extant Bible text is a trustworthy reproduction of the divinely inspired original text? And in the second place, we will begin to wonder why we should not deal with the inspiration of the Bible in the same neutral, naturalistic way in which we have dealt with the Bible text. If it is right to discuss the text of the Bible without *"introducing considerations which could not reasonably be applied to other ancient texts,"* why isn't it right to follow the same policy in our discussions of the authorship and inspiration of the Bible? (Hills)

Before following Hills further, I would like to express my concern regarding this very malaise of neutrality that has entered the halls of power in fundamentalism. Many of the great schools, mission boards, and churches seem insistent that they will take a neutral position on the preservation of the text of Scripture. It is not that they are for Westcott and Hort or against the Received Text. It is just that they must be neutral. And despite the fact that (unlike the earlier part of this century) the world is awash with many different modern versions, there is a strange reluctance to be informed on this matter.

XIII. How Christ Has Kept His Promise to Preserve the New Testament Scriptures

In the Gospels Christ has promised that the same divine providence which has preserved the Old Testament Scriptures will also preserve the New. In the concluding verses of the Gospel of Matthew we find His *"Great Commission"* not only to the twelve Apostles but also to His Church throughout all ages, *"Go ye therefore and teach all nations."* Implied in this solemn charge is the promise that through the working of God's providence the Church will always be kept in possession of an infallible record of Christ's words and works. And, similarly, in His discourses on the last things He assures His disciples that His words not only shall certainly be fulfilled but shall remain available for the comfort of His people during that troubled period which shall precede His second coming. In other words, He promises that they shall be preserved until that time. *"Heaven and earth shall pass away, but My words shall not pass away"* (Matt. 24:35; Mark 13:3; Luke 21:33). Likewise, the word of Christ is to be the foundation of Christian character down through the ages (Matt. 7:24-27; Luke 6:46-49) and the standard by which all men shall be judged at the last day (John 12:48).

How has our Savior fulfilled His promise? Through the usage of His Church. The New Testament Scriptures have been preserved in the New Testament way, not through a divinely appointed order of priests and scribes (as in the Old Testament dispensation), but through the universal priesthood of believers (I Peter 2:9), through the leading of the Holy Spirit in the hearts of individual Christians of every walk of life. A brief survey of the history of the New Testament and its text makes this evident.

1.   How the New Testament Books Were Written

The writing of the New Testament as well as the preservation of it was a fulfillment of the promises of Christ. Chapter 14 of the Gospel of John teaches us this very clearly. As the Savior is about to return to His heavenly Father, He leaves with His Apostles this blessed assurance :

> Jn. 14:25-26--*These things have I spoken unto you, being yet present with you. But the Comforter, which is the Holy Ghost, whom the Father will send in My name, He shall teach you all things and bring all things to your remembrance, whatsoever I have said unto you.*

Here Jesus answers beforehand a question which Bible scholars have been asking down through the ages. Why is it that the first three Gospels Matthew, Mark, and Luke agree together so closely, and why is it that the Gospel of John differs from these first three Gospels so widely? Both these agreements and these differences are due to the inspiration which the Apostles received from the Holy Spirit and the control which He exercised over their minds and memories.

In the Gospels, therefore, Jesus reveals Himself through the story of His earthly ministry. The rest of the New Testament books are His divine commentary on the meaning of that ministry, and in these books also Jesus reveals Himself.   These remaining books were written in accordance with His promise to His Apostles:

> Jn. 16:12-13--*I have yet many things to say unto you, but ye cannot bear them now. Howbeit, when He, the Spirit of truth is come, He will guide you into all truth; for He shall not speak of Himself: but whatsoever He shall hear that shall He speak: and He will shew you things to come.*

It was in fulfillment of this promise that the Holy Spirit descended upon the Apostles at Pentecost, filled their minds and hearts with the message of the risen, exalted Lord, and sent them out to preach this message, first to the Jews at Jerusalem and then to all the world. Then followed the conversion of the Apostle Paul and the Epistles which he wrote under the inspiration of the Holy Spirit. Then James, Peter, John, and Jude were inspired to write their Epistles, and Luke to tell the story of the Acts of the Apostles. Finally, the Revelation proceeded from the inspired pen of John on Patmos, announcing those things that were yet to come. Volumes, of course, could be filled with a discussion of these sacred developments, but here a bare statement of the essential facts must suffice.

2.   The Formation of the New Testament Canon

After the New Testament books had been written, the next step in the divine program for the New Testament Scriptures was the gathering of these individual books into one New Testament canon in order that thus they might take their place beside the books of the Old Testament canon as the concluding portion of His holy Word. Let us now consider how this was accomplished under the guidance of the Holy Spirit.

The first New Testament books to be assembled together were the Epistles of Paul. The Apostle Peter, shortly before he died, referred to Paul's Epistles as Scripture and in such a way as to indicate that at least the beginning of such a collection had already been made (II Peter 3:15-16). Even radical scholars, such as E. J. Goodspeed (1926), agree that a collection of Paul's Epistles was in circulation at the beginning of the second century and that Ignatius (117) referred to it. When the Four Gospels were collected together is unknown, but it is generally agreed that this must have taken place before 170 A.D. because at that time Tatian made his Harmony of the Gospels (*Diatessaron*), which included all four of the canonical Gospels and only these four. Before 200 A.D. The epistles of Paul, the Gospels, Acts, I Peter and I John were recognized as Scripture by Christians everywhere (as the writings of Irenaeus, Clement of Alexandria, and Tertullian prove) and accorded an authority equal to that of the Old Testament Scriptures. It was Tertullian, moreover, who first applied the name New Testament to this collection of apostolic writings.

The seven remaining books, 2 and 3 John, 2 Peter, Hebrews, James, Jude, and Revelation were not yet unanimously accepted as Scripture. By the time the fourth century had arrived, however, few Christians seem to have questioned the right of these disputed books to a place in the New Testament canon. Eminent Church Fathers of that era, such as Athanasius, Augustine, and Jerome include them in their lists of the New Testament books. Thus through the Holy Spirit's guidance of individual believers, silently and gradually--but nevertheless surely, the Church as a whole was led to a recognition of the fact that the twenty-seven books of the New Testament, and only these books, form the canon which God gave to be placed beside the Old Testament Scriptures as the authoritative and final revelation of His will.

This guidance of the Holy Spirit was negative as well as positive. It involved not only the selection of canonical New Testament books but also the rejection of many non-canonical books which were mistakenly regarded as canonical by some of the early Christians. Thus the Shepherd of Hermes was used as holy Scripture by Irenaeus and Clement of-Alexandria, and the same status was wrongly given to the Teaching of the Twelve Apostles by Clement and Origen. Clement likewise commented on the Apocalypse of Peter and the Epistle of Barnabas, to which Origen also accorded the title *"catholic."* And in addition, there were many false Gospels in circulation, as well as numerous false Acts ascribed to various Apostles. But, although some of these non-canonical writings gained temporary acceptance in certain quarters, this state of affairs lasted for but a short time. Soon all Christians everywhere were led by the Holy Spirit to repudiate these spurious works and to receive only the canonical books as their New Testament Scriptures. (Hills)

Having said all this, it must also be acknowledged that there is a deep and sacred mystery in the formation of the Written Word on earth just as there had been in the incarnation and development of the Living Word.

3.   The Preservation of the New Testament Text

Thus the Holy Spirit guided the early Christians to gather their individual New Testament books into one New Testament canon and to reject all non-canonical books. In the same manner also the Holy Spirit guided the early Christians to preserve the New Testament text by receiving the true readings and rejecting the false. Certainly, it would be strange if it had been otherwise. It would have been passing strange if God had guided His people in regard to the New Testament canon but had withheld from them His divine assistance in the matter of the New Testament text. This would mean that Bible-believing Christians today could have no certainty concerning the New Testament text but would be obliged to rely on the hypotheses of modern, naturalistic critics.

But God in His mercy did not leave His people to grope after the true New Testament text. Through the leading of the Holy Spirit He guided them to preserve it during the manuscript period. God brought this to pass through the working of His preserving and governing providence. First, many trustworthy copies of the original New Testament manuscripts were produced by faithful scribes. Second, these trustworthy copies were read and recopied by true believers down through the centuries. Third, untrustworthy copies were not so generally read or so frequently recopied. Although they enjoyed some popularity for a time, yet in the long run they were laid aside and consigned to oblivion. Thus as a result of this special providential guidance the true text won out in the end, and today we may be sure that the text found in the vast majority of the Greek New Testament manuscripts is a trustworthy reproduction of the divinely inspired original text. This is the text which was preserved by the God-guided usage of the Greek Church. Critics have called it the Byzantine text, thereby acknowledging that it was the text in use in the Greek Church during the greater part of the Byzantine period (452-1453). It is much better, however, to call this text the Traditional text. When we call the text found in the majority of the Greek New Testament manuscripts the Traditional text, we signify that this is the text which has been handed down by the God-guided tradition of the Church from the time of the Apostles unto the present day.

A further step in the providential preservation of the New Testament was the printing of it in 1516 and the dissemination of it throughout the whole of Western Europe during the Protestant Reformation. In the first printing of the Greek New Testament we see God's preserving providence working hiddenly and, to the outward eye, accidentally The editor, Erasmus, performed his task in great haste in order to meet the deadline set by the printer, Froben of Basle. Hence this first edition contained a number of errors of a minor sort, some of which persisted in later editions. But in all essentials the New Testament text first printed by Erasmus and later by Stephanus (1550) and Elzevir (1633) is in full agreement with the Traditional Text providentially preserved in the vast majority of the Greek New Testament manuscripts.

This printed text is commonly called the Textus Receptus (Received Text). It is the text which was used by the Protestant Reformers during the Reformation and by all Protestants everywhere for three hundred years thereafter. It was from this Textus Receptus that the King James Version and the other classic Protestant translations were made. In the Textus Receptus God provided a trustworthy printed New Testament text for the Protestant Reformers and for all believing Christians down to the present day. Thus the printing of it was, after all, no accident but the work of God's special providence.

4. The Universal Priesthood of Believers

As we have seen, the study of the Old Testament indicates that the Old Testament Scriptures were preserved through the divinely appointed Old Testament priesthood. The Holy Spirit guided the priests to gather the separate parts of the Old Testament into one Old Testament canon and to maintain the purity of the Old Testament text. Have the New Testament Scriptures been preserved in this official manner? In the New Testament Church has there ever been a special, divinely appointed organization of priests with authority to make decisions concerning the New Testament text or the books that should belong to the New Testament canon? No! Not at all! When Christ died upon the cross, the veil of the Temple was rent in sunder, and the Old Testament priesthood was done away forever. There has never been a special order of priests in the New Testament Church. Every believer is a priest under Christ, the great High Priest (Rev. 1:5-6). Within the New Testament Church there has never been any body of men to whom God has given any special authority to make decisions concerning the New Testament canon or the New Testament text.

Just as the divine glories of the New Testament are brighter far than the glories of the Old Testament, so the manner in which God has preserved the New Testament text is far more wonderful than the manner in which He preserved the Old Testament text. God preserved the Old Testament text by means of something physical and external, namely, the Aaronic priesthood. God has preserved the New Testament text by means of something inward and spiritual, namely, the universal priesthood of believers.

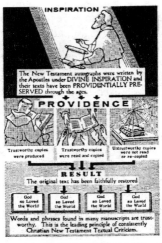

The O.T. was preserved through the Aaronic Priesthood.
The N.T. has been preserved through the Universal Priesthood of Believers.

Hence the preservation of the New Testament text is not due to the decisions of any ecclesiastical organization or council or committee. All such attempts to deal with the New Testament text are bound to fail. God has preserved the New Testament text in the New Testament way which is free from any traces of Old Testament bondage, namely, through the guidance of the Holy Spirit operating in the hearts of individual believers and gradually leading them, by common consent, to reject false readings and to preserve the true. By this God-guided usage of believers the true New Testament text has been, preserved and is now found in the vast majority of the Greek New Testament manuscripts. This is the text which is found in the King James Version and the other classic Protestant translations.

XIV. The Various Kinds of New Testament Manuscripts

It is evident that the New Testament text was preserved publicly rather than privately and in many manuscripts rather than in just a few. The promises of Christ ensure that this is so. For if the New Testament text had been deposited in a box for hundreds of years, or sealed in a pot, or secluded in a cave, or hidden in some forgotten recess of an ancient library, Christ would not have fulfilled His pledged word always to preserve in His Church the true New Testament text. It must be, therefore, that Christ has preserved this true text in the usage of His Church and in the vast majority of the Greek New Testament manuscripts, which are the products of the Church's usage. Such are the convictions with which the believing Bible student approaches the study of the New Testament documents. And through such study his convictions are confirmed, for he soon finds that these convictions agree with the observed facts. As a first step, then, toward such confirmation, let us proceed to an enumeration of the New Testament documents.

How many New Testament manuscripts are there? For information on this point let us turn to the statistics as they are presented by Kurt Aland. Let us begin with the Greek New Testament manuscripts. According to Aland, there are approximately 5,255 known manuscripts which contain all or part of the Greek New Testament.

The earliest of these Greek New Testament manuscripts are the papyri. They are given this name because they are written on papyrus, an ancient type of writing material made from the fibrous pith of the papyrus plant, which in ancient times grew plentifully along the river Nile. Eighty-eight of these papyri have now been discovered, many of them mere fragments. The most important of these papyrus manuscripts are the Chester Beatty Papyri and the Bodmer Papyri. The Chester Beatty Papyri were published in 1933-37. They include Papyrus 45 (Gospels and Acts, c. 225 A.D.), Papyrus 46 (Pauline Epistles, c. 225 A.D.), and Papyrus 47 (Revelation, c. 275 A.D.). The Bodmer Papyri were published in 1956-62. The most important of these are Papyrus 66 (John c. 200 A.D.) and Papyrus 75 (Luke and John 1-15, c. 200 A.D.).

All the rest of the Greek New Testament manuscripts are of Velum. (leather), except for a few late ones in which paper was used. The oldest of the velum manuscripts are written in uncial (capital) letters. These uncial manuscripts now number 267. The three oldest complete (or nearly complete) uncial manuscripts are B (Codex Vaticanus), Aleph (Codex Sinaiticus), and A (Codex Alexandrinus). Codex B was written about the middle of the fourth century. It is the property of the Vatican Library at Rome. When it arrived there is not known, but it must have been before 1475, since it is mentioned in a catalogue of the library made in that year. Codex Aleph was discovered by Tischendorf in 1859 at the Monastery of St. Catherine on Mount Sinai. Tischendorf persuaded the monks to give it as a present (requited with money and favors) to the Czar of Russia. In 1933 it was purchased from the Russian government by the Trustees of the British Museum. It is generally considered by scholars to have been written in the second half of the fourth century. Codex A was for many years regarded as the oldest extant New Testament manuscript. It was given to the King of England in 1627 by Cyril Lucar, patriarch of Constantinople, and is now kept in the British Museum. Scholars date it from the first half of the fifth century. Other important uncial manuscripts are W (Gospels, 4th or 5th century), D (Gospels and Acts, 5th or 6th century), and D, (Pauline Epistles, 6th century).

About the beginning of the ninth century minuscule (small letter) handwriting began to be used for the production of books. Thus all the later New Testament manuscripts are minuscules. According to Metzger, 2,764 minuscule manuscripts have been catalogued. These date from the ninth to the sixteenth century. In 1751 Wettstein introduced the practice of designating the uncial manuscripts by capital letters and the minuscule manuscripts by Arabic numerals. The following are some of the minuscule manuscripts which critics have regarded as the most important: 1, 13, 28, 33, 690, 700.

Another important class of Greek New Testament manuscripts are the lectionaries. These are service books which contain in proper sequence the text of the passages of Scripture appointed to be read at the worship services of the Church. These lectionaries are of two kinds, the synaxaria, which begin the year at Easter, and the menologia, which begin the year at September 1. Aland sets the number of the lectionary manuscripts at 2,143.

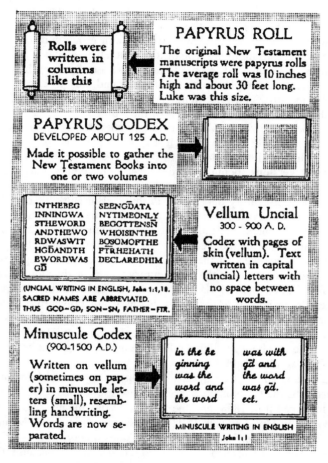

PAPYRUS ROLL

Rolls were written in columns like this

The original New Testament manuscripts were papyrus rolls The average roll was 10 inches high and about 30 feet long. Luke was this size.

PAPYRUS CODEX
DEVELOPED ABOUT 125 A.D.

Made it possible to gather the New Testament Books into one or two volumes

INTHEBEG INNINGWA STHEWORD ANDTHEWO RDWASWIT HGDANDTH EWORDWAS GD

SEENGDATA NYTIMEONLY BEGOTTENSN WHOISINTHE BOSOMOFTHE FTRHEHATH DECLAREDHIM

(UNCIAL WRITING IN ENGLISH, John 1:1,18. SACRED NAMES ARE ABBREVIATED. THUS GOD-GD, SON-SN, FATHER-FTR.

Vellum Uncial
300 - 900 A. D.

Codex with pages of skin (vellum). Text written in capital (uncial) letters with no space between words.

Minuscule Codex
(900-1500 A.D.)

Written on vellum (sometimes on paper) in minuscule letters (small), resembling handwriting. Words are now separated.

in the be ginning was the word and the word

was with gd and the word was gd. ect.

MINUSCULE WRITING IN ENGLISH John 1:1

New Testament Manuscripts From 50-1500 A.D.

New Testament Manuscripts from 50-1500 A.D.

The translation of the New Testament Greek scriptures into the various languages of that day is another major class of manuscript evidence.

When and where the New Testament was first translated into Latin has been the subject of much dispute, but, according to Metzger, most scholars now agree that the first Latin translation of the Gospels was made in North Africa during the last quarter of the second century. Only about 50 manuscripts of this Old Latin version survive. These manuscripts are divided into the African Latin group and the European Latin group according to the type of text which they contain. In 382 A.D. Pope Damasus requested Jerome to undertake a revision of the Old Latin version. Jerome complied with this request and thus produced the Latin Vulgate, the official Bible of the Roman Catholic Church. There are more than 8,000 extant manuscripts of the Vulgate.

Of the Syriac versions the most important is the Peshitta, the historic Bible of the whole Syrian Church, of which 350 manuscripts are now extant. The Peshitta was long regarded as one of the most ancient New Testament versions, being accorded a second century date. In more recent times, however, Burkitt (1904) and other naturalistic critics have assigned a fifth-century date to the Peshitta. But Burkitt's hypothesis is contrary to the evidence, and today it is being abandoned even by naturalistic scholars. All the sects into which the Syrian Church is divided are loyal to the Peshitta. In order to account for this it is necessary to believe that the Peshitta was in existence long before the fifth century, for it was in the fifth century that these divisions occurred.

The Philoxenian Syriac version was produced in 508 A.D. for Philoxenus, bishop of Mabbug, by his assistant Polycarp. In 616 this version was re-issued, or perhaps revised, by Thomas of Harkel, who likewise was bishop of Mabbug. The Philoxenian-Harclean version includes the five books which the Peshitta omits, namely, 2 Peter, 2 and 3 John, Jude and Revelation.

The so-called *"Old Syriac"* version is represented by only two manuscripts, the Curetonian Syriac manuscript, named after W. Cureton who published it in 1858, and the Sinaitic Syriac manuscript, which was discovered by Mrs. Lewis in 1892 at the same monastery on Mount Sinai in which Tischendorf had discovered Codex Aleph almost-fifty years before. These manuscripts are called *"Old Syriac"* because they are thought by critics to represent a Syriac text which is older than the Peshitta. This theory, however, rests on Burkitt's untenable hypothesis that the Peshitta was produced in the fifth century by Rabbula, bishop of Edessa.

The Egyptian New Testament versions are called the Coptic versions because they are written in Coptic, the latest form of the ancient Egyptian language. The Coptic New Testament is extant in two dialects, the Sahidic version of Southern Egypt and the Bohairic version of

Northern Egypt. According to Metzger, the Sahidic version dates from the beginning of the third century. The oldest Sahidic manuscript has been variously dated from the mid-fourth to the sixth century. The Bohairic version is regarded as somewhat later than the Sahidic. It is extant in many manuscripts most of which are late. Recently, however, M. Bodmer has acquired a papyrus Bohairic manuscript containing most of the Gospel of John which is thought by its editor, R. Kasser, to date from the mid-fourth century.

In addition to the Latin, Syriac, and Coptic versions, there are a number of other versions which are important for textual criticism. The Gothic version was translated from the Greek in the middle of the fourth century by Ulfilas, the renowned missionary to the Goths. Of this version six manuscripts are still extant. Of the Armenian version 1,244 manuscripts survive. This version seems to have been made in the fifth century; but by whom is uncertain. Whether it was made from the Greek or from a Syriac version is also a matter of debate among scholars. The Christians of Georgia, a mountainous district between the Black and Caspian seas, also had a New Testament in their own language, several copies of which are still extant.

The New Testament quotations found in the writings of the Church Fathers constitute yet another source of information concerning the history of the New Testament text. Some of the most important Fathers, for the purposes of textual criticism, are the following: the three Western Fathers, Irenaeus (c. 180), Tertullian (150-220), Cyprian (200-258); the Alexandrian Fathers, Clement (c. 200), Origen (182-251); the Fathers who lived in Antioch and in Asia Minor, especially Chrysostom (345-407). Another very important early Christian writer was Tatian, who about 170 A.D. composed a harmony of the Four Gospels called the *Diatessaron*. This had wide circulation in Syria and has been preserved in two Arabic manuscripts and various other sources.

XV. The So-called "Families" of New Testament Manuscripts

Since the 18th century the New Testament documents have been divided into families according to the type of text which they contain. There are three of these families, namely, the Traditional (Byzantine) family, the Western family, and the Alexandrian family.

The Traditional (Byzantine) family includes all those New Testament documents which contain the Traditional (Byzantine) text. The vast majority of the Greek New Testament manuscripts belong-to this family, including A (in the Gospels) and W (in Matthew and the last two thirds of Luke). The Peshitta Syriac version and the Gothic version also belong to the Traditional family of New Testament documents. And the New Testament quotations of Chrysostom and the other Fathers of Antioch and Asia Minor seem generally to agree with the Traditional text.

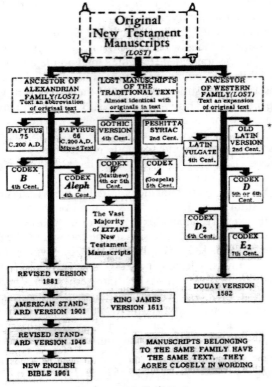

The Ancestry of the English Versions

The Western family consists of those New Testament documents which contain that form of text found in the writings of the Western Church Fathers, especially Irenaeus, Tertullian, and Cyprian. A number of Greek manuscripts contain this text, of which the most important are D and D_2. Two other important witnesses to the Western text are the Old

Latin version, the *Diatessaron* of Tatian, and the Curetonian and Sinaitic Syriac manuscripts.

The Alexandrian family consists of those New Testament documents which contain that form of text which was used by Origen in many of his writings and also by other Church Fathers who, like Origen, lived at Alexandria. This family includes Papyri 46, 47, 66, 75, B, Aleph and about twenty-five other Greek New Testament manuscripts. The Coptic versions also belong to the Alexandrian family of New Testament documents. Westcott and Hort (1881), two noted English critics of the previous century, distinguished between the text of B and the text of the other Alexandrian documents. They called this B text Neutral, thus indicating their belief that it was a remarkably pure text which had not been contaminated by the errors of either the Western or Alexandrian text. Many subsequent scholars, however, have denied the validity of this distinction.

The foregoing survey of the New Testament documents throws light on the early history of the New Testament text and on the manner in which this text has been preserved by the special providence of God. In order to see how this is so, let us consider briefly the characteristic history of each of the major families into which the New Testament text has been divided.

1. The Early Characteristic History of the Traditional Text

In considering the early history of the Traditional text we must note that, contrary to the opinion of many modern critics, it was probably among the poorer and less educated members of the early Christian Church that the true New Testament text was preserved. Such persons could read and write, to be sure, but were not skillful in the use of the pen. For them writing was a chore to be avoided as far as possible. Conscious of their inability to write neatly, they would hesitate to mar their precious copies of the New Testament books by writing notes in the margins. Thus they would tend to keep their copies clean, free, that is, from additions in the form of marginal notes and from subtractions in the form of deletion marks. And the copies made from these clean copies would in their turn be clean, for there would be no marginal notes which the scribe could copy into the text of the new manuscript which he was producing. Also, among the poorer, less educated Christians there would be far less opportunity to compare different types of texts together and note the variant readings. There would even be a positive reluctance to make such a comparison, because the natural tendency of these humbler believers would be to adhere closely to the text to which they were accustomed and ignore texts that varied from it.

For all these reasons, therefore, the New Testament text which circulated among the humbler, less educated Christians was probably free from intentional alterations. The errors would be chiefly accidental ones due to careless copying, and these could be detected and remedied. Thus it was among the poorer, lowlier Christian brethren, we may well believe, that the Traditional (true) New Testament text was preserved during the early Christian centuries, the text which is now found in the vast majority of the Greek New Testament manuscripts.

2.   The Early Characteristic History of the Western Text

In the better educated Christian circles the case would be entirely different. In these higher social brackets there were undoubtedly many who were proficient in the art of writing and who were easily able to note down neatly in the margins of their New Testament manuscripts their own comments and any additional material which seemed to them interesting and important. Then when these annotated manuscripts were copied and new manuscripts made from them, many of these marginal notes were incorporated into the texts of the new manuscripts. It was probably in this manner that the Western text was developed. According to most scholars, this text is characterized by additions and verbal variations, and both these features were probably due either to the incorporation of marginal notes into the texts or to the effect of these notes on the minds of the scribes as they were doing their copying.

3.   The Early Characteristic History of the Alexandrian Text

Among the Christian scribes of Alexandria, developments took another turn. According to Streeter (1924), these learned Christians followed the tradition of Alexandrian classical scholarship, which was always to prefer the shortest reading in places in which the manuscripts differed. The Alexandrians were always ready to suspect and reject New Testament readings which seemed to them to present difficulties. John Burgon (1896), one of England's greatest believing Bible scholars, proved this long ago by pointing out a relevant passage in Origen's Commentary an Matthew.

In this Commentary Origen, the leading Christian critic of antiquity, gives us an insight into the arbitrary and highly subjective manner in which New Testament textual criticism was carried on at Alexandria about 230 A.D. In his comment on Matt. 19:17-21 (Jesus' reply to the rich young man) Origen reasons that Jesus could not have concluded his list of God's commandments with the comprehensive requirement, Thou shalt love thy neighbour as thyself. For the reply of the young man was, All these things have I kept from my youth up, and Jesus evidently accepted this statement as true. But if the young man had loved his neighbour as himself, he would have been perfect, for Paul says that the whole law is summed up in this saying, Thou shalt love thy neighbour as thyself. But Jesus answered, If thou wilt be perfect etc., implying that the young man was not yet perfect. Therefore, Origen argued, the commandment, Thou shalt love thy neighbour as thyself, could not have been spoken by Jesus on this occasion and was not part of the original text of Matthew. The clause had been added, Origen concluded, by some tasteless scribe.

XVI. Are There Really Three (Or More) Families of Manuscripts ?

Though there is truth in the above commonly presented position and we referred to Dr. Hills at length, yet the basic idea of textual types or families has its source in the naturalistic viewpoint and we do not believe that it represents the facts concerning the distribution of MSS in the early centuries. With some 85% or more of the 5000 extant MSS falling into the category of the Received Text, there is in fact only one textual family --the Received. All that remains is so contradictory, so confused, so mixed, that not by the furthest stretch of imagination can they be considered several families of MSS.

Rather than face squarely this preponderance of support for the TR, naturalistic scholars with their ingrained bias against that text have found it convenient to talk of three or four families, as if all were basically equals. This was one of the main pillars in the Westcott and Hort theory which enabled them to construct a new Greek Testament on the fewest possible MSS.

Yet as the following quotations from *The Identity of the New Testament Text*, by Wilbur Pickering show, most present day textual scholars (mainly naturalistic) are prepared to abandon the entire idea.

♦   *"We have reconstructed text-types and families and sub-families and in so doing have created things that never before existed on earth or in heaven."* (Parvis).

♦   *"The major mistake is made in thinking of the old text-types as frozen blocks."* (Colwell).

♦   *"It is still customary to divide MSS into four well-known families. . . This classical division can no longer be maintained."* (Klijn).

♦   *"Was there a fundamental flaw in the previous investigation which tolerated so erroneous a grouping. . . Those few men who have done extensive collating of MSS, or paid attention to those done by others, as a rule have not accepted such erroneous groupings."* (Metzger).

♦   *"I defy anyone, after having carefully perused the foregoing lists . . . to go back to the teaching of Dr. Hort* [regarding text-types] *with any degree of confidence."* (Hoskier).

1. Is There a Unified Western Text?

Codex "D" Bezae is claimed to be the primary representative of this textual family, but--*"What we have called the D-text type (see chart), indeed, is not so much a text as a congeries of various readings, not descending from any one archetype. No one MS can be taken as even approximately representing the D-text."* (Kenyon).

Colwell observes that the Nestle text (25th edition) denies the existence of the Western text as an identifiable group, saying it is *"a denial with which I agree."* Speaking of von Soden's classification of the Western text, Metzger says, *"So diverse are the textual phenomena that von Soden was compelled to posit seventeen sub-groups."* And Klijn, speaking of a pure or original Western text affirms that *"such a text did not exist."*

2. Is There a Unified Alexandrian Text ?

Codex "B" Vaticanus and Codex "Aleph" Sinaiticus are the two famous representatives of the Alexandrian "family" of manuscripts. But the evidence shows that those family members don't get along very well.

Colwell offers the result of an interesting experiment.

After a careful study of all alleged B text-type witnesses in the first chapter of Mark, six Greek MSS emerged as primary witnesses--Aleph, B, L, 33, 892, 2427. Therefore the weaker B type MSS (C, Sangallenses, 157, 517, 579, 1241, and 1342) were set aside. Then on the basis of the six primary witnesses [Note how few, why not more?], an average or mean text was reconstructed including all the readings supported by the majority of the primary witnesses. Even on this restricted basis the amount of variation was dismaying. In this first chapter of Mark, each of the six witnesses differed from the average B text as follows:

◆ L   differed 19 times;
◆Aleph   differed 26 times;
◆2427   differed 32 times;
◆33   differed 33 times;
◆B   differed 39 times;
◆892   differed 41 times.

These results show convincingly that any attempt to reconstruct the text on the basis of B-type MSS is doomed to failure. The text is an artificial entity that never existed.

Hoskier, after filling 450-pages with a detailed and careful discussion of the errors in Codex B and another 400 on the idiosyncrasies of Codex Aleph, affirms that in the Gospels alone these two MSS differ well over 3,000 times, which number does not include minor errors such as spelling, nor variants between certain synonyms which might be due to *"provincial exchange."*

In Hills' chart showing the family tree of manuscripts, Papyrus 66 and Papyrus 75 are listed with the other Alexandrian MSS.

Referring again to *The Identity of the New Testament Text*: Both P66 and P75 have been generally affirmed to belong to the *"Alexandrian text-type."* Klijn offers the results of a comparison of Aleph, B, P45, P66, and P75 in the passages where they are all extant (John 10:7-25, 10:32-11:10, 11:19-33 and 11:43-56). He considered only those places where Aleph and B disagree and where at least one of the papyri joins either Aleph or B. He found eight such places plus 43 where all three of the papyri line up with Aleph or B. He stated the result for the 43 places as follows [to which I have added figures for the Textus Receptus, *BFBS* 1946]:

P45 agrees with Aleph 19 x, with B 24 x, with TR 32 x.
P66 agrees with Aleph 14 x, with B 29 x, with TR 33 x.
P75 agrees with Aleph 09 x, with B 33 x, with TR 29 x.

P45, 66, 75 agree with Aleph 4 x, with B 18 x, with TR 20 x.
P45, 66   agree with Aleph 7 x, with B 03 x, with TR 08 x.
P45, 75   agree with Aleph 1 x, with B 02 x, with TR 22 x.
P66, 75   agree with Aleph 0 x, with B 08 x, with TR 05 x.

As for the eight other places,

P45 agrees with Aleph 2 x, with B 1 x, with TR 1 x.

P66 agrees with Aleph 2 x, with B 3 x, with TR 5 x.
P75 agrees with Aleph 2 x, with B 3 x, with TR 4 x.
60 (Each of the three papyri has other readings as well.)

Is the summary assignment of P66 and P75 to the *"Alexandrian text-type"* altogether reasonable?

If the above confuses you a little, you may be excused. But it demonstrates the knot that naturalistic critics have tied themselves into when refusing to face the fact of the Received Text. Several other examples of the futility of trying to group MSS into families (particularly the Alexandrian) are given on pages 48-58 of *The Identity of the New Testament Text* (Hereafter abbreviated *INTT*).

3.   Is There a Unified Received Text

If the 15% minority of extant MSS is hopeless confusion, what about the 85% majority? What about the text referred to as Majority, Traditional, Byzantine, Syrian, Antiochan or Received?

In sharp contrast to the above two textual "families," the MSS which fall under the category of "Received," though differing in minor details, show a very definite unity. They are family members that get along quite well.

The textual critics have attempted to offset this fact through two arguments: (1) genealogy and close copying and (2) conflation and standardization.

(1)   The Received Text Unity is NOT the result of Genealogy or Close Copying

The textual critic has sought to show that the large number of Textus Receptus MSS are merely copies one of the other. This brings us to another basic "Pillar" in the Westcott and Hort theory known as "Genealogy."

Colwell says of Hort's use of this method: *"As the justification of their rejection of the majority, Westcott and Hort found the possibilities of genealogical method invaluable. **Suppose that there are only ten copies of a document and that nine are all copies of one: then the majority can be safely rejected.** Or suppose that the nine are copied from a lost manuscript and that this lost manuscript and the other one were both copied from the original; then the vote of the majority would not outweigh that of the minority. These are the arguments with which W. and H. opened their discussion of genealogical method. . . . They show* *clearly that a majority of manuscripts is not necessarily to be preferred as correct. It is this a priori possibility which Westcott and Hort used to demolish the argument based on the numerical superiority of the adherents of the Textus Receptus."*

It is clear that the notion of genealogy is crucial to Hort's theory and purpose. He felt that the genealogical method enabled him to reduce the mass of manuscript testimony to four voices--"Neutral," "Alexandrian," "Western," and "Syrian" (*INTT*).

Textual research, however, has shown that the great mass of Textus Receptus MSS are not merely copies one of another, but most are independent offspring of different lines of transmission which go deeply into the past.

The research of Kirsopp Lake into this matter was a collation of Mark, chapter eleven, in all the MSS of Mt. Sinai, Patmos, and the Patriarchal Library and collection of St. Saba at Jerusalem.

This collation covers three of the great ancient collections of MSS; and these are not modern conglomerations, brought together from all directions. Many of the MSS, now at Sinai, Patmos, and Jerusalem must be copies written in the scriptoria of these monasteries. We expected to find that a collation covering all the MSS in each library would show many cases of direct copying. But there are practically no such cases. Moreover, the amount of direct genealogy which has been detected in extant codices is almost negligible. Nor are many known MSS sister codices. The Ferrar group and family 1 are the only reported cases of the repeated copying of a single archetype, and even for the Ferrar group there were probably two archetypes rather than one.

There are cognate groups--families of distant cousins but the manuscripts which we have *are almost all orphan children* without brothers or sisters.

Taking this fact into consideration along with the negative result of our collation of MSS at Sinai, Patmos, and Jerusalem, it is *hard to resist the conclusion that the scribes usually destroyed their exemplars when they had copied the sacred books.*

J. W. Burgon, because he had himself collated numerous minuscule MSS, had remarked the same thing years before Lake.

Now those many MSS were executed demonstrably at different times in different countries. They bear signs in their many hundreds of copies representing the entire area of the Church, except where versions were used instead of copies in the original Greek. And yet, of multitudes of them that survive, hardly any have been copied from any of the rest. On the contrary, they are discovered to differ among themselves in countless unimportant particulars; and every here and there single copies exhibit idiosyncrasies which are altogether startling and extraordinary. There has therefore demonstrably been no collusion--no assimilation to an arbitrary standard--no wholesale fraud. It is certain that every one of them represents a MS, or a pedigree of MSS, older than itself; and it is but fair to suppose that it exercises such representation with tolerable accuracy. (*INTT*)

Let the reader ponder this fact that most of the thousands of MSS in the Received Text grouping represent long lines of independent transmission rather than tightly knitted genealogy or copying among contemporaries.

(2) The Received Text Did Not Develop from Conflation or Official Standardization

"The Syrian text," Hort said, *"must in fact be the result of a 'recension,' in the proper sense of the word, a work of attempted criticism, performed deliberately by editors and not merely by scribes. An authoritative Revision at Antioch . . . was itself subjected to a second authoritative Revision carrying out more completely the purposes of the first. At what date between A.D. 250 and 350 the first process took place, it is impossible to say with confidence. The final process was apparently completed by A.D. 350 or thereabouts."*

Hort tentatively suggested Lucian (who died in 311) as perhaps the leader in this movement [*INTT*].

Because the TR is a generally fuller and longer text than that found among the other "families," Hort postulated that it must have come about through the combining of the shorter readings in the other textual groups.

The passages Hort listed are Mark 6:33; 8:26; 9:38; 9:49; Luke 9:10; 11:54; 12:18; 24:53. Since Hort discusses the first of these passages at great length, it may serve very well as a sample specimen.

Mark 6:33--*And the people saw them departing and many knew Him, and ran together there on foot out of all the cities,*

(Then follow three variant readings.)

    (1)   and came before them and came together to Him.
                         "Traditional" Reading.
    (2)   and came together there.   "Western" Reading.
    (3)   and came before them.   "Alexandrian" Reading.

John Burgon (1882) immediately registered one telling criticism of this hypothesis of conflation in the Traditional text. *"Why,"* he asked, *"if conflation was one of the regular practices of the makers of the*

Traditional text, could Westcott and Hort find only eight instances of the phenomenon? After ransacking the Gospels for 30 years, they have at last fastened upon eight!"

Westcott and Hort disdained to return any answer to Burgon's objection, but it remains a valid one. If the Traditional text was created by fourth century Antiochian editors, and if one of their habitual practices had been to conflate (combine) Western and Alexandrian readings, then surely more examples of such conflation ought to be discoverable in the Gospels than just Hort's eight. But only a few more have since been found to add to Hort's small deposit. Kenyon (1912) candidly admitted that he didn't think that there were very many more. And this is all the more remarkable because not only the Greek manuscripts but also the versions have been carefully canvassed by experts, such as Burkitt and Souter and Lake, for readings which would reveal conflation in the Traditional text.

Moreover, even the eight alleged examples of conflation which Westcott and Hort did bring forward are not at all convincing. At least they did not approve themselves as such in the eyes of Bousset (1894). This radical German scholar united with the conservatives in rejecting the conclusions of these two critics. In only one of their eight instances did he agree with them. In four of the other instances he regarded the Traditional reading as the original reading, and in the three others he regarded the decision as doubtful. *"Westcott and Hort's chief proof,"* he observed, *"has almost been turned into its opposite."*

In these eight passages, therefore, it is just as easy to believe that the Traditional reading is the original and that the other texts have omitted parts of it as to suppose that the Traditional reading represents a later combination of the other two readings [Hills].

Kenyon does refer in passing to *An Atlas of Textual Criticism* by E. A. Hutton (London: Cambridge University Press, 1911) which he says contains added examples of conflation.

Upon inspection, the central feature of the 125-page work proves to be a purportedly complete list of triple variant readings in the New Testament where the "Alexandrian," "Western," and "Byzantine" texts are pitted against each other. Hutton adduces 821 instances. Out of all that, a few cases of possible *"Syrian conflation"* (aside from Hort's eight) may be culled--such as in Matt. 27:41, John 18:40, Acts 20:28, or Rom. 6:12. Twenty years ago a Hortian might have insisted that John 10:31 also has a *"Syrian conflation,"* but now that P66 moves the "Syrian" reading back to 200 A.D., a different interpretation is demanded.

Hutton's list may well be open to considerable question; but if we may take it at face value for the moment, it appears that the ratio of

"Alexandrian-Western-Byzantine" triple variants to possible *"Syrian conflations"* is about 100:1. In other words, for every instance where the "Syrian" text is possibly built on the "Neutral" and "Western" texts, there are a hundred where it is not.

That raises another problem. If the "Syrian" text is eclectic, where did it get the material that is its private property? As Burgon observed at the time, *"It is impossible to 'conflate' in places where B, Aleph and their associates furnish no materials for the supposed conflation. Bricks cannot be made without clay. The materials actually existing are those of the Traditional Text itself"* [INTT].

Coming now to the related argument of an official standardization of the text, Hills asks:

> *"Why is it that the Traditional (Byzantine) text is found in the vast majority of the Greek New Testament manuscripts rather than some other text, the Western text, for example, or the Alexandrian? What was there about the Traditional (Byzantine) text which enables it to conquer all its rivals and become the text generally accepted by the Greek Church?"*

The classic answer to this question was given by Westcott and Hort in their celebrated Introduction (1881). They believed that from the very beginning the Traditional (Byzantine) text was an official text with official backing and that this was the reason why it overcame all rival texts and ultimately reigned supreme in the usage of the Greek Church. They regarded the Traditional text as the product of a thorough-going revision of the New Testament text which took place at Antioch in two stages between 250 and 350 A.D. They believed that this text was the deliberate creation of certain scholarly Christians at Antioch, and that the presbyter Lucian (d. 312) was probably the original leader in this work. According to Westcott and Hort, these Antiochian scholars produced the Traditional text by mixing together the Western, Alexandrian, and Neutral (B-Aleph) texts.

What would be the motive which would prompt these supposed editors to create the Traditional New Testament text? According to Westcott and Hort, their motive was to eliminate hurtful competition between the Western, Alexandrian, and Neutral (B-Aleph) texts by the creation of a compromise text made up of elements of all three of these rival texts. *"The guiding motives of their* [the editors'] *criticism are transparently displayed in its effects. It was probably initiated by the distracting and inconvenient currency of at least three conflicting texts in the same region. The alternate borrowing from all implies that no selection of one was made. Each text may perhaps have found a patron in some leading personage or see, and thus seemed to call for a conciliation of rival claims."*

In other words, Westcott and Hort's theory was that the Traditional text was an official text created by a council or conference of bishops and leading churchmen meeting for the express purpose of constructing a New Testament text on which all could agree, and in their discussion of the history of the Traditional text they continue to emphasize its official character. This text, they alleged, was dominant at Antioch in the second half of the fourth century, *"probably by authority."* It was used by the three great Church Fathers of Antioch, namely, Diodorus (d. 394), Chrysostom (345-407), [This explains why Hort was so anxious to make Chrysostom the first Church Father to use the Received Text.] and Theodore of Mopsuestia (350-428). Soon this text was taken to Constantinople and became the dominant text of that great, imperial city-- perhaps even the official text. Then, due to the prestige which it had obtained at Constantinople, it became the dominant text of the whole Greek-speaking Church. *"Now Antioch,"* Westcott and Hort theorized, *"is the true ecclesiastical parent of Constantinople; so that it is no wonder that the traditional Constantinople text, whether formally official or not, was the Antiochian text of the fourth century. It was equally natural that the text recognized at Constantinople should eventually become in practice the standard New Testament of the East."*

Thus Westcott and Hort bore down heavily on the idea that the Traditional (Byzantine) text was an official text. It was through ecclesiastical authority, they believed, that this text was created, and it was through ecclesiastical authority that this text was imposed upon the Church, so that it became the text found in the vast majority of the Greek New Testament manuscripts. This emphasis on ecclesiastical authority, however, has been abandoned by most present-day scholars. As Kenyon (1912) observed long ago, there is no historical evidence that the Traditional text was created by a council or conference of ancient scholars. History is silent concerning any such gathering. *"We know,"* he remarks, *"the names of several revisers of the Septuagint and the Vulgate, and it would be strange if historians and Church writers had all omitted to record or mention such an event as the deliberate revision of the New Testament in its original Greek."*

Recent studies in the Traditional (Byzantine) text indicate still more clearly that this was not an official text imposed upon the Church by ecclesiastical authority or by the influence of any outstanding leader. Westcott and Hort, for example, regarded Chrysostom as one of the first to use this text and promote its use in the Church. But studies by Geerlings and New (1931) and by Dicks (1948) appear to indicate that

Chrysostom could hardly have performed this function, since he himself does not seem always to have used the Traditional text. Photius (815-897) also, patriarch of Constantinople, seems to have been no patron of the Traditional text, for, according to studies by Birdsall (1956-1958), he customarily used a mixed type of text called the "Caesarean" text.

Thus recent research has brought out more clearly the fact that the true New Testament text has never been an official text. It has never been dependent on the decisions of an official priesthood or convocation of scholars. All attempts to deal with the New Testament text in this way are bound to fail. It was rather through the testimony of the Holy Spirit operating in the hearts of individual Christians and gradually leading them, by common consent, to reject false readings and to preserve the true.

XVII. The Triumph of the Received Text

From what we have seen above, the history of the New Testament Text is not to be seen as three or four textual families, or several streams of transmission but rather as one great stream with numbers of small eddies along the edges. These eddies are more pronounced at the beginning of the stream.

The following illustration from *INTT* gives a simple illustration of the true picture of textual history.

It may be safely said that the greatest spiritual battle that was ever fought on this planet was fought between the powers of Darkness and Light during the first two centuries after our Lord ascended back to Heaven. With the LIVING WORD returned to glory, Satan turned all of his fury upon the WRITTEN WORD.

This is the key to understanding the history of the New Testament Text. Any theory of transmission which does take this into account is totally adrift.

As the evolutionist seeks to explain the geological phenomena of this planet without any cataclysmic intervention (i.e. the Flood), so Hort said *"there are no signs of deliberate falsification of the text for dogmatic purposes."* But, it is the constant declaration of the early Church Fathers to the contrary.

Most tampering of the text took place before 200 A.D. And most was done in the Western areas furthest from the location of the original autographs.

Colwell says, *"The overwhelming majority of variant readings were created before the year 200."* Scrivener says, *"The worst corruptions to which the N.T. has ever been subjected originated within a hundred years after it was composed."* Kilpatrick states, *"The creation of new variants ceased by 200 A.D. because it became impossible to sell them."*

Between 18 and 24 of the 27 New Testament books were written originally to cities in Asia Minor and Greece. None were written to Alexandria. But it was precisely in these Western and Alexandrian areas that corrupted pretenders to the true text became prominent.

John Burgon said, *"Vanquished by THE WORD INCARNATE, Satan next directed his subtle malice against THE WORD WRITTEN. Hence, the extraordinary fate which befell certain early transcripts of Scripture. First, heretical assailants; then, orthodox defenders; lastly and above all, self-constituted critics--each had a hand in the corrupting influences which were actively at work throughout the first hundred years after the death of the Apostle John. Profane literature has never known anything approaching to it--can show nothing at all like it.*

Satan's darts were defeated indeed through the multiplication in every quarter of unadulterated specimens of the inspired text. This provided a sufficient safeguard against the grosser forms of corruption. Did not the Holy Spirit, the Divine Author of Holy Writ pledge Himself to guide his children into all truth? The Church has been perpetually purging herself of those shamefully depraved copies which once everywhere abounded. Never, however, up to the present hour, has there been any complete eradication of all traces of the attempted mischief. These are found to have lingered on anciently in many quarters. The wounds were healed, but the scars remained--nay, the scars are discernible still.

What, in the meantime, is to be thought of those blind guides; those deluded ones, who would now persuade us to go back to those same codices, of which the Church hath already purged herself." [The above has been condensed.]

Coming back to the early centuries:

The true text continued to circulate among the more lowly and humble classes of Christian folk virtually undisturbed by the influence of other texts. Moreover, because it was difficult for these less prosperous Christians to obtain new manuscripts, they put the ones they had to maximum use. Thus all these early manuscripts of the true text were eventually worn out. The papyri which do survive seem for the most part to be prestige-texts which were preserved in the libraries of ancient schools. According to Aland (1963), both the Chester Beatty and the Bodmer Papyri may have been kept at such an institution. But the papyri with the true text were read to pieces by the believing Bible students of antiquity. In the providence of God they were used by the Church. They survived long enough, however, to preserve the true (Traditional) New Testament text during this early period of obscurity and to bring it out into the period of triumph which followed.

The victorious march of the New Testament text toward triumph was realized in the 4th century. The great 4th century conflict with the Arian heresy brought orthodox Christians to a theological maturity which enabled them, under the leading of the Holy Spirit, to perceive the superior doctrinal soundness and richness of the true text. In ever increasing numbers Christians in the higher social brackets abandoned the corrupt prestige-texts which they had been using and turned to the well-worn manuscripts of their poorer brethren, manuscripts which, though meaner in appearance were found in reality to be far more precious, since they contained the true New Testament text. No doubt they paid handsome sums to have copies made of these ancient books, and this was done so often that these venerable documents were worn out through much handling by the scribes. But before these old manuscripts finally perished, they left behind them a host of fresh copies made from them and bearing witness to the true text. Thus it was that the true (Traditional) text became the standard text now found in the vast majority of the Greek New Testament manuscripts.

During the march of the Traditional (Byzantine) text toward supremacy many manuscripts of the Traditional type must have perished. The investigations of Lake (1928) and his associates indicate that this was so. *"Why,"* he asked, *"are there only a few fragments* [even in the two oldest of the monastic collections, Sinai and St. Saba] *which come from a date earlier than the 10th century?"* There must have been in existence many thousands of manuscripts of the gospels in the great days of Byzantine prosperity, between the 4th and the 10th centuries.

As a result of these investigations, Lake found it *"hard to resist the conclusion that the scribes usually destroyed their exemplars when they copied the sacred books."* If Lake's hypothesis is correct, then the manuscripts most likely to be destroyed would be those containing the Traditional text. For these were the ones which were copied most during the period between the 4th and the 10th centuries, as is proved by the fact that the vast majority of the later Greek New Testament manuscripts are of the Traditional type.

By the same token, the survival of old uncial manuscripts of the Alexandrian and Western type, such as B, Aleph, and D, was due to the fact that they were rejected by the Church and not read or copied but allowed to rest relatively undisturbed on the library shelves of ancient monasteries. Burgon (1883) pointed this out long ago, and it is most significant that his observation was confirmed more than forty years later by the researches of Lake.

When we say that the Holy Spirit guided the Church to preserve the true New Testament text, we are not speaking of the Church as an organization but of the Church as an organism. We do not mean that in the latter part of the 4th century the Holy Spirit guided the bishops to the true text and that then the bishops issued decrees for the guidance of the common people. Investigations indicate that the Holy Spirit's guidance worked in precisely the opposite direction. The trend toward the true (Traditional) text began with the common people, the rank and file, and then rapidly built up such strength that the bishops and other official leaders were carried along with it. Chrysostom, for example, does not seem to have initiated this trend, for, as stated above, studies by Geerlings and New and by Dicks indicate that Chrysostom did not always use the Traditional text.

There is evidence that the triumphal march of the Traditional (Byzantine) text met with resistance in certain quarters. There were some scribes and scholars who were reluctant to renounce entirely their faulty Western, Alexandrian, and Caesarean texts. And so they compromised by following sometimes their false texts and sometimes the true (Traditional) text. Thus arose those classes of mixed manuscripts described by von Soden and other scholars. This would explain also the non-Traditional readings which Colwell and his associates have found in certain portions of the lectionary manuscripts. And if Birdsall is right in his contention that Photius (815-897), patriarch of Constantinople, customarily used the Caesarean text, this too must be regarded as a belated effort on the part of this learned churchman to keep up the struggle against the Traditional text. But his endeavor was in vain. Even before his time the God-guided preference of the common people for the true (Traditional) New Testament text had prevailed, causing it to be adopted generally throughout the Greek-speaking Church [Hills].

We conclude this section with several penetrating statements by Zane Hodges:

> *"Herein lies the greatest weakness of contemporary textual criticism. Denying to the TR any claim to represent the actual form of the original text, it is nevertheless unable to explain its rise, its*

comparative uniformity, and its dominance in any satisfactory manner."

He states further, *"All minority text forms are, on this view, merely divergent offshoots of the broad stream of transmission whose source is the autographs themselves."*

He says again, *"Under normal circumstances, the older a text is than its rivals, the greater are its chances to survive in a plurality or a majority of the texts extant at any subsequent period. But the oldest text of all is the autograph. Thus it ought to be taken for granted that, barring some radical dislocation in the history of transmission, a majority of texts will be far more-likely to represent correctly the character of the original than a small minority of texts. This is especially true when the ratio is an overwhelming 8:2. Under any reasonably normal transmission conditions, it would be quite impossible for a later text-form (which critics declare the TR to be) to secure so one-sided a preponderance."*

PART THREE:

WITNESS OF THE EARLY CHURCH FATHERS TO THE RECEIVED TEXT

XVIII. A Key Pillar in the Westcott and Hort Theory

This section seeks to gather what early church leaders had to say about the actual text of the New Testament. What do they say about the attempt to corrupt or preserve it? Did they have a part in this? We are especially interested in what kind of text they quoted from in their numerous writings. Do they bear witness to the text variously referred to as Byzantine, Syrian, Majority, Traditional or Received? Or do these early Fathers quote from a small minority of conflicting manuscripts known as Alexandrian, Western, Neutral, etc., i.e. the kind of manuscripts which Drs. Westcott and Hort used last century to build their revised Greek New Testament? This Greek Testament has been the basis of nearly all 20th century translations.

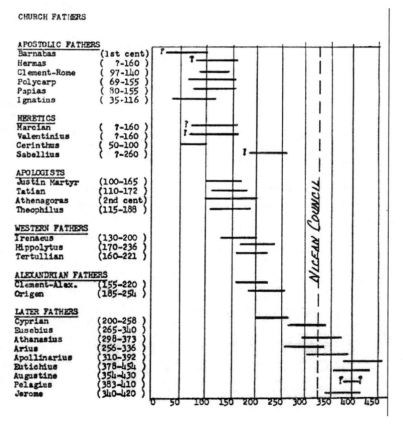

Much of the material in this section has been gathered from *The Identity of the New Testament Text* by Wilbur Pickering.

Without agreeing with all of its conclusions, this book is among the most authoritative to be written on the text of the New Testament in our generation. As D. A. Carson (no friend of the Received Text) has said that it is *"the most formidable defense of the priority of the Byzantine text yet published in our day."*

Many authors and textual critics are quoted in Pickering's book. They have given different names to the various "families" of texts. For the sake of simplicity we will refer to these as either Received Text (TR) or Westcott and Hort (WH).

Dr. Hort claimed that Chrysostom who died in 407 was the first Church Father to characteristically use the TR. He said that the readings characteristic of the Received Text are never found prior to about A.D. 350. This is a fundamental pillar in the Westcott and Hort theory and if shown to be untrue, as Kenyon says *"there would be an end to Hort's theory, for its premises would be shown to be thoroughly unsound."*

XIX. A Survey of Leading Church Fathers

Polycarp (69-155)

For many years he was the pastor of the church of Smyrna in Asia Minor. Irenaeus (130-200) states that he was a disciple of the Apostle John. In writing to the Philippian church (115), he makes about fifty clear quotations from many of the N.T. books. He said, *"Whoever perverts the sayings of the Lord, that one is the firstborn of Satan."*

Justin Martyr (100-165)

He was born in Samaria and died in Rome. Wilkinson stated, *"Beginning shortly after the death of the Apostle John, four names stand out in prominence whose teachings contributed both to the victorious heresy and to the final issuing of manuscripts of a corrupt New Testament. These four are Justin Martyr, Tatian, Clement of Alexandria, and Origen."* Many good things have justifiably been said about him. But he made the fatal mistake of presenting the Christian message in philosophical terms. Newman indicates that to Justin, Christ's work on the cross was not so much to satisfy the Divine justice, but rather through such an example to enlighten men and turn them from the worship of demons to God. Miller says, *"The texts of Hippolytus, Methodius, Irenaeus, and even of Justin, are not of that exclusively western character which Hort ascribes to them. TR readings occur almost equally with others in Justin's works and predominate in the other three."*

Tatian (110-172)

He was a learned teacher who was "converted" to Christianity and studied under Justin Martyr at Rome. He turned to Syrian Gnosticism. He wrote the *Diatessaron* in which he combined the four Gospel narratives into one, eliminating the genealogies and all passages referring to Christ's Jewish descent. According to Metzger, the heretic Marcion (died 160) also did this with his copy of the Gospel of Luke. The *Diatessaron* was so corrupted that in later years a bishop of Syria threw out 200 copies, since church members were mistaking it for the true Gospel.

Dionysius (died 176)

He was Bishop of Corinth. He complained that his own letters had been tampered with, and worse yet, the Holy Scriptures also. Notice how all this contradicts Hort's statement *"There are no signs of deliberate falsification of the text for dogmatic purposes."* During the 2nd century, the battle raged between God and Satan over the preservation of the Written Word. Any theory of textual transmission which does not take this into account and seeks to explain *"natural processes"* is totally adrift.

Metzger states, *"Irenaeus, Clement of Alexandria, Tertullian, Eusebius and many other Church Fathers accused the heretics of corrupting the Scriptures in order to have support for their special views."* Burgon says, *"Even the orthodox were capable of changing a reading for dogmatic reasons. Epiphanius states that the orthodox deleted 'he wept' from Luke 19:41 out of jealousy for the Lord's divinity."*

Irenaeus (130-200)

He was a western Father. He was born in Asia Minor, and in his youth was a disciple of the aged Polycarp. He labored for some years in Lyons (Gaul) and became its bishop in 177. He accused heretics of corrupting the Scriptures. His major work *Against Heretics* (c. 185) is about equal in volume to the writings of all the preceding Church Fathers put together. He quotes the last twelve verses of Mark. He quotes from every N.T. book except Philemon and III John. Thus the dimensions of the New Testament canon recognized by Irenaeus are very close to what we hold today.

Irenaeus said, *"The doctrines of the apostles had been handed down by the succession of bishops being guarded and preserved, without any forging of the Scriptures, allowing neither additions nor curtailment."*

He demonstrates his concern for the accuracy of the text by defending the traditional reading of a single letter. The question is whether John wrote 666 or 616 in Rev. 13:18. Irenaeus asserts that 666 is found *"in all the most approved and ancient copies"* and that *"those men who saw John face to face"* bear witness to it. And he warns *"there shall be no light punishment upon him who either adds or subtracts anything from the Scriptures."*

Considering Polycarp's friendship with John, his personal copy of Revelation would probably have been taken from the Autograph. And considering Irenaeus' veneration for Polycarp, his personal copy was probably taken from Polycarp's.

Since 1881, the word "vinegar" in Mt. 27:34 has been despised as a *"late Byzantine"* reading. There are seven early witnesses against it. Irenaeus is one of the eighteen witnesses for it. Contrary to Hort's view, Miller found that Irenaeus sided with the TR 63 times and with the WH 41 times.

Gaius (f. 175-200)

He was an orthodox Father who wrote between A.D. 175 and 200. He names Asclepiades, Theodotus, Hermophilus and Apolomides as heretics who prepared corrupted copies of the Scriptures and had disciples that multiplied these.

Clement of Alexandria (155-220)

He was a leader in the famous Catechetical School. He speaks of his teacher Pantaenus with the greatest praise, *"the deepest Gnostic."* Though a forerunner of Origen and a prime developer of the corrupt religious system of the era, yet Miller's research shows he quoted more frequently from the TR than from the WH (82 to 72).

Tertullian (160-221)

He was from Carthage in North Africa. He accused heretics of corrupting the Scriptures in order to gain support for their special views. Distinctive TR quotations can be found in his writings. He says of his right to the N.T. Scriptures, *"I hold sure title deeds from the original owners themselves. . . . I am the heir of the apostles. Just as they carefully prepared their will and testament and committed to a trust . . . even so I hold it."*

Around the year 208, he urged the heretics to *"Run over to the apostolic churches, in which the very thrones of the apostles are still pre-eminent in their places, in which their own authentic writings are read. Achaia is very near you, in which you find Corinth. Since you are not far from Macedonia you have Philippi . . . and the Thessalonians. Since you are able to cross to Asia, you get Ephesus. Since, moreover, you are close upon Italy, you have Rome, from which there comes even into our own hands the very authority of the apostles themselves. "*

It seems that Tertullian is claiming that Paul's Autographs were still being read in his day (208); but, at the very least, he must mean they were using faithful copies.

Dr. D. A. Waite states that Tertullian refers to I Jn. 5:7.

Hippolytus (170-236)

He was a western Father, active in the Roman church and greatly influenced by Irenaeus. Hort claimed he quoted from an exclusively western text. Miller states that TR readings predominate in his writings. Hoskier says that his quotations from I Thess. 4:13-17 and I Thess. 2:1-12 are generally on the side of the TR.

Origen (185-254)

He is considered by many to be the most profound mind in the history of the church. But in fact it may be said that he had a greater corrupting influence on the early church and on the Bible itself than any man.

Origen was born in Alexandria, Egypt, the cradle of Gnosticism. He and Clement before him were renowned teachers in Alexandria's famous Catechetical School. This school was a center of philosophical and scientific learning as well as theology.

He practiced rigorous asceticism, memorized large portions of Scripture and wrote commentaries on much of the Bible. *Miller's Church History* states, *"He sought to gather the fragments of truth scattered throughout the pagan philosophies and unite them to Christian teaching so as to present the Gospel in a form that would not offend but rather ensure the conversion of Jews, Gnostics, and cultivated heathen. "*

Origen said, *"Infants are baptized for the forgiveness of sins. "* He did not believe in the resurrection of the body. He believed in universalism, that all including demons would eventually be saved. His theology included a kind of reincarnation of the soul.

He was given to wild allegorizing of Scripture, saying *"The Scriptures are of little use to those who understand them as written. "* Though Origen says, *"There never was a time when the Son was not. "* His attempts to explain the Father's *"begetting"* of the Son have somewhat left this issue in doubt. In the famous dispute that arose in Alexandria between Arius and Athanasius (4th century) over the deity of Christ, Origen was called the father of Arianism.

Adam Clarke says he was the first to teach purgatory. A number of the doctrines which later found their way into Romanism have their source in this man. J. H. Newman who was made a Cardinal after he left the Church of England for the Church of Rome said, *"I love the name of Origen; I will not listen to the notion that so great a soul was lost."* The fact that the Catholic Bibles contain the seven additional books known as the Apocrypha may be traced to Origen's inclusion of these books in his own "doctored" Greek manuscripts. This indicates that he placed tradition and Scripture on about the same footing--a prime tenet in Roman theology.

Reumann in *The Romance of Bible Scripts and Scholars* says that Origen had a team of scribes whose purpose it was to "correct" the manuscripts (pp 50-56).

Westcott refers to his alteration of Mark 6:3. Hills states that he altered Matthew 19:17-21 and Burgon that he altered Luke 2:14. Kilpatrick says, *"The creation of new variants ceased about 200 A.D. because it became impossible to sell them. From the 3rd century onward, even an Origen could not effectively alter the text."*

Origen himself, referred to the tampering of manuscripts in his day. *"Nowadays, as is evident, there is a great diversity between the various manuscripts, either through the negligence of certain copyists, or the perverse audacity shown by some in correcting the text, or through the fault of those, who, playing the part of correctors, lengthen or shorten it as they please."*

Hort stated regarding Origen, *"His Scripture quotations to the best of our belief exhibit no clear and tangible traces of the TR."* However, Edward Miller, in his exhaustive study of the Fathers, found that Origen sided with the TR 460 times and with the WH 491 times. This is a powerful proof that even in Alexandria at this early date, the distinctive readings of the Received Text were almost as common as that of the other.

Hills states, *"In the first fourteen chapters of the Gospel of John (that is, in the area covered by P66) out of 52 instances in which the TR stands alone, Origen agrees with it 20 times and disagrees with it 32 times. Thus to assertions that Origen knew nothing of the TR becomes difficult indeed to maintain."* It is argued that these TR readings are not really Origen's, but represent alterations made by scribes who copied Origen's works to make them conform with the TR. However, a number of these distinctively TR readings in Origen also appear in P66.

Origen spent the later part of his life in Caesarea where his corruptive influence affected later generations, including Eusebius (265-340) and Jerome (340-420). Newman says, *"Palestine, where Origen spent the latter half of his life has always been devoted to his memory and faithful to his teachings."*

Wilkinson says, *"When we come to Origen, we speak the name of him who did the most of all to create and give direction to the forces of apostasy down through the centuries. His corrupted manuscripts of the Scriptures were well arranged and balanced with subtlety. The last one hundred years have seen much of the so-called scholarship of European and English Christianity dominated by the subtle and powerful influence of Origen."*

Eusebius (265-340)

He was from Caesarea. He was known as the Father of Church History because of his 10 volume *Ecclesiastical History*. He was a devoted follower and defender of Origen. Wilkinson says, *"Eusebius worshiped at the altar of Origen's teachings. He claims to have collected 800 of Origen's letters, to have used Origen's six-column Bible, the Hexapla, in his Biblical labors. Assisted by Pamphilus, he restored and preserved Origen's library at Caesarea."*

Eusebius sought to reconcile the heretical Arius of Alexandria (denied the eternal existence of Christ) with the orthodox Athanasius at the Nicean Council in 325. He was highly favorable to Constantine; and as we shall see, was commissioned by the Emperor to produce a version of the Bible based on Origen's manuscripts.

Jerome (340-420)

He was born in Italy. Jerome later presided over monastic institutions in Bethlehem. He and his wife were earnest students of Origen's works. He was the means of powerfully forwarding the cause of celibacy and monasticism, especially among women. In 382, Jerome at the request of Pope Damasus revised the Latin Bible; this new translation became the famous *Latin Vulgate*.

Wilkinson says, *"Jerome was devotedly committed to the textual criticism of Origen, 'an admirer of Origen's critical principles' as Swete says. To be guided aright in his forthcoming translation, Jerome went to the famous library of Eusebius at Caesarea where the voluminous manuscripts of Origen had been preserved. Among these was a Greek Bible of the Vaticanus and Sinaiticus type. It contained the seven books Protestants have rejected as being spurious--Tobit, Wisdom, Judith, Baruch, Ecclesiasticus, First and Second Maccabees. The existence of these books in Origen's Bible is sufficient evidence to reveal that tradition and Scripture were on equal footing in the mind of that theologian. His other doctrines, such as purgatory and transubstantiation had now become as essential to the imperialism of the Papacy as was the teaching that tradition had equal authority with the*

Scripture. "

Thus this "Bible" was designed to give in Latin, the same Romanizing flavor as the "Bible" in Greek sanctioned by Constantine.

Let the reader ponder the above twelve names, for they reveal the titanic struggle that took place between the forces of light and darkness over the text of Scripture during the first three or four centuries of Church history. Its numerical superiority in extant manuscripts shows that the Received Text was the decisive winner, and it held its ground for the next fifteen centuries. But now in our century the battle has been renewed and an even more intense conflict ensues with the proliferation of modern versions based on the text of Origen.

XX. The Research of John Burgon and Edward Miller into Patristic Quotations

Apart from searching through the writings of the Church Fathers individually, a primary source for information has been the massive compilation of John Burgon. He gathered 86,489 patristic Scripture quotations. These are bound in 16 volumes and located at the British Museum. After his death, Edward Miller gathered and edited much of Dr. Burgon's material. He prepared a book entitled *The Traditional Text of the Holy Gospels* (1896). In this work, he undertakes the mammoth task of categorizing the patristic quotations according to textual type. On pp. 99-101 is a table of 76 Church Fathers who died before 400 A.D. The number of times each refers to the TR or WH kind of text is tabulated. The overall ratio was three to two in favor of the TR.

Kenyon says the following about Miller's research: *"The results of his examination are stated by him as follows. Taking the Greek and Latin (not the Syriac) Fathers who died before A.D. 400 their quotations are found to support the TR in 2,630 instances (that is the distinctive TR readings), the WH text in 1753. Nor is this majority due solely to the writers who belong to the end of this period. On the contrary, if only the earliest writers be taken, from Clement of Rome to Irenaeus and Hippolytus (A.D. 97-236), the majority in favor of the TR is proportionately even greater, 151 to 84. Only in the Western and Alexandrian writers do we find approximate equality of votes on either side. Further, if a select list of thirty important passages be taken for detailed examination, the preponderance of early patristic evidence in favour of the TR is seen to be no less than 530 to 170, a quite overwhelming majority."*

Kenyon attempted to refute this evidence by stating that later editors "doctored" the patristic quotations to align them with the TR.   See Pickering for a refutation of this totally unworthy objection If this did occur, a wide variation among different editions of a given Father's quotations should be the norm. Miller's research did not find very much variation., Kenyon admitted as much when he said, *"The errors arising from this source would hardly affect the general result."*

Edward Miller's survey and tabulation is according to Pickering limited to the four Gospels.   In this day of the computer, it would be interesting to see a complete tabulation. However, surveys since Miller's time in the remainder of the N.T. show the-same preponderance of support for the TR.

It should also be noted that Miller's tabulations included only those readings which were either accepted as being a part of the TR tradition, or were accepted by Westcott and Hort in their critical text.   Variant readings outside of those were not included.

Wilbur Pickering gives the following abbreviated summary:

"TR readings are recognized most notably by"

100-150 A.D.   The Didache, Diognetus, Justin Martyr
150-200 A.D.   Gospel of Peter, Athenagorus, Hegesippus, Irenaeus
200-250 A.D.   Clement of Alexandria:, Tertullian, Clementines, Hippolytus, Origen
250-300 A.D.   Gregory of Thaumaturgus, Novatian, Cyprian, Dionysius of Alexandria, Archelaus
300-400 A.D.   Eusebius, Athanasius, Macarius Magnus, Hilary, Didymus, Basil, Titus of Bostra, Cyril of Jerusalem, Gregory of Nyssa, Apostolic Canons and Constitutions, Epiphanius, Ambrose.

Some Very Important Things to Remember

1. **Most tampering of the text took place before 200 and most was done in the Western areas furthest from the location of the original autographs.**

    Colwell says, *"The overwhelming majority of variant readings were created before the year 200."* Scrivener says, *"The worst corruptions to which the N.T. has ever been subjected, originated within a hundred years after it was composed."*   Kilpatrick states, *"The creation of new variants ceased by 200 A.D. because it became impossible to sell them."*

    Between 18 and 24 of the 27 New Testament books were written originally to cities in Asia Minor and Greece. *None* was written to

Alexandria. But it was the Western and Alexandrian Fathers who became the most prominent and prolific in their writings and being far from the autographs could take greater liberties and were more susceptible to a corrupted text. Most patristic quotations are from precisely these fathers. Yet even with this disadvantage, the TR has a 3:2 majority. After this period of disruption is passed, textual history shows the TR regaining an overwhelming advantage.

The above is borne out by Miller's research. *"The advantage of the TR over the WH before Origen was 2:1, setting aside Justin Martyr, Heracleon, Clement of Alexandria and Tertullian. If these four are included, the advantage of the TR drops to 1.33:1, since the confusion which is most obvious in Origen is already observable in these men. From Origen to Macarius Magnus (early 300's), the advantage drops to 1.24:1 while from Macarius to 400 A.D. it is back up to 2:1."*

2.   There is the Scripture principle, *that "God hath chosen the weak things of the world to confound the things which are mighty"* (I Cor. 1:27).

Regarding the preservation and transmission of the N.T. Scriptures, it is believed that when all the evidence is in this principle will have been shown to be upheld. In speaking to Dr. Tom Strouse, he felt that John Burgon erred at this point--that it was not primarily through the famous bishops and fathers that the Word was preserved, but rather the humble believer. The priesthood of the believer was the means, not ecclesiastical authority.

A survey of the leading Fathers shows much doctrinal deviation. Consider our own day; is it the famous church leaders who contend for the preservation and purity of God's Word, or humble believers scattered around the world. It has always been, *"the common people heard Him gladly."* Luther called the Church Fathers the Church "Babies"!

3.   Pre 400 A.D. patristic citations favour the TR over the WH by a 3:2 margin.

But this gives the impression that the WH represents a unified kind of text. It does not! Whereas the TR is reasonably unified, the WH is a hopeless grouping of conflicting readings. The only thing they have in common is their disagreement with the TR, but conflict among themselves is almost as great. There is only one textual family, the TR. Everything else is confusion.

Thus the main pillar of the Westcott and Hort theory (*"Readings characteristic of the Received Text are never found prior to 350."*) has completely crumbled in the light of the evidence.

Miller concludes: *"As far as the writers who died before 400 A.D. are concerned, the question may now be put and answered. Do they witness to the TR as existing from the first, or do they not? The results of the evidence, both as regards the quantity and the quality of the testimony, enable us to reply, not only that the TR was in existence, but that it was predominant, during the period under review. Let anyone who disputes this conclusion make out for the Western Text, or the Alexandrian, or the text of Vaticanus and Sinaiticus, a case from the evidence of the Fathers which can equal or surpass that which has now been placed before the reader."*

XXI. Specific Examples of the Early Patristic Support for Received Text Readings

ASSERTION: *"There is no unambiguous evidence that the Byzantine Text-type was known before the middle-of the fourth century."* D. A. Carson.

DOCUMENTATION:

KJV **Mk. 1:1-2**	*"The beginning or the gospel of Jesus Christ, the Son of God; as it in written In the prophets. . . "*
Irenaeus (130-202)	*"Mark does thus commence his Gospel narrative 'The beginning of the Gospel of Jesus, Christ, the Son of God, as it is written in the prophets.' . . . Plainly does, the commencement of the Gospel quote the words of the holy prophets, and point out Him . . . whom they confessed as God and Lord."* (Against Heresies III: 10:5, :11:4, :16:3)
KJV **Mk. 16:19**	*"So then after the Lord had spoken unto them, he was received up into heaven, and sat on the right-hand of God."*
Irenaeus (130-202)	*"Also towards the conclusion of his Gospel, Mark says: 'So then, after the Lord Jesus had spoken to them., He was received up into heaven, and sitteth on the right hand of God.'"* (Against Heresies III: 10:6)
KJV **Lk 22:44**	*"And being in an agony he prayed more earnestly: and his sweat was as it were great drops of blood falling down to the ground."*
Justin (100-165)	*"For in the memoirs which I say were drawn up by His apostles and those who followed them, it is recorded that*

His sweat fell down like drops of blood while He was praying, and saying, 'If it be possible, let this cup pass'" (*Trypho* 103:24).

KJV **Jn. 1:18**	*"No man hath seen God at any time; the only begotten Son, which is in the bosom of the Father, he hath declared him."*
Irenaeus (130-202)	*"the only begotten Son of God, which is in the bosom of the Father." (Against Heresies* III:11:6), *"the only begotten Son, who" (IV:20:6), "the only begotten God, which" (IV: 20:11).*

KJV **Jn. 3:13**	*"And no man hath ascended up to heaven, but he that came down from heaven, even the Son of man which is in heaven."*
Hippolytus (170-236)	*"No man hath ascended up to heaven, but He that came down from heaven, even the Son of Man which is in heaven." (Against the Heresy of One Noetus* I: 1:4)

KJV **Jn. 5:3-4**	*"waiting for the moving of the water, For an angel went down at a certain season unto the pool, and troubled the water: whosoever then first after the troubling of the water stepped in was made whole of whatsoever disease he had."*
Tertullian (160-221)	*"If it seems a novelty for an angel to be present in waters, an example of what was to come to pass has*

forerun. An angel, by his intervention, was want to stir the pool at Bethsaida. They who were complaining of ill-health used to watch for him; for whoever had been the first to descend into them, after his washing ceased to complain." (*On Baptism* I: 1:5)

KJV **Jn. 6:69**	*"And we believe and are sure that thou art that Christ, the Son of the living God."*
Irenaeus (130-202)	*"By whom also Peter, having been taught, recognized Christ as the Son of the living God." (Against Heresies* III: 11:6)

KJV **Jn. 14:17**	*"but ye know him; for he dwelleth with you, and shall be in you."*
P66 (c. 200)	*"shall be in you."*

KJV **Acts 8:36-37**	*"See, here is water; what doth hinder me to be baptized? And Philip said, If thou believest with all thine heart, thou mayest. And he answered and said, I believe that Jesus Christ is the Son of God."*

Cyprian (200-258)	*"In the Acts of the Apostles: Lo, here is water; what is there which hinders me from being baptized? Then said Phillip, If thou believest with all thine heart thou mayest."* (*The Treatises of Cyprian* I: 1:17)

KJV **I Tim 3:16**	*"And without controversy great is the mystery of godliness: God was manifest in the flesh."*
Ignatius (35-116)	*"God was in the flesh."* (*To the Ephesians* 1:1:7)
Hippolytus (170-236)	*"God was manifested in the flesh."* (*Against the Heresies of Noetus* I: 1:17)
Dionysius (3rd cent.)	*"For God was manifested in the flesh."* (*Conciliations* I: 1:853)

KJV **I Jn. 5:7-8**	*"For there are three that bear record in heaven, the Father, the word, and the Holy Ghost: and these three are one. And there are three that bear witness in earth, the Spirit, and the water, and the blood: and these three agree in one."*
Cyprian (200-258)	*"The Lord says, 'I and the Father are one,' and again it is written of the Father, and of the Son, and of the Holy Spirit, 'and these three are one.'"* (The Treatises of Cyprian I: 1:6)

KJV **Rev. 22:14**	*"Blessed are they that do his commandments, that they may have right to the tree of life, and may enter in through the gates into the city,"*
Tertullian (160-221)	*"Blessed are they who act according to the precepts, that they may have power over the tree of life, and over the gates, for entering into the holy city."* (*On Modesty* I: 19:2)

CONCLUSION:

KJV **II Pet. 3:16**	*"As also in all his epistles, speaking in them of these things; in which are some things hard to be understood, which they that are unlearned and unstable wrest, as they do also the other Scriptures, unto their own destruction."*
Tertullian (160-221)	*"Now this heresy of yours does not receive certain Scriptures; and whichever of them it does receives it perverts by means of additions and diminutions, for the accomplishment of its own purposes."* (*On Prescriptions Against Heresies* I: 17:1)

Thomas M, Strouse, Ph.D.
Maranatha Baptist Graduate School of Theology
Watertown, WI 53094

PART FOUR:

A SURVEY OF THE NEW TESTAMENT DOCUMENTS

We now come to a survey of the New Testament documents themselves. In our survey of the MSS, as explained above, it will often be a survey of corruption for many of the earlier MS have remained solely because of their corruption and subsequent disuse by the early Christians.

XXII. A Survey of the Papyrus Fragments

1. What Is Papyrus

Papyrus is the source of our word "paper." It was made from the papyrus plant which grew along the water's edge. It is to be distinguished from vellum or parchment which was made from animal skins, though Herodotus (484-425 B.C.) is quoted as saying that parchment was papyrus. This, however, refers to what is called vegetable parchment. Though not cheap, it was a lot less expensive to use than vellum (the word for fine parchment).

2. A List of the Papyrus Fragments

Over the past one hundred years, some eighty-eight papyrus fragments of the New Testament have been discovered in Egypt. Many of them were found at Oxyrhynchus, 120 miles South of Cairo in the Libyan Desert.

The following is a complete list taken originally from the 26th Edition of the *Nestle-Aland Greek New Testament*. (This appeared in the *Truth About King James Version Controversy* by Stewart Custer.)

Symbol	Century	City	Contents
P01	III	Philadelphia	Portions of Matthew
P02	VI	Florence	Portions of John
P03	VI, VII	Vienna	Portions of Luke
P04	III	Paris	Portions of Luke
P05	III	London	Portions of Luke
P06	IV	Strasbourg	Portions of John
P07	IV-VI(?)	Kiev	Portions of Luke
P08	IV	Berlin	Portions of Acts
P09	III	Cambridge, MA	Portions of I John
P10	IV	Cambridge, MA	Portions of Romans
P11	VII	Leningrad	Portions of I Corinthians
P12	III	New York	Portions of Hebrews

Symbol	Century	City	Contents
P13	III/IV	London & Florence	Portions of Hebrews
P14	V	Sinai	Portions of I Corinthians
P15	III	Cairo	Portions of I Corinthians
P16	III/IV	Cairo	Portions of Philippians
P17	IV	Cambridge	Portions of Hebrews
P18	III/IV	London	Portions of Revelation
P19	IV/V	Oxford	Portions of Matthew
P20	III	Princeton	Portions of James
P21	IV/V	Allentown, PA	Portions of Matthew
P22	III	Glasgow	Portions of John
P23	III	Urbana, IL	Portions of James
P24	IV	Newton Center, MA	Portions of Revelation
P25	IV	Berlin	Portions of Matthew
P26	ca. 600	Dallas	Portions of Romans
P27	III	Cambridge	Portions of Romans
P28	III	Berkeley	Portions of John
P29	III	Oxford	Portions of Acts
P30	III	Ghent	Portions of I & II Thess.
P31	VII	Manchester	Portions of Romans
P32	ca. 200	Manchester	Portions of Titus
P33	VI	Vienna	Portions of Acts
P34	VII	Vienna	Portions of I and II Cor.
P35	IV(?)	Florence	Portions of Matthew
P36	VI	Florence	Portions of John
P37	III/IV	Ann Arbor, MI.	Portions of Matthew
P38	ca. 300	Ann Arbor, MI	Portions of Acts
P39	III	Chester, PA.	Portions of John
P40	III	Heidelberg	Portions of Romans
P41	VIII	Vienna	Portions of Acts
P42	VII/VIII	Vienna	Portions of Luke
P43	VI/VII	London	Portions of Revelation
P44	VI/VII	New York	Portions of Matthew & John
P45	III	Dublin	Parts of Mt, Mk, Lk, Jn, Act
P46	ca. 200	Dublin	Ro/1Co/Gal/Eph/Col/1Th/ Heb
P47	III	Dublin	Portions of Revelation
P48	III	Florence	Portions of Acts
P49	III	New Haven, CN	Portions of Ephesians
P50	IV/V	New Haven, CT	Portions of Acts
P51	ca. 400	Oxford	Portions of Galatians
P52	II	Manchester	Portions of John
P53	III	Ann Arbor, MI	Portions of Matthew & Acts

Symbol	Century	City	Contents
P54	V/VI	Princeton	Portions of James
P55	VI/VII	Vienna	Portions of John
P56	V/VI	Vienna	Portions of Acts
P57	IV/V	Vienna	Portions of Acts
P59	VI	New York	Portions of John
P60	VII	New York	Portions of John
P61	ca. 700	New York	Rom/1Co/Phi/Col/1Th/Tit/Plm
P62	IV	Oslo	Portions of Matthew
P63	ca. 600	Berlin	Portions of John
P64	ca. 200	Oxford & Barcelona	Portions of Matthew
P65	III	Florence	Portions of I Thess.
P66	ca. 200	Cologne	Portions of John
P68	VII(?)	Leningrad	Portions of I Corinthians
P69	III	Oxford	Portions of Luke
P70	III	Oxford	Portions of Matthew
P71	IV	Oxford	Portions of Matthew
P72	III/IV	Cologne	Portions of I, II Pet, & Jde
P73	?	Cologne	Portions of Matthew
P74	VII	Cologne	Act/1Pe/2Pe/Jam/1Jn/2Jn/3Jn/Jde
P75	III	Geneva	Portions of Luke
P76	VI	Vienna	Portions of John
P77	II/III	Oxford	Portions of Matthew
P78	III/IV	Oxford	Portions of Jude
P79	VII	Berlin	Portions of Hebrews
P80	III	Barcelona	Portions of John
P81	IV	Barcelona	Portions of I Peter
P82	IV/V	Strasbourg	Portions of Luke
P83	VI	Louvain	Portions of Matthew
P84	VI	Louvain	Portions of Mark & John
P85	IV/V	Strasbourg	Portions of Revelation
P86	IV	Cologne	Portions of Matthew
P87	III	Cologne	Portions of Philemon
P88	IV	Milan	Portions of Mark

The above gives the student a good overview of the date and location of the papyri. It has the disadvantage of giving the impression that these "Portions" are fairly sizeable. In fact, in most cases, they are only fragments. For example, the Portions of John in P52 is only the one small fragment below

Therefore much of the papyri is often too fragmentary to show whether it supports the characteristic differences found in the Received Text or those found in Vaticanus and Sinaiticus (the two pillars of the revised text of Westcott and Hort). Given the close proximity of the papyri finds to Alexandria, where much of the early corruption of MSS took place, it is to be expected that this same corruptive influence is to be found in a number of the more substantial papyri portions. This is the case, but to the consternation of textual critics who would have us think that the TR is a late text, the papyri give quite a lot of support to the TR also.

A small papyrus fragment of the Gospel
of John (p52), c. AD 125 (Jn. xviii. 31–33, 37, 38).

papyrus fragment of the Gospel of John (P52), c. AD 124 (Jn 18:31-33, 37).

3.   Papyri Support for the Alexandrian and Received Text Types

In his desire to demonstrate early support for the Alexandrian text, Stewart Custer lists nine papyri which manifest that text:

> P20--3rd century, James
> P23--4th century, James
> P45--3rd century, Acts
> P46--3rd century, Epistles of Paul
> P47--3rd century, Revelation
> P50--4th century, Acts
> P52, 2nd century, John (see above)
> P66--2nd century, John
> P75--2nd or 3rd century, John

I find it remarkable that after listing the eighty-eight papyri, he is only prepared to list nine which support the Vaticanus kind of text (and when we use the word "support," please keep in mind what was said about the so-called "families.")

Many years ago, Kenyon made a similar list and to those of Custer he would add:

P04--3rd century, 16 verses of Luke
P05--3rd century, 30 verses of John
P08--4th century, 27 verses of Acts
P13--3rd or 4th century, longer portions of Hebrews

These MSS and those listed after P66 (The list in *Our Bible and the Ancient Manuscripts* goes to P66.) apparently did not give enough firm support to the Vaticanus or Alexandrian type of MS for Custer to list them. But what I want the reader to see here is that (+/-) 13 papyri out of 88 is hardly overwhelming support for that text type.

Among the above, those which are most important, and the ones which scholars spend most of their time with--the ones that have had the greatest influence on the modern critical text of the New Testament are P45 and P46 (known as the Chester Beatty Papyri, named after their discoverer), and P66 and P75 (known as *"Bodmer Papyrus II,"* named after their owner M. M. Bodmer).

But, upon examination of these four *"most important"* papyri, it is no wonder why they were left on the shelf and not used. In them we see a manifest example of the hand of Satan in corrupting the text in that part of the world (far off from the location of the autographs).

Refer back to Part Two, where the amount of agreement between these four papyri and Sinaiticus, Vaticanus and the TR was demonstrated. With regard to the distinctive differences of each, the four papyri gave greater support to the TR than to Vaticanus or Sinaiticus. By adding the figures we see the following instances of support.

Sinaiticus	60 times
Vaticanus	124 times
Received Text	139 times

Now, please remember these four papyri are the "favorite sons" of the modern textual critic. (All were listed by Custer.) Remember too, that they came from that part of the world where the forces of corruption were greatest. And then consider their dates--3rd century, 200 A.D., 200 A.D., 3rd century. (Thus the earliest of the papyri.) Therefore, though marred, the traditional text base is clearly attested in the papyri of Egypt.

4.   Several Examples of Doctrinal Deviation in the Papyri

There are serious errors in Papyrus 66. For example, in John 19:5,

Papyrus 66 omits the following famous sentence, *"And he saith unto them, Behold the, Man."* Four Old Latin manuscripts and one Coptic manuscript also omit this reading. This omission seems to be a mutilation of the sacred text at the hands of heretics, probably Gnostics. They seem to have disliked the idea that Christ, whom they regarded as exclusively a heavenly Being, actually became a man and was crucified.

John 1:34 *"And I saw, and bare record that this is the Son of God."*
P5 and P77 change this to read *"God's chosen One."*

John 3:13 *"The Son of Man who is in heaven"*
Removed from P66 and P75.

John 6:69 *"Thou art the Christ the Son of the Living God."*
P75 changes to, *"The Holy One."*

John 9:35 *"Dost thou believe on the Son of God?"*
P66 and P75 change to *"Son of Man."*

Jn 9:38-39 *"And he said, Lord, I believe. And he worshiped Him."*
P75 omits.

John 1:18 *"only begotten Son"*
P66 and P77 change to *"only begotten God."* This is a Gnostic perversion! They taught that there were various levels of Spiritual beings (i.e. lesser gods) between God and man.

There are many examples of this. See 200 Omissions in Modern Versions. Many of these can be traced back to the Egyptian Papyri.

5.   "Strange" Copying in the Papyri

In general, P75 copies letters one by one; P66 copies syllables, usually two letters in length; P45 copies phrases and clauses.

The accuracy of these assertions can be demonstrated. That P75 copied letters one by one is shown in the pattern of the errors. He has more than sixty readings that involve a single letter, and not more than ten careless readings that involve a syllable. But P66 drops sixty-one syllables (twenty-three of them in "leaps") and omits as well a dozen articles and thirty short words. In P45 there is not one omission of a syllable in a "leap" nor is there any list of "careless" omissions of syllables. P45 omits words and phrases.

As an editor the scribe of P45 wielded a sharp axe. The most striking aspect of his style is it conciseness. The dispensable word is dispensed with. He omits adverbs, adjectives, nouns, participles, verbs, personal pronouns--without any compensating habit of addition. He frequently omits phrases and clauses. He prefers the simple to the compound word. In short, he favors brevity. He shortens the text in at least fifty places in singular readings alone. But he does not drop syllables or letters. His shortened text is readable.

Enough of these have been cited to make the point that P66 editorializes as he does everything else--in a sloppy fashion. He is not guided in his changes by some clearly defined goal which is always kept in view. If he has an inclination toward omission, it is *not "according to knowledge"* but is whimsical and careless, often leading to nothing but nonsense. (Colwell in *INTT*)

And yet this is the very kind of source material that modern "experts" would have us go back to in the "reconstruction" of the New Testament Text.

The image of the true text was marred in Egypt, but it cannot be emphasized too strongly that the distinctive TR readings abound in the papyri.

6.   A Summary of the Evidence

Referring again to *INTT*.

Many other studies are available, but that of H.A. Sturz sums it up. He surveyed all the available papyri to discover how many papyrus-supported Byzantine readings exist. In trying to decide which were distinctively Byzantine, he made a conscious effort to err on the conservative side, so the list is shorter than it might be.

He found and listed the evidence for more than 150 distinctive Byzantine readings that have early [before 300 A.D.] papyrus support. He found a further 700 Byzantine readings which had been altered by Western and Alexandrian influence.

The magnitude of this vindication can be more fully appreciated by recalling that only about 30 percent of the New Testament has early papyrus attestation, and much of that 30 percent has only one papyrus. Where more than one covers a stretch of text, each new MS discovered vindicates added Byzantine readings. Extrapolating from the behavior of those in hand, if we had at least 3 papyri covering all parts of the New Testament, almost all the 5000+ Byzantine readings rejected by the critical [eclectic] texts would be vindicated by an early papyrus.

P45 Chester Beatty Gospels Papyrus--early third century. John 10:7-25
(Actual size 6.25 in. x 5.75 in.)

P46 Chester Beatty Papyrus of Pauline Epistles. Galatians 6:10- Philippians 1:1.
(Actual size 8.5 in x 6 in)

XXIII. A Survey of the Uncial Manuscripts

1. The Number of Uncials

　　According to Kurt Aland, there are now 267 extant uncial (large lettered) MSS dating from the 4th to 10th centuries. The later minuscule or small lettered MSS were used from the 9th to 16th centuries. As with the papyri, a number of the earlier ones survive solely through their lack of use because of a tampered text. Yet still the vast majority of uncial MSS support the TR against the other textual "types."

2. A Description of This Kind of Manuscript

The word "uncial" comes from *uncia*, meaning the 12th part. Each letter would take up the 12th part of a column. Count the letters per column in the picture of the Sinaiticus MS below. Further, there was generally no space between the words. (GODSOLOVEDTHEWORLD.)

Papyri was used until about the third century. From the 4th to the 14th centuries, most surviving MSS are written on parchment--tanned animal skins. A finer kind of parchment was usually made from calfskin and known as vellum. Constantine had a least 50 official Bibles made on this high quality parchment or vellum. [Perhaps Vaticanus and Sinaiticus are examples.] A palimpsest is a parchment that has been scraped and re-written upon. Codex Ephraemi Rescriptus is the earliest example.

Until about the 3rd century, the Scriptures were written on separate sheets which varied in size from 6" x 9 "to 12" x 15". The sheets were then pasted together and made into rolls of 20 sheets each. One roll was called a "biblos." Several rolls were called a "tome." The roll was wound around a stick. For Greek and Latin it was unwound horizontally from left to right. For Hebrew, it went from right to left. The longest books in the New Testament were from 30-55 feet.

Obviously the scroll was very awkward to use. Thus a proverb developed, *"A great book is a great evil."* Christianity and the desire to spread the Word was the greatest force that brought about the change from the scroll to the codex or book form. [The above is taken from Tom Strouse.] Peter Ruckman says, *"Papyri constituted a cheap paper, similar to modern day 'newsprint' . . . It is highly probable that the Codex (with papyri sheets) was invented by soul winning personal workers, who carried New Testaments with them."* Then in his characteristically expressive manner he says, *"It is certain that no real 2nd century Christian would have been caught dead with 'vellum scrolls' on him , or the high-class 'revised Versions' put out by Alexandria. Rather, the 1rst and 2nd century Bible-believing people used papyrus rolls and codices which they copied."* The explains why few papyrus copies of the TR survived the first three centuries of Roman Persecution.

3. "The Five Old Uncials"

Though there are now know to be 267 extant uncial MSS containing substantial portions of the N.T., and several hundreds more fragments; the interest of scholars has been centered on *"The Five Old Uncials"* which date back to the 4th and 5th centuries. These are as follows:

Name	Cen	Location	Contents
א Sinaiticus	IV	London	Gospels, Acts, Epistles, Revelation
A Alexandrinus	V	London	Gospels, Acts, Epistles (Minus parts of Mat., John, & 2 Cor)
B Vaticanus	IV	Rome	Gospels, Acts, Epistles (Minus parts of 1 Tim, Plm, & Heb)
C Ephraemi Rescriptus	V	Paris	Parts of all the New Testament books
D Bezae Cantabrigiensis	V	Cambridge	Parts of the Gospels, Acts, James, Jude

These five are the primary reason why we have so many modern versions today *"based on older and better manuscripts than the Authorized Version."*

(1) Sinaiticus (Aleph), British Museum

Sinaiticus was written about 350-370 A.D. It contains part of the O.T. and all [?] of the N.T. plus the Epistle of Barnabas and Shepherd of Hermes. It has four columns per page and forty-eight lines per column. It is written on vellum. This famous MS was discovered by Constantine Tischendorf in 1844 in the Monastery of St. Catherine on Mt. Sinai. It was found in a load of wastepaper about to be burned. Tischendorf suggested that it was one of 50 copies prepared by Constantine in 331 and sent by Justinian to this convent named after his mother. It was sold to the Russians and then to the British Museum in 1933. Its text is a mixture of Alexandrian and Western. (Strouse)

However, with regard to its place of origin, Kenyon says: *"Caesarea, Rome, southern Italy, have all been advocated, but the preponderance of opinion is in favor of Egypt. Every detail in its writing can be paralleled in Egyptian papyri. . . . Its kinship in text with Vaticanus, which also has instances of these peculiar forms, and with the Coptic versions is a further argument for an Egyptian origin; and if Egypt, then Alexandria is the most probable home for so splendid a piece of book production. "*

It is commonly said to be the only uncial MSS which contains the entire N.T. But it must be remembered that it omits John 5:4; 8:1-14; Matt. 16:2-3; Rom. 16:24; Mark 16:9-20 and hundreds of other words and phrases which are commonly removed from the Alexandrian Text. As with other corrupted MSS, it still shows its Received Text base and in a number of cases, agrees with the TR against the Vaticanus. (Based on Ruckman)

Hort conceded that the scribe of Vaticanus *"reached by no means a high standard of accuracy." "Sinaiticus is acknowledged on every side to be worse than B in every way." (INTT)*

Using the TR as a basis of comparison, Burgon found that Sinaiticus in the four Gospels alone omitted 3,455 words, added 839, substituted 1114, transposed 2299, modified 1265. Thus in all 8972 words are affected (Dr D. A. Waite in *An Answer to Stewart Custer*).

Waite says further, *"It is found that at least ten revisers, between the 4th and the 12th centuries busied themselves with the task of correcting its many and extraordinary perversions of the truth of Scripture."*

Yet this is one of the two main pillars of our modern versions!

Codex Sinaiticus - fourth century
British Museum
(Actual size 15 in. × 13½ in.)

Codex Sinaiticus--fourth century, British Museum (Actual size 15 in. x 13.5 in.)

(2)   Vaticanus (B), Vatican Library

This is the chief pillar of our modern critical Greek Testaments--whether they be called Westcott and Hort, Nestle, Nestle-Aland, United Bible Society, etc, etc. It is common today to read that a given modern translation (See N.I.V. preface.) or Greek text is based on an "eclectic" text. This is to give the impression that the "best readings" from many sources were used including the TR. This must be exposed as being totally misleading. When the critical text was first produced by Westcott and Hort, so also today the primary pillar is Codex B and it is only departed from with the greatest reluctance.

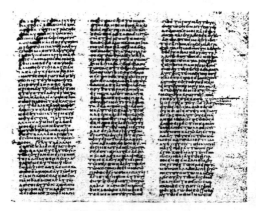

Codex Vaticanus - fourth century
Vatican Library
(Actual size 10½ in. × 10 in.)

Codex Vaticanus--fourth century, Vatican Library (Actual size 10.5 in. x 10 in.)

Vaticanus was also written around 350-370 A.D. and has been in the Vatican Library since 1481. It contains most of the O.T. and most of the N.T., except for part of Hebrews, the Pastoral Epistles, and Revelation. Strouse says its text is mixed but in the main Alexandrian.

It survived those eleven centuries before being placed in the Vatican Library because Christians didn't use it. Its reading in John 1:18 *"only begotten God"* showed every Christian exactly what it was--a Gnostic perversion.   It contains the *"Epistle to Barnabas"* and the O.T. Apocrypha.   Tischendorf claimed it was copied by the same man as Sinaiticus (doubtful considering the differences). The Pope insisted that it must be earlier than Sinaiticus, because of the way divisions are placed in the Gospels.

Scholars have called it *"the best text," "the most perfectly preserved text," "a remarkably pure text," "a beautifully preserved text," "highly legible,"* etc. According to Westcott and Hort it was written in Italy. They called it a *"neutral text preserved on an island of purity."* (How Italy fits this description is a little difficult to see!) However, modern scholars have abandoned the theory that Vaticanus was written there, as they also have that it was written by or copied from Eusebius in Caesarea. (Ruckman)

On this last point, Kenyon said, *"Hort was inclined to assign it to Rome, and others to southern Italy or Caesarea; but the association of its text with the Coptic (Egyptian) Versions and with Origen, and the style of writing (notably the Coptic forms used in some of the titles), point rather to Egypt and Alexandria."* (*The Text of the Greek Bible*)

The writing is small and neat, but its appearance has been spoilt by a later scribe, who finding the ink faded went over every letter, except those which he thought incorrect. (Kenyon)

Again using the Received Text as the basis of comparison, in the four Gospels; B is found to omit at least 2877 words, to add 536, to substitute 935, to transpose 2098 and to modify 1132--for a total of 7578 words that have in some way been altered. (Waite quoting Burgon)

With primarily Vaticanus followed by Sinaiticus, you have the *"two main pillars"* of the modern Greek Text, and yet not only have they departed from the Received Text, but also there is the sharpest disagreement between them. Herman Hoskier in *Codex B and its Allies* said, *"There are over 3000 real differences between Aleph and B in the Gospels alone!"* This is the kind of "foundation" that one has in the new versions.

Burgon, who spent years examining both MSS said, *"It is in fact easier to find two consecutive verses in which these two MSS differ, than two consecutive verses in which they entirely agree."*

And yet these are the two MSS on which Westcott and Hort and all subsequent editors--Nestle, Aland, Souter and the United Bible Society text put their greatest reliance. (Waite)

The reader will begin to see the frequent omissions in these two manuscripts (actually the tip of the iceberg) by looking at our paper *"Two Hundred Omissions in Modern Versions."*

(3)   Alexandrinus (A), British Museum

Kenyon says it was written early in the 5th century with the writing being later in character than B or Aleph. It is missing much of Matthew and part of John and II Corinthians. It attaches the two *"Epistles of Clement"* to the end of the canonical books. With regard to its place or origin, everything points to Alexandria Egypt. (Kenyon)

It has the Byzantine Text in the Gospels and the Alexandrian elsewhere. (Strouse) Kenyon is typical of scholars who are uncomfortable with this Byzantine presence and says, *"In the Gospels it shows signs of the Antiochian revision."*

Though not relied upon as heavily as Aleph and B, the arrival of this text in Europe sixteen years after the publication of the Authorized Version gave the first stimulus-towards the criticism of the text. (Kenyon) The naturalistic critic considers this a tragedy that *"it arrived sixteen years too late."* However, in this the Bible believer can see the providence of God delaying its arrival until the Authorized Version was safely in the hands of His people.

Codex Alexandrinus–fifth century
British Museum
(Actual size 12¾ in. × 10¼ in.)

Codex Alexandrinus--fifth century British Museum (Actual size 12.75" x 10.25")

(4) Ephraemi Rescriptus (C), Bibliotheque Nationale in Paris

Written originally in the 5th century and containing the whole of both Testaments, it was in the 12th century converted into a palimpsest.

That is, the original writing was washed out, and some works of a certain Ephraim Syrus were written over it. Many leaves also were thrown away. It now contains parts of all the N.T. books except for II Thessalonians and II John. Much of the original writing has been discerned. (Kenyon) Strouse says the text is mixed but pro-Byzantine. Kenyon (as we would expect) speaks of this Byzantine presence being due to *"its correctors."*

Burgon would rank this codex behind Alexandrinus as having the fewer corruptions among the *"five old uncials."*

(ii) Codex Ephraemi Rescriptus–fifth century
Bibliothèque Nationale, Paris
(Actual size of part reproduced 7¼ in. x 9 in.

(ii) Codex Ephraemi Rescriptus--fifth century, Biblotheque Nationale, Paris
(Actual size of part reproduced 7.25 in. X 9 in.)

(5)   Bezae (D), University Library at Cambridge

This is the worst of the lot. It is the reason, and practically the only reason (There is nothing else quite like it, except, a few Old Latin MSS. *INTT*) why the so-called Western Text is said to be an expansion of the original text. Kenyon calls it the chief representative of the Western Text. Unlike the usual Alexandrian MS which abbreviates, this one in the most curious of ways enlarges the text. It is placed in either the 5th or 6th centuries.

It was presented to Cambridge by the great Reformation Scholar Theodore Beza. But it is a case of a good man with a very bad MS.

Kenyon says, *"Codex Bezae is the most peculiar manuscript of the New Testament, showing the widest divergences, both from the*

Alexandrian and Received type text.

Its format is different than the others above. The page size is much smaller, measuring 10 by 8 inches. And then it is the first extant example of a N.T. being written in two languages--Greek and Latin.

It only contains the Gospels and Acts and III John 11-15. The Gospels are arranged in what Kenyon calls, "the order common in the Western Church--Matthew, John, Luke, Mark."

The existence of a Latin text is sufficient proof by itself that the manuscript was written in the West of Europe, where Latin was the language of literature and daily life.

The extent of its corruption can be seen in the ways that it agrees with Aleph and B (against the TR), in omitting key passages, but then expanding passages in many other places.

Codex Bezæ--sixth century
Cambridge University Library
(Actual size of each page 10 in. × 8½ in.)

Codex Bezae--sixth century, Cambridge University Library
(Actual size of each page 10 in x 8.5 in.)

As one example, notice its addition <u>between</u> Matt. 20:28 and 29:

"But seek ye to increase from that which is small, and to become less from that which is greater. When ye enter into a house and are summoned to dine, sit not down in the highest places, lest perchance a more honorable man than thou shall come in afterwards, and he that bade thee come and say to thee, go down lower; and thou shall be ashamed. But if thou sittest down in the worst place, and one worse than thee come in afterwards, then he that bade thee will say

to thee, go up higher; and this shall be advantageous for thee. "

(6)   The "Five Old Uncials" Summarized

Here then are the *"five old uncials"* that modern scholarship would have us base our Bibles upon.

Burgon gives the following summary:

The serious deflections from the Received Text in

Alexandrinus	0842
Ephraemi Rescriptus	1798
Vaticanus	2370
Sinaiticus	3392
Bezae	4697

Each deflection may include anything from one word, to a phrase, to a verse, to several verses, etc. In the previous comparison between B, Aleph and the TR, the total number of words were counted. Also as each of these uncials do not have in every instance the same portion of Scripture remaining; the comparison is drawn only from those portions where all are extant.

Notice how the above graphically proves not only their conflict with the TR but also with each other.

Burgon's comment on this evidence sums up the sordid state of affairs that modern textual criticism has brought us to.

"We venture to assure you, without a particle of hesitation, that Aleph, B, and D are three of the most scandalously corrupt copies extant. They have become the depositories of the largest amount of fabricated readings, ancient blunders, and intentional perversions of Truth, which are discoverable in any known copies of the Word of God."

How does Stewart Custer's statement *"the Alexandrian text is older and better attested than the others"* (namely the TR) square with the above evidence?

4.   Other Important Uncial Manuscripts

Sir Frederick Kenyon's *Our Bible and the Ancient Manuscripts* is an authoritative presentation of the transmission of Scripture from the naturalistic position. It first came out in 1895 and has gone through a number of revisions and editions. The copy that I am referring to is the fifth edition that was revised and enlarged by A. W. Adams D.D. in 1958.

Along with its sister volume *The Text of the Greek Bible*, it is the classic text book on the subject.

The Bible believer will be very interested to hear what Kenyon (or his reviser) has to say on Page 213. After discussing in detail *"the five old uncials,"* he first discusses three others:

1) Claromontanus (D2), 6th century. It has the epistles of Paul in Greek and Latin. Containing as it does the Latin, it falls into the Western camp, but does not have the striking type of additions that Bezae does.

2) Basiliensis (E), 8th century, 4 Gospels, Byzantine (Received) Text.

3) Laudianus (E2), 7th century, Acts in Greek and Latin; the Greek is Byzantine.

We now come to the statement: *"Of the remaining manuscripts, we shall notice only those which have some value or interest. Many of them consist of fragments only, and their texts are for the most part less valuable. Most of them contain texts of the Syrian (Received) type, and are of no more importance than the great mass of cursives. They prove that the Syrian text was predominant in the Greek world."*

Despite his bias against the Received Text ("less valuable," "not important"), he is forced to concede that "most" of the uncials are of that kind of text. In fact of the 267 extant uncials, it is overwhelmingly so.

To be more specific, in surveying both of Kenyon's books I could only find that the following MSS were said by him to be of the Alexandrian Type (i.e. in basic alignment with Aleph, B, or A).

1) Aleph, Sinaiticus, 4th century.

2) B, Vaticanus, 4th century.

3) A, Alexandrinus, 5th century, Epistles, Gospels are TR.

4) I, Washingtonianus, 7th century, Fragments of Epistles, *"Agrees with Aleph and A more than B."*

5) L, Regius, 8th century, Gospels, *"Often agrees with B."*

6) R, Nitriensis, 6th century, Palimpsest of half of Luke, *"Akin in character to Aleph and B."*

7) T, Borgianus, 5th century, Portions of Luke and John, *"Closely associated with Aleph and B."*

8) Z, Dublinensis, 6th century, Palimpsest containing 295 verses of Matthew, *"Many agreements with Aleph."*

9) Xi, Zacynthius, 8th century, Palimpsest containing most of Luke 1 - 11, *"Its text is akin to B."*

Now there may be others and there were one or two instances where a smaller portion of a MS had some Alexandrian readings (i.e. Codex Laurensis). But out of well over two hundred uncials, these were all that Kenyon and his later revisers were prepared to mention. Further, the very marked conflict between Aleph, B, and A is magnified much further when support is sought from these other six uncials.

Nine conflicting MSS, which early Christians didn't bother to use, out of over two hundred uncials doesn't present any stronger use than the nine papyri that Custer mentions, or the eight conflations that Hort talks about.

At Marquette Manor Baptist Church in Chicago (1984), Dr. Custer said that God preserved His Word *"in the sands of Egypt."* No! God did not preserve His Word in the sands of Egypt, or on a library shelf in the Vatican Library, or in a wastepaper bin in a Catholic Monastery at the foot of Mt. Sinai. God did not preserve His Word in the "disusing," but in the "using." He did not preserve the Word by it being stored away or buried, but rather through its use and transmission in the hands of humble believers. The good copies were worn out, the corrupted ones were put on the shelf. And to repeat what Kirsopp Lake said, *"It is hard to resist the conclusion that the scribes usually destroyed their exemplars when they had copied the sacred books."*

Yet despite this, there is the same clear evidence from the earlier Uncials as there is from the Papyri. Kenyon's books list the following pre-7th century MSS as being on the side of the Received Text. Though as his statements show, he doesn't seem to be very happy to admit it.

1) A, Alexandrinus, 5th century, *"The Gospels,"* says Kenyon, *"show signs of the Antiochian revision."* Hills says, *"Another witness to the early existence of the Traditional text is Codex A [Codex Alexandrinus]. This venerable manuscript, which dates from the fifth century, has played a very important role in the history of New Testament textual criticism. It was given to the King of England in 1627 by Cyril Lucar, patriarch of Constantinople, and for many years was regarded as the oldest extant New Testament manuscript. In Acts and the Epistles Codex A agrees most closely with the Alexandrian text of the B and Aleph type, but in the Gospels it agrees generally with the Traditional text. Thus in the Gospels Codex A testifies to the antiquity of the Traditional text."*

2) C, Ephraemi, 5th century, Strouse speaks of its mixed text, but also describes it as being *"pro-Byzantine."* Kenyon speaks of its Byzantine portions as being due to its "correctors."

3) W, Washingtonianus, 4th or 5th centuries. It is now housed in the Freer Gallery of Art in Washington, D.C. It contains the four Gospels in the Western order, Matthew, John, Luke, Mark. In John and the first third of Luke the text is Alexandrian in character. In Mark the text is of the Western type in the first five chapters and of a mixed "Caesarean" type in the remaining chapters. The especial value of W, however, lies in Matthew and the last two thirds of Luke. Here the text is Traditional (Byzantine) of a remarkably pure type. According to Sanders, in Matthew the text of W is of the Kappa 1 type, which von Soden (1906) regarded as the oldest and best form of the Traditional (Byzantine) text.

The discovery of W tends to disprove the thesis of Westcott and Hort that the Traditional text is a fabricated text which was put together in the fourth century by a group of scholars residing at Antioch. For Codex W is a very ancient manuscript. B .P. Grenfell regarded it as *"probably fourth century."* Other scholars have dated it in the 5th century. Hence W is one of the oldest complete manuscripts of the Gospels in existence, possibly of the same age as Aleph. Moreover, W seems to have been written in Egypt, since during the first centuries of its existence it seems to have been the property of the Monastery of the Vinedresser, which was located near the third pyramid. If the Traditional text had been invented at Antioch in the 4th century, how would it have found its way into Egypt and thence into Codex W so soon thereafter? Why would the scribe of W, writing in the 4th or early 5th century, have adopted this newly fabricated text in Matthew and Luke in preference to other texts which (according to Hort's hypothesis) were older and more familiar to him? Thus the presence of the Traditional text in W indicates that this text is a very ancient text and that it was known in Egypt before the 4th century. (Hills)

4) N, Purpureus, 6th century, Portions of the four Gospels, *"The text is of Byzantine type, in a rather early stage of its evolution."* (Kenyon)

5) O, Sinapensis, 6th century, Matthew 13-24, Byzantine, *"Akin to N."*

6) Sigma, Rossanensis, 6th century, Matthew and Mark, Byzantine, *"A sister MS of N."*

7) Phi, Beratinus, 6th century, Matthew and Mark, Byzantine.

To these we may add the vast majority of the remaining uncial MSS (latest total number is 267) and most of several hundreds of uncial fragments. I believe the number was 320 in 1950.

Washington Codex of Gospels–late fourth or fifth century
Freer collection, Washington
(Actual size 8¾ in. × 5¾ in.)

Washington Codex of Gospels--late fourth or fifth century, Freer collection,
Washington (Actual size 8.75 in. x 5.75 in.)

XXIV. A Survey of the Cursive (Minuscule) Manuscripts

1. The Transition

In the 9th century, Greek began to be written in a small-lettered script. In the study of how God transmitted and preserved the Greek New Testament, there is an important consideration at this point which is usually overlooked.

Dr. Jakob van Bruggen (quoted in *INTT*) says: *"In the codicology the great value of the transliteration-process in the 9th century and thereafter is recognized. At that time the most important New Testament manuscripts written in majuscule script were carefully transcribed into minuscule script. It is assumed that after this transliteration-process the majuscule was taken out of circulation."* The import of this datum has not been taken into account enough in the present New Testament textual criticism. For it implies that just the oldest, best, and most customary manuscripts come to us in the new uniform of the minuscule script, does it not? This throws a totally different light on the situation that we are confronted with regarding the manuscripts. Why do the surviving ancient manuscripts show another text-type? Because they are the only survivors of their generation, and because their survival is due to the fact that they were of a different kind. Even though one continues to maintain that the copyists at the time of the transliteration handed down the wrong text-type to the Middle Ages, one can still never prove this codicologically with the remark that older majuscules have a different text. This would be circular reasoning. There certainly were majuscules just as venerable and ancient as the surviving Vaticanus or Sinaiticus, which, like a section of the Alexandrinus, presented a Byzantine text. But they have been renewed into minuscule script and their majuscule-appearance has vanished.

At latest count, there were 2764 Cursive MSS. Kenyon says, *"Only a small minority of these contain the complete New Testament and those of the four Gospels are by far the most numerous. An overwhelming majority contain the common ecclesiastical text* [one of his names for the Received Text]. *"*

Reverting to the classic means of attempted escape from this evidence, Kenyon says, *"The common ecclesiastical text, which, originating in a revision which seems to have begun in Syria at the end of the 4th century, was generally adopted throughout the Church."*

He then seeks to try and list these cursive MSS which *"appear to have in some degree escaped this revision."*

In 1948 he said that the number of minuscules were 2401. He then lists those which *"in some degree"* differ from the Received Text. Below are those which would give some support to the Alexandrian text:

1)   1 and its allies 118, 131, 209. They are now recognized as the *"Caesarean text type."*
2)   The Ferrar group, 13, 69, 124, 346. And 543, 713, 788, 826, 828, 983 "have been shown to have *traces* of the same type of text." "It forms part of the Caesarean group."
3)   28 contains many non-Byzantine readings in Mark. Also Caesarean.
4)   33 Hort said it was the best of the minuscules, for its Gospel portions agree with Vaticanus. It is called the Queen of the Cursives.

5) 157, "same class as 33"--Hort.
6) 81, "best of the minuscules in Acts."
7) 274, "contains in the margin the shorter ending to Mark" 579 is similar in this respect.
8) 565, "Has a good text with ancient readings, and in Mark is akin to the Caesarean type."
9) 1108, "A good text of the Pauline Epistles."
10) 2040, "A good text of the Apocalypse."

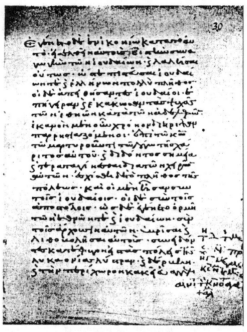

Cursive Greek MS. - 1054
British Museum
(Actual size 7 in. x 5 in.)

Cursive Greek MS--1054, British Museum (Actual Size 7 in. x 5 in.)

Assuming that when Kenyon says, "A good text of . . . ," he means that there is a fair amount of agreement with Vaticanus or the Alexandrian text, and assuming that there are some similarities between the so-called Caesarean text and Alexandrian (Origen went to Caesarea after he left Alexandria.), Kenyon is prepared to list only 22 that give even partial support to the "best" text. Twenty-two out of 2401!!

Are we to believe that in the language in which the New Testament was originally written (Greek), that only twenty-two examples of the true Word of God are to be found between the 9th and 16th centuries? How does this fulfil God's promise to preserve His Word? Why at that juncture when the uncial script was replaced by the minuscule were an overwhelming number of copies of the Received Text made, but practically none of the Alexandrian? We answer with a shout of triumph: God has been faithful to His promise. Yet in our day, the world has become awash with translations based on MSS similar to the twenty-two rather than the two and a half thousand.

XXV. History's Witness to the Spread of the Greek Received Text Amid Corrupting Influence

Referring to Benjamin Wilkinson: *"The Textus Receptus was the Bible of early Eastern Christianity. Later it was adopted as the official text of the Greek Catholic Church. There were local reasons which contributed to this result. But, probably, far greater reasons will be found in the fact that the Received Text had authority enough to become, either in itself or by its translation, the Bible of the great Syrian Church; of the Waldensian Church of northern Italy; of the Gallic Church in southern France; and of the Celtic Church in Scotland and Ireland; as well as the official Bible of the Greek Catholic Church. All these churches, some earlier, some later, were in opposition to the Church of Rome and at a time when the Received Text and these Bibles of the Constantine type were rivals. They, as represented in their descendants, are rivals to this day. The Church of Rome built on the Eusebio-Origen type of Bible; these others built on the Received Text. Therefore, because they themselves believed that the Received Text was the true apostolic Bible, and further, because the Church of Rome arrogated to itself the power to choose a Bible which bore the marks of systematic depravation, we have the testimony of these five churches to the authenticity and the apostolicity of the Received Text."*

The following quotation from Dr. Hort is to prove that the Received Text was the Greek New Testament of the East. Note that Dr. Hort always calls it the Constantinopolitan or Antiochian text:

"It is no wonder that the traditional Constantinopolitan text, whether formally official or not, was the Antiochian text of the fourth

century. It was equally natural that the text recognized at Constantinople should eventually become in practice the standard New Testament of the East."

1. Fundamentally, There Are Only Two Streams of Bibles

Anyone who is interested enough to read the vast volume of literature on this subject, will agree that down through the centuries there were only two streams of manuscripts.

The first stream which carried the Received Text in Hebrew and Greek, began with the apostolic churches, and reappearing at intervals down the Christian Era among enlightened believers, was protected by the wisdom and scholarship of the pure church in her different phases: precious manuscripts were preserved by such as the church at Pella in Palestine where Christians fled, when in 70 A.D. the Romans destroyed Jerusalem; by the Syrian Church of Antioch which produced eminent scholarship; by the Italic Church in northern Italy; and also at the same time by the Gallic Church in southern France and by the Celtic Church in Great Britain; by the pre-Waldensian, the Waldensian, and the churches of the Reformation.

This first stream appears, with very little change, in the Protestant Bibles of many languages, and in English, in that Bible known as the King James Version, the one which has been in use for three hundred years in the English-speaking world.   These manuscripts have in agreement with them, by far the vast majority of copies of the original text. So vast is this majority that even the enemies of the Received Text admit that nineteen-twentieths of all Greek manuscripts are of this class.

The second stream is a small one of a very few manuscripts. These last manuscripts are represented:

(a) In Greek: The Vatican MS, or Codex B, in the library at Rome; and the Sinaitic, or Codex Aleph, its brother.

(b) In Latin: The Vulgate or Latin Bible of Jerome.

(c) In English: The Jesuit Bible of 1582, which later with vast changes is seen in the Douay, or Catholic Bible.

(d) In English *again*: In many modem Bibles which introduce practically all the Catholic readings of the Latin Vulgate which were rejected by the Protestants of the Reformation; among these, prominently, are the Revised

Versions.

These two great families of Greek Bibles are well illustrated in the work of that outstanding scholar, Erasmus. Before he gave to the Reformation the New Testament in Greek, he divided all Greek manuscripts into two classes: those which agreed with the Received Text and those which agreed with the Vaticanus manuscript. (Nolan)

So the present controversy between the King James Bible in English and the modern versions is the same old contest fought out between the early church and rival sects; and later, between the Waldenses and the Papists from the fourth to the thirteenth centuries; and later still, between the Reformers and the Jesuits in the sixteenth century.

2.   The Final Labors of the Apostle Paul

In his later years, the apostle Paul spent more time in preparing the churches for the great future apostasy than in pushing the work farther on. He foresaw that this apostasy would arise in the West. Therefore, he spent years laboring to anchor the Gentile churches of Europe to the churches of Judea. The Jewish Christians had back of them 1500 years of training. Throughout the centuries God had so molded the Jewish mind that it grasped the idea of sin; of an invisible Godhead; of man's serious condition; of the need for a divine Redeemer.

But throughout these same centuries, the Gentile world had sunk lower and lower in frivolity, heathenism, and debauchery. It is worthy of notice that the apostle Paul wrote practically all of his epistles to the Gentile churches--to Corinth, to Rome, to Philippi, and so on. He wrote almost no letters to the Jewish Christians. Therefore, the great burden of his closing days was to anchor the Gentile churches of Europe to the Christian churches of Judea. They were to be the base. Therefore, at the end of his ministry, when fresh fields and splendid prospects were opening up for him in the West, Paul went to Jerusalem.

"There is not a word here of the church of Rome being the model after which the other churches were to be formed; it had no such preeminence--this honor belonged to the churches of Judea; it was according to them, not the church at Rome, that the Asiatic churches were modeled.

The purest of all the apostolic churches was that of the Thessalonians, and this was formed after the Christian churches in Judea. Had any preeminence or authority belonged to the church of Rome, the apostle would have proposed this as a model to all those which he formed, either in Judea, Asia Minor, Greece, or Italy" (Adam Clarke).

3.   The Early Corruption of Manuscripts

Some of this we have previously seen, but it is needful to re-emphasize certain points.

The last of the apostles to pass away was John. His death is usually placed about 100 A.D. In his closing days, he co-operated in the collecting and forming of those writings we call the New Testament. (Eusebius).

While John lived, heresy could make no serious headway. He had hardly passed away, however, before perverse teachers infested the Christian Church. These years were times which saw the New Testament books corrupted in abundance.

Eusebius is witness to this fact. He also relates that the corrupted manuscripts were so prevalent that agreement between the copies was hopeless; and that those who were corrupting the Scriptures, claimed that they really were correcting them.

This rising flood, as we shall see, had multiplied in abundance copies of the Scriptures with bewildering changes in verses and passages within one hundred years after the death of John (100 A.D.). As Irenaeus said concerning Marcion, the Gnostic: *"Wherefore also Marcion and his followers have betaken themselves to mutilating the Scriptures, not acknowledging some books at all; and, curtailing the Gospel according to Luke, and the epistles of Paul, they assert that these alone are authentic, which they have themselves shortened."*

When the warring sects had been consolidated under the iron hand of Constantine, this heretical potentate adopted the Bible which combined the contradictory versions into one, and so blended the various corruptions with the bulk of pure teachings as to give sanction to the great apostasy, now seated on the throne of power.

Beginning shortly after the death of the apostle John, four names stand out in prominence whose teachings contributed both to the victorious heresy and to the final issuing of manuscripts of a corrupt New Testament. These names are (1) Justin Martyr, (2) Tatian, (3) Clement of Alexandria, and (4) Origen. We shall speak first of Justin Martyr.

The year in which the apostle John died, 100 A.D., is given as the date in which Justin Martyr was born. Justin, originally a pagan and of pagan parentage, afterward embraced Christianity and although he is said to have died at heathen hands for his religion, nevertheless, his teachings were of a heretical nature. Even as a Christian teacher, he continued to wear the robes of a pagan philosopher.

In the teachings of Justin Martyr, we begin to see how muddy the stream of pure Christian doctrine was running among the heretical sects fifty years after the death of the apostle John. It was in Tatian, Justin Martyr's pupil, that these regrettable doctrines were carried to alarming lengths, and by his hand committed to writing. After the death of Justin Martyr in Rome, Tatian returned to Palestine and embraced the Gnostic heresy. This same Tatian wrote a Harmony of the Gospels which was called the *Diatessaron*, meaning four in one. The Gospels were so notoriously corrupted by his hand that in later years a bishop of Syria, because of the errors, was obliged to throw out of his churches no less than two hundred copies of this *Diatessaron*, since church members. were mistaking it for the true Gospel.

We come now to Tatian's pupil known as Clement of Alexandria, 200 A.D. He went much further than Tatian in that he founded a school at Alexandria which instituted propaganda along these heretical lines. Clement expressly tells us that he would not hand down Christian teachings, pure and unmixed, but rather clothed with precepts of pagan philosophy. All the writings of the outstanding heretical teachers were possessed by Clement, and he freely quoted from their corrupted manuscripts as if they were the pure words of Scripture. His influence in the depravation of Christianity was tremendous.   But his greatest contribution, undoubtedly, was the direction given to the studies and activities of Origen, his famous pupil.

When we come to Origen, we speak the name of him who did the most of all to create and give direction to the forces of apostasy down through the centuries. It was he who mightily influenced Jerome, the editor of the Latin Bible known as the Vulgate. Eusebius worshiped at the altar of Origen's teachings. He claims to have collected eight hundred of Origen's letters, to have used Origen's six-column Bible, the *Hexapla*, in his Biblical labors. Assisted by Pamphilus, he restored and preserved Origen's library. Origen's corrupted manuscripts of the Scriptures were well arranged and balanced with subtlety. The last one hundred years have seen much of the so-called scholarship of European and English Christianity dominated by the subtle and powerful influence of Origen.

Origen had so surrendered himself to the furore of turning all Bible events into allegories that he, himself, says, "The Scriptures are of little use to those who understand them as they are written." In order to estimate Origen rightly, we must remember that as a pupil of Clement, he learned the teachings of the Gnostic heresy and, like his master, lightly esteemed the historical basis of the Bible.   As Schaff says, "His predilection for Plato [the pagan philosopher] led him into many grand and fascinating errors." He made himself acquainted with the various heresies and studied under the heathen Annonius Saccas, founder of Neo-Platonism.

He taught that the soul existed from eternity before it inhabited the body, and that after death, it migrated to a higher or a lower form of life according to the deeds done in the body; and finally all would return to the state of pure intelligence, only to begin again the same cycles as before. He believed that the devils would be saved, and that the stars and planets had souls, and were, like men, on trial to learn perfection. In fact, he turned the whole Law and Gospel into an allegory.

Such was the man who from his day to this has dominated the endeavors of destructive textual critics. One of the greatest results of his life was that his teachings became the foundation of that system of education called Scholasticism, which guided the colleges of Latin Europe for nearly one thousand years during the Dark Ages.

Origenism flooded the Catholic Church through Jerome, the father of Latin Christianity. *"I love . . . the name of Origen,"* says the most distinguished theologian of the Roman Catholic Church since 1850. *"I will not listen to the notion that so great a soul was lost."* (Newman)

A final word from the learned Scrivener will indicate how early and how deep were the corruptions of the sacred manuscripts: *"It is no less true to fact than paradoxical in sound, that the worst corruptions to which the New Testament has ever been subjected, originated within a hundred years after it was composed; that Irenaeus (A.D. 150), and the African Fathers, and the whole Western, with a portion of the Syrian Church, used far inferior manuscripts to those employed by Stunica, or Erasmus, or Stephens thirteen centuries later, when molding the Textus Receptus."*

The basis was laid to oppose a mutilated Bible to the true one. How these corruptions found their way down the centuries and reappear in our revised and modern Bibles, the following pages will tell.

4. The Bible Adopted by Constantine

Miller's Church History states, *"The Epistle to the Church in Pergamos (Rev. 2:12-17) exactly describes, we believe, the state of things in Constantine's time.*

In Ephesus, we see the first point of departure, leaving their 'first love' the heart slipping away from Christ, and from the enjoyment of His love. In Smyrna, the Lord allowed the saints to be cast into the furnace, that the progress of declension might be stayed. They were persecuted by the heathen. By means of these trials Christianity revived; the gold was purified; the saints held fast the Name and the faith of Christ. Thus was Satan defeated; and the Lord so ruled that the Emperors, one after the other, in the most humiliating and mortifying circumstances, publicly confessed their defeat. But in Pergamos, the enemy changes his tactics. In place of persecution from without, there is seduction from within. Under Diocletian, Satan was the roaring lion; under Constantine he is the deceiving serpent. Pergamos is the scene of Satan's flattering power; he is within the Church."

On October 28, 312, Constantine defeated Maxentius, a rival claimant to the throne, near Rome. As they approached the battle, it is said that Constantine and his soldiers saw a glittering cross in the sky. Above it was the inscription BY THIS CONQUER. That night, it is claimed, Christ appeared to Constantine in a dream, bearing in his hand the same cross and directing him to make a banner after the same pattern.

After this "conversion," his life was a strange mixture of Christianity and paganism. He issued the Edict of Milan which legalized Christianity and put an end to the persecution of Christians.

"Constantine now took his place more openly to the whole world as the head of the church; but at the same time, retained the office of the Pontifex Maximus (the high priest of the heathen). Thus we see for the first time the unholy union, of Church and State. Bishops appeared as regular attendants upon the court; the internal matters of Christianity became affairs of the State."

According to Wilkinson (quoting from Hort and Swete in the earlier part of this paragraph), *"Constantine found three types of manuscripts, or Bibles, vying for supremacy: the Textus Receptus, the Palestinian (Eusebio-Origen), and the Egyptian. Particularly was there earnest contention between the advocates of the Textus Receptus and those of the Eusebio-Origen text. The defenders of the TR were of the humbler class who earnestly sought to follow the Scriptures. The Eusebio-Origen text was the product of the intermingling of the pure Word of God and Greek philosophy in the mind of Origen. It might be called the adaptation of the Word of God to Gnosticism.*

As Constantine embraced Christianity, it became necessary for him to choose which of these Bibles he would sanction. Quite naturally he preferred the one edited by Eusebius and written by Origen. The philosophy of Origen was well-suited to serve Constantine's religio-political theocracy."

Kenyon says, *"The Emperor himself instructed Eusebius of Caesarea, the great historian of the early church to provide fifty copies of the Scriptures for the churches of Constantinople; and the other great towns of the Empire must have required many more for their own wants."*

More specifically Ira Price says, *"Eusebius assisted by Pamphilus issued with all its critical remarks the fifth column of Origen's Hexapla."* This then was the source of the Emperor's Bible *in the O.T.* Vaticanus and Sinaiticus are examples of this "Bible."

The Latin Vulgate, the Sinaiticus, the Vaticanus, the *Hexapla,* Jerome, Eusebius, and Origen, are terms for ideas that are inseparable in the minds of those who know. The type of Bible selected by Constantine has held the dominating influence at all times in this history of the Catholic Church.   This Bible was different from the Bible of the Waldenses, and, as a result of this difference, the Waldenses were the object of hatred and cruel persecution, as we shall now show. In studying this history, we shall see how it was possible for the pure manuscripts, not only to live, but actually to gain the ascendancy in the face of powerful opposition.

Attentive observers have repeatedly been astonished at the unusual phenomenon exhibited in the meteoric history of the Bible adopted by Constantine. Written in Greek, it was disseminated at a time when Bibles were scarce, owing to the unbridled fury of the pagan emperor, Diocletian. We should naturally think that it would therefore continue long. Such was not the case.

The echo of Diocletian's warfare against the Christians had hardly subsided, when Constantine assumed the imperial purple. Even as far as Great Britain, that far had the rage of Diocletian penetrated. One would naturally suppose that the Bible which had received the promotion of Constantine, especially when disseminated by that emperor who was the first to show favor to that religion of Jesus, would rapidly have spread everywhere in those days when imperial favor meant everything. The truth is, the opposite was the outcome.

It flourished for a short space. The span of one generation sufficed to see it disappear from popular use as if it had been struck by some invisible and withering blast.

Through the providence of God the Textus Receptus was the Bible in use in the Greek Empire, in the countries of Syrian Christianity, in northern Italy, in southern France, and in the British Isles in the second century. This was a full century and more before the Vaticanus and the Sinaiticus saw the light of day. When the apostles of the Roman Catholic Church entered these countries in later centuries, they found the people using the Textus Receptus.

XXVI. A Survey of Early Versions

Having looked at the primary sources, the MSS of the Greek New Testament itself, we now look at the various foreign language versions into which it was translated during the early centuries. Here again the promise of Christ to preserve His Word and the malicious intent of Satan to corrupt that same Word came into titanic conflict. This warfare must ever be kept before the believer who would rightly understand the early translation of the Scriptures into other languages.

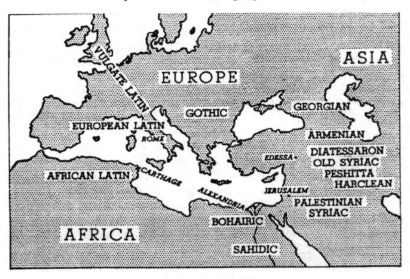

A Map of the Ancient New Testament Versions.

A Map of the Ancient New Testament Versions.

It was the Greek-speaking Church especially which was the object of God's providential guidance regarding the New Testament text, because this was the Church to which the keeping of the Greek-New Testament had been committed. But this divine guidance was by no means confined to those ancient Christians who spoke Greek. On the contrary, indications can be found in the ancient New Testament versions of this same God-guided movement of the Church away from readings which were false and misleading and toward those which were true and trustworthy.

1. The Old Latin Version

In approaching this and the other versions, we begin on the premise that God was actively superintending the translation of His Word into the other languages. Inspiration deals only with the Hebrew and Greek. But in that eventually so few could speak these languages, God's promise of preservation has no practical meaning unless he superintends the translation process.

(1) Its Origin and Character

History accords very little information about the beginnings of the Old Latin Version. And most who have written about it do so from the naturalistic position. But several key facts can be gleaned.

Tertullian speaks of an apparently complete Latin Bible circulating in North Africa (Carthage is the important city.) as far back as 190 A.D. *Ruckman speaks of it being the "spontaneous effort of African Christians."* He refers to Augustine's *"angry comment"* (354-430) :

"In the earliest days of the faith, when a Greek manuscript came into anyone's hands and he thought he possessed a little facility in both languages [i.e. Greek and Latin]*, he ventured to make a translation."*

This comment, though meant in the negative sense, may in fact point to the translation of this version.

Though looked upon with disdain by the "scholarly" Augustine, it was in fact the spontaneous effort of African Christians, and it was God who made it spontaneous. Scrivener says that *"the Latin Bible, the Italic, was translated from the Greek not later than 157."* More specifically, the Italic may refer to the particular type of the Old Latin used in northern Italy.

The International Standard Bible Encyclopedia takes us back a step further. *"The Old Latin was written in Antioch by missionaries to Africa* [north]*; it was then copied out by the common Christians in North Africa."* This would be one strong indication that the Old Latin (at least in its beginnings) was of the Received Text type, for Antioch in Syria was the chief focal point for that text.

This fact throws a great deal of light on Kenyon's statement, *"They* [many of the MSS of the Old Latin] *certainly represent a different type of text from that which we have found domiciled in Egypt of which the foremost representatives are Aleph and B."*

In dealing with the fact that Tertullian (160 221) often quotes from the Old Latin, Kenyon says, *"Tertullian writing in Africa in Latin, quotes the Scriptures freely, but he is by no means an accurate writer, and he seems often to have made his own translations from the Greek, so that his quotations have to be used with caution."*

But why is Kenyon *really* so wary of Tertullian's Old Latin quotations? The reason is not hard to find. Tertullian frequently quotes from the Received Text! It is also claimed that he quotes I John 5:7 (Dr. D. A. Waite).

Thus, though Kenyon cannot bring himself to admit it, there is a strong case to be made for the Received Text in the Old Latin Version. In scanning through the two books by Kenyon and one by Bruce, I did not see any reference to the Old Latin supporting the Alexandrian kind of text. Knowing their sympathies, if it did, they would be quick to say so!

It is true that many of the extant MSS show corruption. Wilkinson says, *"Much but by no means all of the Old Latin evidence is favorable to the Received Text."* Several of the North African MSS show an affinity to Codex Bezae.

Ruckman says that the Old Latin bears witness to the Syrian Text type where it has not been tampered with. He states that both Augustine and Tertullian testify that the scribes in Africa continually tampered with Bible MSS and that this *"explains satisfactorily the confused condition of the Old Latin by the time of Jerome."* Kenyon also says, *"As a rule, the larger divergences in the Old Latin are found in the African form, the smaller in the European."*

At this point, it should be noted that many scholars divide the Old Latin MSS into two or three families--African, European and Italian. This division though is disputed.

The Apocrypha is affixed to many copies of the Old Latin. However, those used by the Waldensians do not contain it. The Apocrypha was added to many Old Latin copies by the followers of Origen and Augustine (Ruckman from *International Standard Bible Encyclopedia*).

As is usually the case, the corrupted copies remain because they were put on a shelf. The pure form was preserved and disseminated throughout North Africa and Western Europe.

Wilkinson says, *"The word Vulgate means 'commonly used,' or 'current.' This word has been appropriated from the Bible to which it rightfully belongs. it took hundreds of years before the common people would call Jerome's Latin Bible, the 'Vulgate.'"*

(2) Manuscripts of the Old Latin

There are now about 35 extant MSS most of which are fragments. The following of the earlier ones is from Kenyon.

1) Vercellensis (a), 4th century, Gospels (mutilated) in Western order.
2) Bobiensis (k), 4th or 5th century, Mark with shorter ending.
3) Veronensis (b), 5th century, Gospels.
4) Palatinus (e), 5th century, Gospels.
5) Saretianus (j), 5th century, Fragments of John.
6) The Old Latin text in parallel, Codex Bezae (o), 5th or 6th centuries.
7) Corbeiensis II (ff2), 5th or 6th centuries, Gospels (mutilated).
8) Bobiensis (s), 5th or 6th centuries, Acts 23- 28, James, I Peter.
9) Brixianus (f), 6th century, Gospels.
10) Claramentanus (h), 6th century, Gospels but only Matthew is in Old Latin.
11) Vindobonensis (i), 6th century, Fragments of Luke and Mark.
12) Guelferbytanus (gue), 6th century, Fragments of Romans.
13) Palimpsestus Floriacensis (h), 6th or 7th centuries, Fragments of Acts, I, II Peter, I John, Revelation.
14) The Old Latin in parallel, Codex Laudianus (E), 7th century.
15) Rehdigeranus (1), 7th century, John 17-21.
16) Sangermanensis I (gi), 8th or 9th century, Gospels, but only Matthew is Old Latin.
17) Bodleianus (X2), 9th century, Nearly complete.
18) Corbeiensis I (ff1), 10th century, Matthew (mixed with Vulgate).
19) Corbeiensis (ff), 10th century, James, Epistle of Barnabas, Vulgate admixture.
20) Sangermanensis II, 10th century, Gospels, Vulgate admixture
21) Colbertinus (c), 12th century, Gospels in Old Latin, rest of N.T. added later.
22) Gigas (g), 13th century, Entire Bible, but only Acts and Revelation are Old Latin.

The above list demonstrates how copies of the Old Latin continued to be made after the translation of the Vulgate in 380. Ruckman, quoting *ISBE* says, *"The Albigenses continued to use the Old Latin long after Jerome's Vulgate came out and their preservation of this text is attributed* (according to Burkitt) *to the fact that they were 'heretics.'"*

(3) History's Witness to the Spread of the Old Latin Version

Referring to Wilkinson: Since Italy, France and Great Britain were once provinces of the Roman Empire, the first translations of the Bible by the early Christians in these parts were made into Latin. The early Latin translations were very dear to the hearts of those primitive churches. God in His wisdom invested this Bible with a charm that outweighed the learned artificiality of Jerome's Vulgate, the Bible adopted by the papacy (380). For 900 years the Old Latin held its own, and was only replaced when Latin ceased to be a living language.

Codex Vercellensis–fourth century. Vercelli, North Italy
(Actual size as reproduced, without margins, 7¼ in. ×4¼ in.)

Codex Vercellensis--fourth century, Vercelli, North Italy (Actual size as reproduced, without margins, 7.25 in. x 4.25 in.)

(a) The Old Latin in England

Onward then pushed those heroic bands of evangelists to England, to southern France, and northern Italy. The Mediterranean was like the trunk of a tree with branches running out to these parts, the roots of the tree being in Judea or Asia Minor, from whence the sap flowed westward to fertilize the distant lands. History does not possess any record of heroism superior to the sacrifices and sufferings of the early Christians in the pagan West. The first believers of ancient Britain nobly held their ground when the pagan Anglo-Saxons descended on the land like a flood. Dean Stanley holds it against Augustine, the missionary sent by the Pope in 596 A.D. to convert England, that he treated with contempt the early Christian Britons. Yes, more, he connived with the Anglo-Saxons in their frightful extermination of that pious people. And after Augustine's death, when those same pagan Anglo-Saxons so terrified the papal leaders in England that they fled back to Rome, it was the British Christians of Scotland who occupied the forsaken fields. It is evident from this that British Christianity did not come from Rome. Furthermore, Dr. Adam Clarke claims that the examination of Irish customs reveals that they have elements which were imported into Ireland from Asia Minor by early Christians.

As Rome did not send any missionaries toward the West before 250 A.D., the early Latin Bibles were well established before these churches came into conflict with Rome. Not only were such translations in existence long before the Vulgate was adopted by the Papacy, and well established, but the people for centuries refused to supplant their old Latin Bibles by the Vulgate. *"The Old Latin versions were used longest by the western Christians who would not bow to the authority of Rome-- e.g., the Donatists; the Irish in Ireland, Britain, and the Continent; the Albigenses, etc."*

Famous in history among all centers of Bible knowledge and Bible Christians was Iona, on the little island of Hy, off the northwest coast of Scotland. Its most historic figure was Columba. Upon this island rock, God breathed out His Holy Spirit and from this center, to the tribes of northern Europe. When Rome awoke to the necessity of sending out missionaries to extend her power, she found Great Britain and northern Europe already professing a Christianity whose origin could be traced back through Iona to Asia Minor. About 600 A.D., Rome sent missionaries to England and to Germany, to bring these simple Bible Christians under her dominion, as much as to subdue the pagans D'Aubigne has furnished us this picture of Iona and her missions:

"Columba esteemed the cross of Christ higher than the royal blood which flowed in his veins, and that Precious manuscripts were brought to Iona, where a theological school was founded and the Word was studied. 'Ere long a missionary spirit breathed over this ocean rock, so justly named the light of the Western world!' British missionaries carried the light of the gospel to the Netherlands, France, Switzerland, Germany, yea, even into Italy, and did more for the conversion of central Europe than the half-enslaved Roman Church."

(b) The Old Latin in France

In southern France, when in 177 A.D. the Gallic Christians were frightfully massacred by the heathen, a record of their suffering was drawn up by the survivors and sent, not to the Pope of Rome, but to their brethren in Asia Minor. Milman claims that the French received their Christianity from Asia Minor.

These apostolic Christians in southern France were undoubtedly those who gave effective help in carrying the Gospel to Great Britain. And as we have seen above, there was a long and bitter struggle between the Bible of the British Christians and the Bible which was brought later to England by the missionaries of Rome. And as there were really only two Bibles--the official version of Rome, and the Received Text--we may safely conclude that the Gallic (or French) Bible, as well as the Celtic (or British), were translations based on the Received Text. Neander claims that the first Christianity in England, came not from Rome, but from Asia Minor, probably through France.

(c)   The Old Latin amongst the Waldenses in Northern Italy

That the messengers of God who carried manuscripts from the churches of Judea to the churches of northern Italy and on brought to the forerunners of the Waldenses a Bible different from the Bible of Roman Catholicism, I quote the following :

"The method which Allix has pursued, in his History of the Churches of Piedmont, is to show that in the ecclesiastical history of every century, from the fourth century, which he considers a period early enough for the enquirer after apostolical purity of doctrine, there are clear proofs that doctrines, unlike those which the Romish Church holds, and conformable to the belief of the Waldensian and Reformed Churches, were maintained by theologians of the north of Italy down to the period when the Waldenses first came into notice. Consequently, the opinions of the Waldenses were not new to Europe in the eleventh or twelfth centuries, and there is nothing improbable in the tradition, that the Subalpine Church persevered in its integrity in an uninterrupted course from the first preaching of the Gospel in the valleys. It is held that the pre-Waldensian Christians of northern Italy could not have had doctrines purer than Rome unless their Bible was purer than Rome's; that is, their Bible was not of Rome's falsified manuscripts."

In the fourth century, Helvidius, a great scholar of northern Italy, accused Jerome, whom the Pope had empowered to form a Bible in Latin for Catholicism, with using corrupt Greek manuscripts. How could Helvidius have accused Jerome of employing corrupt Greek manuscripts if Helvidius had not had the pure Greek manuscripts? And so learned and so powerful in writing, and teaching was Jovinian, the pupil of Helvidius, that it demanded three of Rome's most famous fathers--Augustine, Jerome, and Ambrose--to unite in opposing Jovinian's influence. Even then, it needed the condemnation of the Pope and the banishment of the Emperor to prevail. But Jovinian's followers lived on and made the way easier for Luther.

There are modern writers who attempt to fix the beginning of the Waldenses from Peter Waldo who began his work about 1175. This is a mistake. The historical name of this people, as properly derived from the valleys where they lived, is Vaudois. Their enemies, however, ever sought to date their origin from Waldo. Waldo was an agent, evidently raised up of God to combat the errors of Rome. Gilly, who made extensive research concerning the Waldenses, pictures Waldo in his study at Lyon, France, with associates, a committee, *"like the translators of our own Authorized Version."* Nevertheless, the history of the Waldenses, or Vaudois, begins centuries before the days of Waldo.

There remains to us in the ancient Waldensian language *The Noble Lesson (La Nobla Leycon)*, written about the year 1100 A.D. which assigns the first opposition of the Waldenses to the Church of Rome to the days of Constantine the Great, when Sylvester was Pope.

Thus when Christianity, emerging from the long persecutions of pagan Rome, was raised to imperial favor by the Emperor Constantine, the Italic Church in northern Italy--later the Waldenses--is seen standing in opposition to papal Rome. Their Bible was of the family of the renowned Itala. It was that translation into Latin which represents the Received Text. Its very name, "Itala" is derived from the Italic district, the regions of the Vaudois.

Of the purity and reliability of this version, Augustine, speaking of different Latin Bibles (about 400 A.D.) says:

"Now among translations themselves the Italian [Itala] is to be preferred to the others, for it keeps closer to the words without prejudice to clearness of expression."

The old Waldensian liturgy which they used in their services down through the centuries contained *"texts of Scripture of the ancient Version called the Italick."*

The Reformers held that the Waldensian Church was formed about 120 A.D. from which date on, they passed down from father to son the teachings they received from the apostles. The Latin Bible, the Italic, was translated from the Greek not later than 157 A.D. We are indebted to Beza, the renowned associate of Calvin, for the statement that the Italic Church dates from 120 A.D. From the illustrious group of scholars which gathered round Beza, 1590 A.D., we may understand how *the Received Text was the bond of union* between great historic churches.

That Rome in early days corrupted the manuscripts while the Italic Church handed them down in their apostolic purity, Allix, the renowned scholar, testifies. He reports the following as Italic articles of faith: *"They receive only, saith he, what is written in the Old and New Testament. They say, that the Popes of Rome, and other priests, have depraved the Scriptures by their doctrines and glosses."*

It is recognized that the Itala was translated from the Received Text (Syrian, Hort calls it); that the Vulgate is the Itala with the readings of the Received Text removed.

Where did this Vaudois Church amid the rugged peaks of the Alps secure these uncorrupted manuscripts? In the silent watches of the night, along the lonely paths of Asia Minor where robbers and wild beasts lurked, might have been seen the noble missionaries carrying manuscripts, and verifying documents from the churches in Judea to encourage their struggling brethren under the iron heel of the Papacy. The sacrificing labors of the apostle Paul were bearing fruit. His wise plan to anchor the Gentile churches of Europe to the churches of Judea provided the channel of communications which defeated continually and finally, the bewildering pressure of the Papacy. Or, as the learned Scrivener has beautifully put it:

"Wide as is the region which separates Syria from Gaul, there must have been in very early times some remote communication by which the stream of Eastern testimony, or tradition, like another Alpheus, rose up again with fresh strength to irrigate the regions of the distant West."

We have it now revealed how Constantine's *Hexapla* Bible was successfully met. A powerful chain of churches, few in number compared with the manifold congregations of an apostate Christianity, but enriched with the eternal conviction of truth and with able scholars, stretched from Palestine to Scotland. If Rome in her own land was unable to beat down the testimony of apostolic Scriptures, how could she hope, in the Greek-speaking world of the distant and hostile East, to maintain the supremacy of her Greek Bible?

The Scriptures of the apostle John and his associates, the traditional text--the Textus Receptus, if you please--arose from the place of humiliation forced on it by Origen's Bible in the hands of Constantine and became the Received Text of Greek Christianity. And when the Greek East for one thousand years was completely shut off from the Latin West, the noble Waldenses in northern Italy still possessed in Latin the Received Text.

To Christians such as these, preserving apostolic Christianity, the world owes gratitude for the true text of the Bible. It is not true, as the Roman Church claims, that she gave the Bible to the world. What she gave was an impure text, a text with thousands of verses so changed as to make way for her unscriptural doctrines. While upon those who possessed the veritable Word of God, she poured out through long centuries her stream of cruel persecution. Or, in the words of another writer:

"The Waldenses were among the first of the peoples of Europe to obtain a translation of the Holy Scriptures. Hundreds of years before the Reformation, they possessed the Bible in manuscript in their native tongue. They had the truth unadulterated, and this rendered them the special objects of hatred and persecution. . . . Here for a thousand years, witnesses for the truth maintained the ancient faith. . . . In a most wonderful manner it [the Word of Truth] was preserved uncorrupted through all the ages of darkness."

The struggle against the Bible adopted by Constantine was won. But another warfare, another plan to deluge the Latin West with a corrupt Latin Bible was preparing. We hasten to see how the world was saved from Jerome and his Origenism.

2. The Latin Vulgate of Jerome

(1) A History of the Times

Referring to Benjamin Wilkinson.

The Papacy, defeated in her hope to control the version of the Bible in the Greek world when the Greek New Testament favored by Constantine was driven into retirement, adopted two measures which kept Europe under its domination. First, the Papacy was against the flow of Greek language and literature to Western Europe. All the treasures of the classical past were held back in the Eastern Roman Empire, whose capital was Constantinople. For nearly one thousand years, the western part of Europe was a stranger to the Greek tongue. As Doctor Hort says:

"The West became exclusively Latin, as well as estranged from the East; with local exceptions, interesting in themselves and valuable to us but devoid of all extensive influence, the use and knowledge of the Greek language died out in Western Europe."

When the use and knowledge of Greek died out in Western Europe, all the valuable Greek records, history, archaeology, literature, and science remained untranslated and unavailable to Western energies. No wonder, then, that this opposition to using the achievements of the past brought on the Dark Ages (476 A.D. to 1453 A.D.).

This darkness prevailed until the half-century preceding 1453 A.D. when refugees, fleeing from the Greek world threatened by the Turks, came west introducing Greek language and literature. After Constantinople fell in 1453, thousands of valuable manuscripts were secured by the cities and centers of learning in Europe. Europe awoke as from the dead, and sprang forth to newness of life. Columbus discovered America. Erasmus printed the Greek New Testament. Luther assailed the corruptions of the Latin Church. Revival of learning and the Reformation followed swiftly.

The second measure adopted by the Pope which held the Latin West in his power was to stretch out his hands to Jerome (about 400 A.D.), the monk of Bethlehem, reputed the greatest scholar of his age, and appeal to him to compose a Bible in Latin similar to the Bible adopted by Constantine in Greek. Jerome, the hermit of Palestine, whose learning was equaled only by his boundless vanity, responded with alacrity. Jerome was furnished with all the funds that he needed and was assisted by many scribes and copyists.

By the time of Jerome, the barbarians from the north who later founded the kingdoms of modern Europe, such as England, France, Germany, Italy and other countries, were overrunning the Roman Empire. They cared nothing for the political monuments of the empire's greatness, for these they leveled to the dust. But they were overawed by the external pomp and ritual of the Roman Church. Giants in physique, they were children in learning. They had been trained from childhood to render full and immediate submission to their pagan gods. This same attitude of mind they bore toward the Papacy, as one by one they substituted the saints, the martyrs, and the images of Rome for their former forest gods. But there was danger that greater light might tear them away from Rome.

If, in Europe, these children fresh from the north were to be held in submission to such doctrines as the papal supremacy, transubstantiation, purgatory, celibacy of the priesthood, vigils, worship of relics, and the burning of daylight candles, the Papacy must offer, as a record of revelation, a Bible in Latin which would be as Origenistic as the Bible in Greek adopted by Constantine. Therefore, the Pope turned to Jerome to bring forth a new version in Latin.

Thus, in contrast to what the naturalistic critics say, it was not the matter of variations in the Old Latin which brought about this Version; but the desire to produce a Bible more compatible with the teachings of Rome. The same device was used by the revisers of 1881.

(2) The Philosophy of Jerome

Jerome was devotedly committed to the textual criticism of Origen, *"an admirer of Origen's critical principles,"* as Swete says. To be guided aright in his forthcoming translation, by models accounted standard in the semi-pagan Christianity of his day, Jerome repaired to the famous library of Eusebius and Pamphilus at Caesarea, where the voluminous manuscripts of Origen had been preserved. Among these was a Greek Bible of the Vaticanus and Sinaiticus type (Price). Both these versions retained a number of the seven books which Protestants have rejected as being spurious. This may be seen by examining those manuscripts. These manuscripts of Origen influenced Jerome more in the New Testament than in the Old, since finally he used the Hebrew text in translating the Old Testament. Moreover, the Hebrew Bible did not have these spurious books. Jerome admitted that these seven books--Tobit, Wisdom, Judith, Baruch, Ecclesiasticus, 1st and 2nd Maccabees--did not belong with the other writings of the Bible. Nevertheless, the Papacy endorsed them, and they are found in the Latin Vulgate and in the Douay, its English translation.

The existence of those books in Origen's Bible is sufficient evidence to reveal that tradition and Scripture were on an equal footing in the mind of that Greek theologian. His other doctrines, such as purgatory and transubstantiation, had now become as essential to the imperialism of the Papacy as was the teaching that tradition had equal authority with the Scriptures. Doctor Adam Clarke indicates Origen as the first teacher of purgatory.

The Latin Bible of Jerome, commonly known as the Vulgate, held authoritative sway for one thousand years. The services of the Roman Church were held at that time in a language which still is the sacred language of the Catholic clergy, the Latin.

Jerome in his early years had been brought up with an enmity to the Received Text, then universally known as the Greek Vulgate. The word

Vulgate means "commonly used"or "current." This word Vulgate has been appropriated from the Bible to which it rightfully belongs, that is, to the Received Text, and given to the Latin Bible. In fact, it took hundreds of years before the common people would call Jerome's Latin Bible, the Vulgate. The very fact that in Jerome's day the Greek Bible, from which the King James is translated into English, was called the Vulgate, is proof in itself that, in the church of the living God, its authority was supreme. Diocletian (302-312 A.D.), the last in the unbroken line of pagan emperors, had furiously pursued every copy of it, to destroy it. The so-called first Christian emperor, Constantine, chief of heretical Christianity, now joined to the state, had ordered (331 A.D.) and under imperial authority and finances, had promulgated a rival Greek Bible. Nevertheless, so powerful was the Received Text that even until Jerome's day (383 A.D.) it was called the Vulgate (Swete).

The hostility of Jerome to the Received Text made him necessary to the Papacy. The Papacy in the Latin world opposed the authority of the Greek Vulgate. Did it not see already this hated Greek Vulgate, long ago translated into Latin, read, preached from, and circulated by those Christians in northern Italy who refused to bow beneath its rule? For this reason it sought help from the great reputation which Jerome enjoyed as a scholar. Moreover, Jerome had been taught the Scriptures by Gregory Nazianzen, who, in turn, had been at great pains with two other scholars of Caesarea to restore the library of Eusebius in that city. With that library Jerome was well acquainted; he describes himself as a great admirer of Eusebius. While studying with Gregory, he had translated from Greek into Latin the Chronicle of Eusebius. And let it be remembered, in turn, that Eusebius in publishing the Bible ordered by Constantine, had incorporated in it the manuscripts of Origen (Price).

(3) How the Vulgate was Translated and Its General Character

Unger's Bible Dictionary states the following:

"After long and self-denying studies in the East and West, Jerome went to Rome A.D. 382, probably at the request of Pope Damasus to assist in an important synod. His active Biblical labors date from this epoch."

Jerome had not been long in Rome, when Damasus applied to him for a revision of the current Latin version of the New Testament by the help of the Greek original. *"There were,"* he says, *"almost as many forms of text as copies."* (See above; there was something greater than this that led to the revision.)

From Unger, the steps may be enumerated as follows:

(a) He began by revising the Old Latin Version of the New Testament. Some of the changes he introduced were made purely on linguistic grounds, but it is impossible to ascertain on what principle he proceeded in this respect. Others involved questions of interpolations. But the greater number consisted in the *removal* of the interpretations by which the synoptic *gospels especially were disfigured. This revision, however, was hasty.* [NOTE: The naturalistic critics have long spoken of removing the interpolations from the Received Text.]

(b) Jerome next undertook the revision of the Old Testament from the *Septuagint.* He apparently finished the entire O.T. using this method.

(c) Through dissatisfaction with the general result, he then made a complete translation of the O.T. from the Hebrew which was completed in 404. [This is to Jerome's credit, and here I believe we can see the hand of God.]

Coming back to the New Testament, Kenyon says, though it was a revision of the Old Latin, Jerome had *"recourse to the best available Greek manuscripts."* Now what kind of Greek MSS did he use?

"The conclusion to which Wordsworth and White come with regard to the Gospels, after most careful investigation, is that while he sometimes followed Greek MSS differing from any that we know, in the main he used MSS of the class represented by Aleph, B, L [i.e. Sinaiticus, Vaticanus and Regius], and especially a MS or MSS closely resembling Aleph. In Jerome's hands then, the Old Latin Version, already considerably modified from its African form . . . took on a distinctly Alexandrian color."

Kenyon also says, *"Large elements of the Old Latin remain in the Vulgate, but he selected the variants which agreed with the Greek MSS."* [i.e. Aleph and B].

From time to time, attempts were made to revise the Vulgate, notably by Alcuin and Theodulf about the beginning of the 9th century, by Hartmut towards the end of the 9th century, and by the University of Paris in the 13th. But these rested on no firm basis of textual criticism, and did little to delay the general progress of deterioration. It was consequently in a far from correct form that the Vulgate appeared as the first book produced by the printing press, the famous Gutenberg or Mazarin Bible of 1456.

Regarding further its corruptive element, Wilkinson says,

"In preparing the Latin Bible, Jerome would gladly have gone all the way in transmitting to us the corruptions in the text of Eusebius, but he did not dare. Great scholars of the West were already exposing him and the corrupted Greek manuscripts" (W. H. Green). Jerome especially mentions Luke 2:33 [where the Received Text reads: 'And Joseph and his mother marveled at those things which were spoken of him,'" while Jerome's text reads: 'His father and his mother marveled,' etc.] *to say that the great scholar Helvidius, who from the circumstances of the case was probably a Vaudois, accused him of using corrupted Greek manuscripts.*

Although endorsed and supported by the power of the Papacy, the Vulgate--which name we will now call Jerome's translation--did not gain immediate acceptance everywhere. It took nine hundred years to bring that about. Purer Latin Bibles than Jerome's had already a deep place in the affections of the West. Yet steadily through the years, the Catholic Church has uniformly rejected the Received Text wherever translated from the Greek into Latin and exalted Jerome's Vulgate. So that for one thousand years, Western Europe, with the exception of the Waldenses, Albigenses, and other bodies pronounced heretics by Rome, knew of no Bible but the Vulgate. As Father Simon, that monk who exercised so powerful an influence on the textual criticism of the last century, says: *"The Latins have had so great esteem for that father [Jerome] that for a thousand years they used no other version."*

Therefore, a millennium later, when Greek manuscripts and Greek learning were again general, the corrupt readings of the Vulgate were noted. Even Catholic scholars of repute, before Protestantism was fully under way, pointed out its thousands of errors. As Doctor Fulke in 1583 writing to a Catholic scholar, a Jesuit, says:

"Great friends of it and your doctrine, Lindanus, bishop of Ruremond, and Isidorus Clarius, monk of Casine, and bishop Fulginatensis: of which the former writeth a whole book, discussing how he would have the errors, vices, corruptions, additions, detractions, mutations, uncertainties, obscurities, pollutions, barbarisms, and solecisms of the vulgar Latin translation corrected and reformed; bringing many examples of every kind, in several chapters and sections: the other, Isidorus Clarius, giving a reason of his purpose, in castigation of the said vulgar Latin translation, confesseth that it was full of errors almost innumerable; which if he should have reformed all according to the

Hebrew verity, he could not have set forth the vulgar edition, as his purpose was. Therefore in many places he retaineth the accustomed translation, but in his annotations admonisheth the reader, how it is in the Hebrew. And, notwithstanding this moderation, he acknowledgeth that about eight thousand places are by him so noted and corrected."

Jerome's reaction to the often hostile initial reception of the Vulgate is given in our Old Testament survey.

(4)   The Hand of God in the Vulgate

While much of what is said above is justifiably critical; there is another side, and to some extent we can see God's overruling providence in the Vulgate.

Its Old Testament was translated directly from the Hebrew (albeit under the influence of Origen's *Hexapla*), whereas the Old Latin was translated from the Greek. In the New Testament *"large elements of the Old Latin remain."* (Kenyon) It was the first Bible to be printed, and though it has always been an integral part of the Catholic Church, many of the classic salvation verses are clearly translated.

Most importantly, John Wycliffe, *"The morning star of the reformation,"* became the first to produce the complete Bible in the English language and this from the Vulgate.

Terrence Brown says,

"Wycliffe knowing no Hebrew or Greek, translated from the Latin Vulgate which was far from perfect, but the English Version nevertheless showed only too clearly how far the doctrines of the Roman Church were removed from the plain teaching of God's Word. Wycliffe was accused of heresy and excommunicated, but continued with his task until his death in 1384. Every copy of his translation had to be written by hand, but so many were written that a Bill was enacted in Parliament to forbid its circulation." Archbishop Arundel complained to the Pope of *"that pestilent wretch Wycliffe"* The convocation of Oxford under Arundel in 1408 decreed *"that no man hereafter by his own authority translate any text of the Scripture into English or any other tongue, by way of book, pamphlet or treatise; and that no man read any such book, pamphlet or treatise, now lately composed in the time of John Wycliffe or since . . . publicly or privately, upon pain of greater excommunication. . . . He that shall do contrary to this shall likewise be punished as a favorer of heresy and error."* During the next hundred years, many Christian martyrs were burned to death with Wycliffe's Bible tied around their necks, but 170 copies remain to this day to testify to his faithfulness and the diligence of

his helpers.

The Mazarin, *or* Gutenberg Bible of 1456
British Museum
(Actual size 15 in. × 11 in.)

Mazarin, or Gutenberg Bible of 1456, British Museum (Actual size 15" x 11")

Finally, we consider the surprising findings of Edward F. Hills, Among the Latin-speaking Christians of the West, the substitution of Jerome's Latin Vulgate for the Old Latin version may be fairly regarded as a movement toward the Traditional (Byzantine) text. The Vulgate New Testament is a revised text which Jerome (384) says that he made by comparing the Old Latin version with *"old Greek"* manuscripts. According to Hort, one of the Greek manuscripts which Jerome used was closely related to Codex A, which is of the Traditional text-type. *"By a curious and apparently unnoticed coincidence the text of A in several books agrees with the Latin Vulgate in so many peculiar readings devoid of Old Latin attestation as to leave little doubt that a Greek manuscript largely employed by Jerome in his revision of the Latin version must have had to a great extent a common original with A."*

In this instance, Hort's judgement seems undoubtedly correct, for the agreement of the Latin Vulgate with the Traditional text is obvious, at least in the more important passages, such as, Christ's agony (Luke

22:43), Father, forgive them (Luke 23:24), the ascension (Luke 24:51). Kenyon (1937) lists 24 such passages in the Gospels in which the Western text (represented by D, Old Latin) and the Alexandrian text (represented by B Aleph) differ from each other. In these 24 instances the Latin Vulgate agrees 11 times with the Western text, 11 times with the Alexandrian text, and 22 times with the Traditional text (represented by the Textus Receptus). In fact, the only important readings in regard to which the Latin Vulgate disagrees with the Traditional New Testament text are the conclusion of the Lord's Prayer (Matt. 6:13), certain clauses of the Lord's Prayer (Luke 11:2-4), and the angel at the pool (John 5:4). In this last passage, however, the official Roman Catholic Vulgate agrees with the Traditional text. Another telltale fact is the presence in the Latin Vulgate of four of Hort's eight so-called *"conflate readings."* Although these readings are not at all "conflate," nevertheless, they do seem to be one of the distinctive characteristics of the Traditional text, and the presence of four of them in the Latin Vulgate is most easily explained by supposing that Jerome employed Traditional (Byzantine) manuscripts in the making of the Latin Vulgate text.

Later, we will look further at the question of Vulgate readings in the Received Text.

(5)   The Vulgate Manuscripts

Manuscripts of the Latin Vulgate far exceed those of the Greek New Testament with over 8000 being extant.   They are found by their hundreds in the libraries of Europe.   They are not as old as the Greek MSS though.

In Kenyon's list of the more important ones, only ten were written before the 8th century. These are,

1) Sangallensis (Sigma), 6th century, half of Gospels, the oldest MS.
2) Fuldenensis (F), 541-546 A.D., Harmony of the Gospels.
3) Harleienus (Z), 6th or 7th century, Gospels.
4) Lindisfarnensis (Y), c 700 A.D., Gospels.
5) Cantabrigiensis (X), 7th century, Gospels.
6) Stonyhurstensis (S), 7th century, John.
7) Oxoniensis (O), 7th century, Gospels in mixed text.
8) Amiatinus (A), Presented to Pope Gregory in 716, Entire Bible, generally regarded as the best MS of the Vulgate.
9) Lichfeldensis (L), 7th or 8th centuries, portions of Gospels.
10) Dunelmensis (Delta), 7th or 8th centuries, Gospels, Traditionally said to have been written by Bede.

Codex Amiatinus–circa 715
Laurentian Library, Florence
(Actual size of complete page 19½ in. x 13½ in.)

Codex Amiatinus--circa 715; Laurentian Library , Florence (Actual size of complete page 19.5 in. x 13.5 in.)

Though some positive things may be said about this version, it was nevertheless the Bible of Rome. That is of the priests of Rome, for it was kept away from the common people. This explains why its MSS remain in such abundance. Further, we must never forget that the warfare waged against those whose Bible was not the Vulgate!

Wilkinson summarizes:

"For nine hundred years, we are told, the first Latin translations held their own after the Vulgate; appeared. The Vulgate was born about 380 A.D. Nine hundred years later brings us to about 1280 A.D. This accords well with the fact that at the famous Council of Toulouse, 1229 A.D., the Pope gave orders for the most terrible crusade to be waged against the simple Christians of southern France and northern Italy who would not bow to his power. Cruel, relentless, devastating, this war was waged, destroying the Bibles, books and every vestige of documents telling the story of the Waldenses and Albigenses."

Since then, some authorities speak of the Waldenses as having their Bible, the Vulgate. We regret to dispute these claims. When we consider that the Waldenses were, so to speak, in their mountain fastnesses, on an island in the midst of a sea of nations using the Vulgate, it is no wonder that they knew and possessed the Vulgate. But the Italic, the earlier Latin, was their own Bible, the one for which they lived and suffered and died. Moreover, to the east was Constantinople, the center of Greek Catholicism, whose Bible was the Received Text; while a little farther east was the noble Syrian Church which also had the Received Text. In touch with these, northern Italy could easily verify her text.

3. The Syriac Peshitta

Regarding the Aramaic language of this version, see Old Testament portion of the Peshitta.

(1) The Importance and Advantage of the Syrian Church

The Syrian Version is more interesting than its Latin counterparts for several reasons. The virtual center of 1st century Christianity was Antioch, an important commercial city in Syria. *"The disciples were called Christians first in Antioch"* (Acts 1-1:26). Paul's great church-planting ministries had their base in Antioch. Syrian Christianity had a close proximity to, and linkage with many of the churches that had received the inspired New Testament Letters. The Syrian church had direct contact with the Apostles and writers of the Scriptures. Therefore the Syrian version may have been written with direct access to the original autographs themselves (based on Ruckman).

Tom Strouse says, *"It was probably translated from the original N.T. MSS."*

Bishop Ellicott in 1870 wrote, *"It is no stretch of imagination to suppose that portions of the Peshitta might have been in the hands of St. John."*

Wilkinson says, *"As time rolled on, the Syrian-speaking Christians could be numbered by the thousands. It is generally admitted that the Bible was translated from the original languages into Syrian about 150 A.D."* (Burgon). This version is known as the Peshitta (the correct or simple). This Bible even today generally follows the Received Text!!

Edward Miller states further:
The rise of Christianity and the spread of the Church in Syria was startling in its rapidity. Damascus and Antioch shot up suddenly into prominence as centers of Christian zeal, as if they had grown whilst men slept.

The arrangement of places and events which occurred during our Lord's Ministry must have paved the way to this success, at least as regards principally the nearer of the two cities just mentioned. Galilee, the scene of the first year of His Ministry, 'the acceptable year of the Lord'--through its vicinity to Syria was admirably calculated for laying the foundation of such a development.

This development saw its full realization after the destruction of Jerusalem in A.D. 70.

(2)   The Question Raised About the Date of the Peshitta

The Peshitta Syriac version, which is the historic Bible of the whole Syrian Church, agrees closely with the Traditional text found in the vast majority of the Greek New Testament manuscripts. Until about one hundred years ago it was almost universally believed that the Peshitta originated in the second century and hence was one of the oldest New Testament versions. Thus because of its agreement with the Traditional text the Peshitta was regarded as one of the most important witnesses to the antiquity of the Traditional text. In more recent times, however, naturalistic critics have tried to nullify this testimony of the Peshitta by denying that it is an ancient version. Burkitt (1904), for example, insisted that the Peshitta did not exist before the fifth century but *"was prepared by Rabbula, bishop of Edessa* [the capital city of Syria] *from 411-435 A.D., and published by his authority."*

Burkitt's theory was once generally accepted, but now scholars are realizing that the Peshitta must have been in existence before Rabbula's episcopate, because it was the received text of both the two sects into which the Syrian Church became divided. Since this division took place in Rabbula's time and since Rabbula was the leader of one of these sects, it is impossible to suppose that the Peshitta was his handiwork, for if it had been produced under his auspices, his opponents would never have adopted it as their received New Testament text. Indeed A. Voobus, in a series of special studies (1947-1954), has argued not only that Rabbula was not the author of the Peshitta but even that he did not use it, at least not in its present form. If this is true and if Burkitt's contention is also true, namely, that the Syrian ecclesiastical leaders who lived before Rabbula also did not use the Peshitta, then why was it that the Peshitta was received by all the mutually opposing groups in the Syrian Church as their common, authoritative Bible? It must have been that the Peshitta was a very ancient version and that because it was so old the common people within the Syrian Church continued to be loyal to it regardless of the factions into which they came to be divided and the preferences of their leaders. It made little difference to them whether these leaders quoted the Peshitta or not. They persevered in their usage of it, and because of their steadfast devotion this old translation retained its place as the received text of the Syriac-speaking churches (Edward F. Hills).

With regard to the above and the contention that the Peshitta was merely a Byzantine revision of another Syrian version called the Old Syriac or Curetonian, Pickering says,

"Because the Peshitta does witness to the "Byzantine" text, Hort had to get it out of the second and third centuries. Accordingly, he posited a late recension to account for it. F. C. Burkitt went further than Hort and specified Rabbula, Bishop of Edessa from A.D. 411-435, as the author of the revision".

Both ideas have had a wide acceptance. H. C. Thiessen's statement is typical, both in content and dogmatism.

"This [Peshitta] was formerly regarded as the oldest of the Syrian versions; but Burkitt has shown that it is in reality a revision of the Old Syriac made by Rabbula, Bishop of Edessa, about the year 425. This view is now held by nearly all Syriac scholars. The text of the Peshitta is now identified as the Byzantine text, which almost certainly goes back to the revision made by Lucian of Antioch about A.D. 300. "

As to the Syrian Peshitta, Burgon protested the complete lack of evidence for Hort's assertions. A. Voobus says of Burkitt's effort:

Burkitt has tried to picture the life-span of Bishop Rabbula as a decisive period in the development of the New Testament text in the Syrian church.

Regardless of the general acceptance of the axiom, established by him, that *"the authority of Rabbula secured an instant success for the new revised version." . . .* and that *"copies of the Peshitta were rapidly multiplied; it soon became the only text in ecclesiastical use"*--this kind of reconstruction of textual history is pure fiction without a shred of evidence to support it.

Voobus finds that Rabbula himself used the Old Syriac type of text. His researches show clearly that the Peshitta goes back at least to the mid-fourth century and that it was not the result of an authoritative revision.

Here again there is an added historical difficulty.

The Peshitta is regarded as authoritative Scripture by both the Nestorians and the Monophysites. It is hard to see how this could have come to pass on the hypothesis that Rabbula was the author and chief promoter of the Peshitta. For Rabbula was a decided Monophysite and a determined opponent of the Nestorians. It is almost contrary to reason, therefore, to Suppose that the Nestorian Christians would adopt so quickly and so unanimously the handiwork of their greatest adversary.

It is hard to understand how men like F. F. Bruce, E. C. Colwell, F.

G. Kenyon, etc. could allow themselves to state dogmatically that Rabbula produced the Peshitta.

"Literary history," says Scrivener, *"can hardly afford a more powerful case than has been established for the identity of the Version of the Syriac now called the 'Peshitta' with that used by the Eastern Church long before the great schism had its beginning, in the native land of the blessed Gospel. The Peshitta is referred by common consent to the 2nd century of our era."*

"We now come to the position," says Miller, *"resting upon the supposed posteriority of the so-called Syrian Text. Here again we are in the region of pure speculation unsustained by historical facts. Dr. Hort imagines first that there was a recension of the early Syrian Version, which this School maintains was represented by the Curetonian Version [see below], somewhere between 250 A.D. and 350 at Edessa, or Nisibis, or Antioch."*

Well indeed may Dr. Hort add, *"Even for conjecture the materials are scanty."* It would have been truer to the facts to have said, *"For such a conjecture there are no materials at all, and therefore it must be abandoned."*

(3) The Questions Raised by the Discovery of the Curetonian (Old Syriac) MSS

Until about the middle of the last century, no Syriac translation of the New Testament was known to be earlier than the Peshitta. However, in 1842, a great mass of Syriac MSS reached the British Museum from the monastery of St. Mary Deipara in the Nitrian desert of Egypt. Many were copies of the ordinary Syriac Peshitta Bible. But among them were eighty leaves of a copy of the Gospels in Syriac which W. Cureton (thus the name), one of the officers of the Museum, recognized as containing a completely different text from any MSS previously known. These leaves were edited by him, with a preface in which he contended that in this version we have the very words of our Lord's discourses, in the identical language in which they were originally spoken. The MSS itself is of the 5th century, practically contemporary with the earliest MSS which we possess of the Peshitta Syriac. But Cureton argued that the character of the translations showed that the original must go back before the Peshitta. He then stated that the Peshitta was a revision of the Old Syriac (its other name), just as the Latin Vulgate was a revision of the Old Latin.

Many scholars, though, strongly disagreed. However, in 1892, two enterprising Cambridge ladies, Mrs. Lewis and her sister, Mrs. Gibson, visited the monastery of St. Catherine on Mount Sinai, the place where Tischendorf made his celebrated discovery of Codex Sinaiticus. They photographed a number of MSS, among them a Syriac palimpsest. When they brought their photographs home, the underlying text was recognized by F. C. Burkitt (there he is again) as belonging to the Old Syriac version, hitherto known only in Cureton's MSS. Fairly substantial portions of the four Gospels were deciphered (Kenyon).

Lining up against the 250 (in 1949) extant MSS of the Peshitta we now have two of the old Syriac!!

Quoting Kenyon further,

"It is clear that the Sinaitic MS does not represent precisely the same text as the Curetonian. The differences between them are made much more marked than, say, between any two manuscripts of the Peshitta or Greek. One striking proof is that in Matthew 1 the Curetonian emphasizes the Miraculous Conception, saying,"

"Jacob begat Joseph, to whom was betrothed Mary the Virgin, who bare Jesus Christ."

Whereas the Sinaitic MS appears to deny this,

"Jacob begat Joseph, and Joseph to whom was betrothed Mary the Virgin, begat Jesus, who is called Christ."

No wonder this MS which dates back to the 4th century became a palimpsest. But these two (often conflicting) MSS provided Westcott, Hort, and Burkitt with a convenient vehicle to move the Peshitta from the 2nd to the 5th century. It sounded very agreeable to say that just as the Vulgate was a revision of the Old Latin, so the Peshitta was of the Old Syriac. The problem with this is that there is strong MS and historical testimony to the Old Latin, but these two MSS are all we have of the so-called Old Syriac.

They are simply another example of a corrupted offspring that was placed on the shelf for long centuries, until it could be taken down and used as a "proof" against God's Word.

Kenyon says regarding its (the two combined!!) agreement with Aleph & B as against D (Codex Bezae),

"In general, however, it is evident that, while the version cannot be reckoned wholly with either the Aleph & B group or the D group, it shows a preponderance of agreement with the latter." This is a nice scholarly way of saying that there is total confusion when these MSS are compared. What Kenyon fails to mention is that the Old Syriac does contain some of the key Received Text readings.

Hills says,

"Critics assign an early third century date to the text of the Sinaitic Syriac manuscript. If they are correct in this, then this manuscript is remarkable for the unexpected support which it gives to the Traditional text found in the vast majority of the Greek New Testament manuscripts. For Burkitt (1904) found that 'not infrequently' this manuscript agreed with the Traditional text against the Western and Alexandrian texts. One of these Traditional readings thus supported by the Sinaitic Syriac manuscript is found in the angelic song of Luke 2:14. Here the Traditional text and the Sinaitic Syriac read, 'good will among [toward] men,' while the Western and Alexandrian texts read, 'among men of good will.'"

Thus again in the corrupted copies of scripture, the Received Text base can still be discerned.

Quoting again from Miller,

"Dr. Hort was perfectly logical when he suggested, or rather asserted dogmatically, that such a drastic revision as was necessary for turning the Curetonian into the Peshitta was made in the third century at Edessa or Nisibis. The difficulty lay in his manufacturing history to suit his purpose, instead of following it. The fact is, that the internal difference between the text of the Curetonian and the Peshitta is so great. . . ."

Thus the differences are too great to speak of one being a revision of the other.

(4) The Witness of History and the Manuscripts to the Early Date of the Peshitta

Miller says,

"The commanding position thus occupied leads back virtually a long way. Changes are difficult to introduce in "the unchangeable East." Accordingly, the use of the Peshitta is attested in the 4th century by Ephraem Syrus and Aphraates. Ephraem "in the main used the Peshitta text"--is the conclusion drawn by Mr. F. H. Woods in the third volume of Studio Biblica. And as far as I may judge from a comparison of readings, Aphraates witnesses for the Traditional Text, with which the Peshitta mainly agrees, twenty-four times as against four. The Peshitta thus reckons as its supporters the two earliest of the Syrian Fathers."

It can be traced by facts of history or by actual documents to the beginning of the golden period of Syriac Literature in the fifth century, when it is found to be firm in its sway, and it is far from being deserted by testimony sufficient to track it into the earlier ages of the Church.

The Peshitta in our own days is found in use amongst the Nestorians who have always kept to it, by the Monophysites on the plains of Syria, the Christians of St. Thomas in Malabar, and by the Maronites on the mountain-terraces of Lebanon. Of these, the Maronites take us back to the beginning of the 8th century when they as Monothelites separated from the Eastern Church; the Monophysites to the middle of the 5th century; the Nestorians to an earlier date in the same century. Hostile as the two latter were to one another, they would not have agreed in reading the same Version of the New Testament if that had not been well established at the period of their separation. Nor would it have been thus firmly established, if it had not by that time been generally received in the country for a long series of years.

In 1950, Kenyon stated that there were 250 extant Peshitta MSS, of which more than 100 were in the British Museum. He mentions that two belong to the 5th century (about 450) and that few others belong to the 6th century. However, Miller at the turn of the century refers to a total of 11 or 12 Peshitta MSS dating before the end of the 6th century. Notice how this compares with the ten or so crucial MSS which date to the end of the 6th century. If Miller's enumeration is correct, then the actual weight of evidence from the Peshitta is greater than that from the older uncials. And as the Peshitta is a TR type text, no wonder the naturalistic critics have done all in their power to *"move it forward in time."*

(5)   Other Syrian Versions

(a) Tatian's *Diatessaron*

Tatian was a native of the Euphrates Valley, but lived for many years in Rome as a disciple of Justin Martyr. After the martyrdom of Justin in 165 he was charged with heresy (Kenyon). Wilkinson says that he *"carried the regrettable doctrine of Justin Martyr to alarming lengths and embraced the Gnostic heresy. About 172 he left Rome for Palestine and then back to his native land where he died in 180."* (Kenyon) [Others say he died 8 years earlier.]

He is famous for his Harmony of the Gospels, in which he combines the four Gospels into one running account. *Diatessaron* is a Greek word meaning *"harmony of four."* Kenyon believes that he wrote it originally in Greek while still at Rome, but took it with him to Syria and there translated it into Syriac. Of course one reason why Kenyon must say this, is to rule out any possibility of a 2nd century Peshitta which Tatian might have had before him.

The *Diatessaron* had many corruptions. We are told that the genealogies and all passages referring to Christ's Jewish descent are removed. The fact of the incarnation was opposed to the teachings of the Gnostics which viewed Christ as merely a heavenly being, i.e. one of the *"heavenly ranks between God and man."*

Though Eusebius referred to it as a kind of *"patchwork Gospel,"* it was widely spread and translated. Ephrem, the famous Syriac Father, made a commentary of the Gospels from it. And for many it practically seemed to be their Bible. But Theodotus, bishop of Cyrrhus near the Euphrates from c. 423-457, records that he collected and removed more than 200 copies from the churches in his area, replacing them by *"the Gospels of the Four Evangelists,"* no doubt the Peshitta. Rabbula himself seems to have taken similar steps in his neighboring diocese of Edessa. He gave instructions that all the churches have copies of the *"Gospel of the separated ones."* This refers to the four Gospels being presented separately rather than in a harmony (Kenyon and Bruce).

Though this is clearly a "doctored" translation, yet the Received text base remains. Ruckman says, *"Readers will be surprised to find that it reads with the King James Version on Luke 2:33 and John 9:35, upholding the Deity of Christ and the Virgin Birth. This gives a definite Syrian witness to the A.V. readings 200 years older than Vaticanus or Sinaiticus."*

Kenyon admits as much when he says, *"Since we now possess it only in late copies of translations, Latin, Armenia, Arabic and Dutch, which have been subject to the universal tendency towards containing strange texts to that generally received . . ."*

(b) The Philoxenian and Harkleian Syriac

Kenyon says:
"In the year 508, Philoxenus, bishop of Mabbug, in eastern Syria, thinking the current Peshitta version did not represent the original Greek accurately enough [The same thing is said about the K.J.V.], *caused it to be revised throughout by one Polycarp. In 616 this version was itself revised, with the assistance of some Greek MSS in Alexandria, by Thomas of Harkel, himself also subsequently bishop of Mabbug."*

There are now about fifty extant MSS of the Harkleian text. The dates of the more notable ones are,

1)   7th century at Rome,
2)   8th century at Rome,
3)   757 A.D. at Florence,
4)   10th century, British Museum,

5) 10th century, British Museum,
6) 1170, Cambridge University Library. This is considered to be the best.

The Philoxenian apparently has survived only in a few MSS of II Peter, II and III John, Jude, and Revelation.

Bruce is typical when he says that the original Peshitta version of the New Testament did not include the above five books. And these were not added to any Syriac version until the Philoxenian Version was produced in 508.

In response to this and the above revisions, it can be said (based on Ruckman),

Corruptions did not enter the Peshitta until the middle of the 3rd century, when Origen moved from Alexandria to Caesarea, bringing his publishing company with him. Further corruption took place during the time of Eusebius and Pamphilus (260-340), and at the time of the revisions known as Philoxenian, Harkleian, and the Jerusalem Syriac.

The omission of Revelation can be traced, undoubtedly, to the work of Origen and Eusebius at Caesarea. Rabulla's edition which omits II Peter, II John, Jude, and Revelation was NOT the original Syriac Bible, as is evident from the findings of Voobus in *Investigations into the Text of the N.T. Used by Rabbula.* Eusebius and Origen are definitely collaborators in the alteration of the Syrian Text (Reumann).

Despite this, though, Strouse says that the Harkleian Syriac contains the Byzantine Text.

(c) The Palestinian Syriac

This is known only to us in fragments in a dialect of Syriac designated as Western or Jewish Aramaic. It is believed to have been made at Antioch in the 6th century, and to have been used exclusively in Palestine.

Nearly all the surviving MSS are in the form of lectionaries (Scripture lessons), the two most important being a pair of Gospel lectionaries, dated 1104 and 1118.

Kenyon says it has "elements" of Aleph, B, and the D type text. This probably means that in the main it is Byzantine.

We conclude our study of the Syriac Peshitta with a comment by Hills,

> *"In the Syrian Church this God-guided trend away from false New Testament texts and toward the true is clearly seen. According to all investigators from Burkitt (1904) to Voobus (1950), the Western*

> text, represented by Tatian's Diatessaron (Gospel Harmony) and the Curetonian and Sinaitic Syriac manuscripts, circulated widely in the Syrian Church until about the middle of the 4th century. After this date, however, this intrusive Western text was finally rejected, and the whole Syrian Church returned to the use of the ancient Peshitta Syriac version, which is largely of the Traditional (Byzantine) text-type. In other words, the Syrian Church as well as the Greek was led by God's guiding hand back to the true text."

Having gone into considerable detail in our study of the three major versions of the New Testament, it will only be necessary to give a brief review of the remaining ones. These versions are presented in a geographic sequence.

4.   The Egyptian Coptic Version

As we saw in our survey of the Old Testament versions, Coptic was the ancient language of Egypt, written originally in hieroglyphics, but in N.T. times written in Greek letters, with the addition of six letters to represent sounds not used in Greek.

There are the two main dialects: Sahidic, the dialect of Upper or Southern Egypt; and Bohairic, the dialect of Lower or Northern Egypt.

The New Testament seems to have been translated into the Sahadic dialect around 200 A.D. Kenyon says, *"It survives only in fragments, but these are now very numerous indeed, so that it has been possible to put together a practically complete New Testament. It is fundamentally and predominantly of the same family as Sinaiticus and Vaticanus."* With this conclusion, Strouse agrees. The oldest MS dates back to about 350 A.D. (shown below).

The Bohairic New Testament of Northern Egypt was somewhat later. This was the more developed and literary dialect and ultimately spread throughout the country superseding the other dialects. Over 100 MSS have been discovered, though none of them is very early. The oldest is dated 1173 A.D. There is one page from Ephesians which may go back as far as the 5th century. As expected with the influence of Alexandria so near, *"the Bohairic text is definitely Alexandrian"* (Kenyon).

Again Strouse concurs.

There is another side though. Ruckman is prepared to say that the Coptic along with several other early versions *"were originally true and trustworthy copies of the original New Testament documents."*

Sahidic Codex of Acts--fourth century

Sahidic Codex of Acts--fourth century

Referring to the detailed research of Kenyon on these versions, Hills says:

"Thus during the fourth and fifth centuries among the Syriac-speaking Christians of the East, the Greek-speaking Christians of the Byzantine empire, and the Latin-speaking Christians of the West the same tendency was at work, namely, a God-guided trend away from the false Western and Alexandrian New Testament texts and toward the true Traditional text. At a somewhat later date, moreover, this tendency was operative also among the Coptic Christians of Egypt. An examination of Kenyon's 24 passages, for example, discloses 12 instances in which some of the manuscripts of the Bohairic (Coptic) version agree with the Textus Receptus against B, Aleph, and the remaining Bohairic manuscripts. This indicates that in these important passages the readings of the Traditional Text had been adopted by some of the Coptic scribes."

5.　The Ethiopic Version

Many would date this translation around the year 600.　Bruce says, *"The translation appears to have been a gradual process, carried out between the late 4th or early 5th centuries.　The translation was made from Greek.　Though influenced by the Coptic Church, the text is mainly Byzantine."*　The MSS are quite late, with the earliest going back to the 13th century (Kenyon).

Ethiopic MS.–seventeenth century
British Museum
(Actual size 14¾ in. × 14 in.)

Ethiopic MS.--seventeenth century; British Museum (Actual size 14.75" x 14 ")

6.　The Arabic Version

The Scriptures do not seem to have been extant in an Arabic version before the time of Muhammad (570-632), who knew the Gospel story only in an oral form and mainly from Syriac sources.　These Syriac sources were marked by Docetism (meaning "deviation"; it said that Christ only appeared to be human and did not really die).　This explains the source of the same teaching in the Muslim religion (Bruce).

Kenyon says, *"Several Arabic versions are known to exist, some being translated from the Greek, some from Syriac, and some from Coptic."* The earliest translation would be in the 7th century.

7.   The Armenian Version

Armenia is a country lying to the east of Asia Minor and north of Mesopotamia, sandwiched between the Roman and Persian Empires It was evangelized in the 3rd century by Syriac-speaking missionaries. However, it was not until the early 5th century that they possessed a version of their own. Armenian traditions themselves differ as to whether this version was translated from Syriac or Greek.

As to the actual translation, it is recorded by Armenian writers of the 5th century that *"under order of Patriarch Saholc and a certain Mesrop this work was performed around 400.   But that after the Council of Ephesus (431) at which Nestorianism was condemned, they received correct copies of the Greek Bible from Constantinople, and revised their translation accordingly . . . this revision after 431 would probably have been from MSS of the Byzantine type, and this seems to be confirmed by the existing MSS"* (Kenyon).

The earliest MS is dated 887. There are probably two others of the 9th century and six of the 10th (Kenyon).

8.   The Georgian Version

North of Armenia lies Georgia, in the Caucasus. They were the next to be evangelized after the Armenians, about the close of the third century. Their version seems to be based on the Armenian Version. *The great majority of MSS show the Byzantine text*; but a few, especially one dated 897 known as the Adysh MS, show a Caesarean text (the town Origen went to when he left Alexandria).

The Armenian alphabet probably, and the Georgian alphabet certainly, were expressly devised in order that the Scriptures might be written in these two languages. These two missionary versions are thus the precursors of many more of a later date, which required that the language concerned should be reduced to writing before the Bible could be written in it (Bruce). Ulfilas also did this when he prepared an alphabet for the Gothic Version.

9.   The Gothic Version

The Roman Empire was subjected to continuous and increasing

pressure on its northern frontier from Germanic tribes. Chief among these were the Goths who sacked Rome in 410. Augustine, at that time, reflects the general feeling of thankfulness that the Goths had been Christianized before the sack of Rome (Bruce).

The Gothic version indicates that the Traditional text is not a late text. This New Testament translation was made from the Greek into Gothic shortly after 350 A.D. by Ulfilas, missionary bishop to the Goths. *"The type of text represented in it,"* Kenyon tells us, *"is for the most part that which is found in the majority of Greek manuscripts."* The fact, therefore, that Ulfilas (means "little wolf") in A.D. 350 produced a Gothic version based on the Traditional text proves that this text must have been in existence before that date. In other words, there must have been many manuscripts of the Traditional type on hand in the days of Ulfilas, manuscripts which since that time have perished (Hills).

The oldest MS dates back to the 5th or 6th century; it contains more than half the Gospels, and is now at Upsala, Sweden (Kenyon).

10. The Slavonic Version

In the 9th century, two brothers, Constantine and Methodius, were sent by Byzantium (Constantinople) to the Slavonic people in East Central Europe. They devised a Slavonic alphabet and translated the Scriptures from Greek into that language. This was also in the Byzantine Text.

In addition, Strouse mentions that a Frankish Version (West Central Europe) was translated in the 8th century; and a Persian Version was translated from the Syriac in the 14th century.

This completes our survey of the versions and manuscripts of the New Testament. Every attempt has been made to present the material accurately, fairly and most importantly, in a way that believes the promise of God to preserve His Word through the centuries.

We have surveyed the four major areas of manuscript evidence: the papyri, uncials, cursives and versions. And, often in quoting from the research of scholars who would deny the Received Text its rightful place, we have seen the overwhelming advantage it enjoys over any other "text type." We have even noted a strong Received Text presence in those places where it was not supposed to be at all (that is, not in the view of Westcott and Hort and company). We have seen a clear Received Text presence in Egypt and Alexandria--in the very backyard of Origen, in the papyri, in the *"five old uncials,"* and in the Coptic. We have also seen a dominant Received Text witness in the writings of the early church

Fathers.

We have surveyed the greatest warfare in history as the forces of Satan sought to thwart God's promise to preserve His Holy Word during the first three centuries. We have seen the casualties of this warfare--the corrupted manuscripts. But we have seen that God was faithful to His Holy Word, that the Father watched over it just as He watched over the Living Word.

Benjamin Wilkinson wrote in 1930, *"Down through the centuries, the pure Bible, the living Word of God, has often faced the descendants of this corrupt version* [the one promulgated by Constantine], *robed in splendor and seated on the throne of power. It has been a battle and a march, a battle and a march. God's Holy Word has always won. And now, once again in these last days, the battle is being renewed, the affections and the control of the minds of men are being contended for by these two rival claimants."*

PART FIVE:

A SURVEY OF ENGLISH BIBLE HISTORY

The ten early versions listed above will give you a good picture of how God dispersed His Word to the population centers of that day. But the most important later developments in Bible History center in England and the Continent. The following pages survey the major epochs in England and Europe leading up to the translation of the Authorized Version of 1611.

XXVII. A Historical Outline of the English People and Their Language

In order to trace the history of the English Scriptures, it is necessary to remember a little of the history of the English people and their language.

1. The Early Settlers

In the millenniums B.C., people from Spain and Brittany in north western France settled on hilltops in southern England. These were followed by settlers from the Rhine and Danube river regions of mainland Europe. This latter group built large circular monuments with stones, of which Stonehenge is an example.

2. The First Invaders

The first invaders of England were the Celts. They began crossing the English Channel in the 700's B.C. The Celts, a warlike people, were divided into various tribes and invaded in several waves. The earliest invading tribe, the Gaels, settled in the western mid-northern areas of the island. The second wave, the Britons or Brythons, occupied most of what is now England and Wales. The Celts worshiped native gods through priests known as Druids. They used iron and mined tin. They traded with the Gauls in what is now France.

3. The Roman Conquest

In 55 B.C. Julius Caesar conquered the Gauls in France and then a year later invaded Britain and defeated some of the Celts. He withdrew after forcing the Celts to give him money.

In A.D. 3 Claudius conquered Britannia (as the island was then called). The Celtic tribes were easily defeated, and Rome ruled England for 400 years. History records how England prospered under Roman rule. It was a Roman province and protected from the warlike peoples of Scotland by forts and walls.

4. The Germanic Invasion

The Roman soldiers left England in the early 400's to help defend Rome against barbarian invaders. With the Romans gone, the Britons could not protect themselves against invasion by tribesmen from Scotland called Picts and people from Ireland called Scots. But the greatest danger came from seafaring Germanic tribes, especially the Angles, Saxons and Jutes. They first raided the coast. In the mid 400's, they began to establish permanent settlements. The Jutes settled in south eastern England. The Angles and Saxons set up kingdoms throughout southern and eastern England. The whole country became known as Angle-land. The native Britons held only the mountain areas of extreme western and northern England.

In 596 Pope Gregory I sent Augustine to Kent. Thousands were "converted," including Ethelbert, King of the Jutes. Augustine built a monastery near Canterbury, and became the first archbishop of Canterbury--the religious center of England. The Picts and Scots in the north were also converted to this Roman type of Christianity. The Latin Vulgate became their Bible. From this point onward until 1534, England was officially a Catholic nation.

However, as we saw earlier, the native Britons (Celts) had had a different and truer form of Christianity and purer Bible--the Old Latin. Stanley in *Historic Memorials of Canterbury* records on pp. 33-34 how Augustine treated with contempt the early Christian Britons and connived with the Angles and Saxons in their frightful extermination. However, after Augustine's death, when these same Anglo-Saxons began to terrify the papal leaders in England to the extent that they fled back to Rome, it was the British or Celtic Christians of Scotland who occupied the forsaken fields. It is evident from this that the original roots of British Christianity was not Rome but the missionaries who came into that land in the early centuries from Judea or Asia Minor.

5. The Anglo-Saxon Period

The Saxons occupied four separate "nations" in the south, and the Angles three in the north and east. These seven kingdoms became known as the "Heptarchy." From 500 to 800 in successive stages, one of the seven would rule the other six.

King Egbert of Wessex (West Saxon), the last "nation" to control the Heptarchy, is often considered to be the first king of England.

During the 800's, Danish raiders attacked England and easily conquered all the Anglo-Saxon kingdoms except Wessex. Their King Alfred the Great resisted and then in 886 defeated the Danes and forced them to withdraw to the northeastern third of England. This became known as Danelaw. However, in the 100 years after Alfred's death in 899, Danish power increased. In 1016 Canute, a brother of the King of Denmark defeated the king of Wessex (Ethelred II) and became king of England. Danish rule collapsed though after his death in 1035.

Under Edward the Confessor, the son of Ethelred II the Saxons again came to power, but it was to be short-lived. He built the first church building on the site of what is now Westminster Abbey.

6.   The Norman Conquest

Edward the Confessor died without a direct heir to the throne. The English nobles chose Harold of Wessex as king. But a french nobleman, William Duke of Normandy, claimed that Edward had promised him the throne. William invaded England and defeated the forces of Harold in the Historic Battle of Hastings. On Christmas Day, 1066, William the Conqueror was crowned king of England.

He divided England among the Normans and forced most of the Anglo-Saxons to become serfs. His survey of land and property owners to determine taxes is known as the *Domesday Book*.

The Normans spoke French at first, but gradually their language blended with that of the Anglo-Saxons. In time they became a united people.

This brings us to the matter of the English language itself.

7.   The Development of the English Language

The history of the English language is divided into three periods.

(1)   Old English or Anglo-Saxon--until c. 1100

As we have seen, until about A.D. 450, England was not called England, nor was English spoken there. Before that time, the country was called Britain, and the people were known as Britons. Most of these spoke Celtic. The Celtic dialects include Breton, Irish, Scottish, Gaelic, and Welsh. Being under Roman rule for 400 years, Latin was also spoken.

The basis and origin of the actual English language is to be found with the Germanic invaders--Angles, Saxons and Jutes. As we have seen, the very word England is from Angle. The language developed with many words evolving from Latin but few from Celtic. The Danish invaders also contributed to the language's development. Also through Latin, many Greek words have come into English.

(2)   Middle English--c. 1100 to 1450

With William the Conqueror, almost overnight Normans replaced Englishmen as the chief landowners and church leaders. The Norman dialect of French became the language of the ruling class, and the literary language, whereas English continued as the language of the common people.

Three hundred years later, during the mid-1300's, English again became the chief literary language and the usual language of the ruling class. But by that time, it had changed greatly--thousands of French words had come into the English language. This transference of French into English continued into the 1400's.

(3)   Modern English--c. 1450 to Present

Words still were and are borrowed from other languages. But with the advent of so-called Modern English, the period of rapid change and development had ended and the language had stabilized into the basic form that we know it today.

The believer should also see the hand of God in this development of the English language, for beside being the most prominent form of communication in the world, it has been the foremost vehicle of God spreading His Word.

With this summary of the origins of the English peoples and language, it will only be necessary to list the further important dates of English History.

8.   Further Important Dates of English History

1215   English barons force King John to agree to the *Magna Carta*.
1282   England conquers Wales.
1295   Edward I calls together the Model Parliament.

1314   Scotland is assured of its independence from England by winning the Battle of Bannockburn.

1337-1453 England fights the Hundred Years' War with France and loses its lands on the European mainland.

1455-1485 Two royal families fight for the throne in the Wars of the Roses.

1534   Henry VIII has Parliament pass a law decreeing that the King and not Pope is head of the church in England. This ended the thousand year reign of Catholicism and led to the formation of the Church of England as we now know it.

1588   The English fleet defeats the Spanish Armada.

1603   England and Scotland are joined in a union under one king, James I.

1649-1659 England becomes a Commonwealth and then a Protectorate.

(The above is taken mainly from the *World Book Encyclopedia*.)

XXVIII. Important Dates in the History of Bible Translation
(From *Which Bible*)

A.D.

35-65   Date of the Copper Scroll from Cave III at Qumran

70   Romans destroy Jerusalem.

73   Masada falls.

73   Latest date possible of a scroll found at Masada, containing some Psalms

100   Death of John

100   Birth of Justin Martyr

120   Birth of Italic Church

135   Death of Rabbi Aquiba

150   Irenaeus (circa)

150   Date of Peshitta, the Syrian Bible

157   Date of the Italic Bible

170   Irenaeus (circa)

175-225 Assigned date of P-75

177   Heathen massacre of Gallic Christians

190   Date of Clement of Alexandria

200   The tract *Yoma*

200   Date of some Aramaic words claimed couldn't have been used

	400-700 years earlier
200	Vast mutilations in many copies of Scriptures have already occurred.
200	Date or clement of Alexandria
200-450	Date of active use of Codex B
250	Earliest date that Rome sent missionaries toward the West
302-312	Dates of Diocletian, last pagan emperor of Rome
312	Constantine becomes emperor of Rome
312-1453	Byzantine Period
321	Constantine's Sunday Law
331	Constantine orders and finances a Rival Greek Bible.
350-400	Textus Receptus is dominant Gracco-Syrian text (same period as that of the production of "B" and "Aleph").
363	Council of Laodicea
363	Council names the 39 books as canonical.
380	Jerome's Vulgate
383	Received (Traditional) Text is still called the Vulgate.
400	Church Fathers up to this date testify that the Traditional Text was in existence, and that it was the predominant one.
400	Augustine prefers the Italic Text.
400	Date of Jerome
400	Roman Empire is breaking up into modern kingdom; diffusion of pure Latin.
450	Codex B falls into discredit and disuse.
476-1453	Dark Ages
500-1881	Codex B abandoned
640	Benedictines founded
600	Rome sends missionaries to England and Germany.
600	Gregory I begins to destroy Waldensian records.
1100	*The Noble Lesson* written
1175	Peter Waldo begins his work.
1179	Lateran Council
1229	Council of Toulouse
1229	Pope orders crusade against those of Southern France and Northern Italy who won't bow to him.
1229	Council condemns the Waldensian New Testament.
1280	Asserted date that Latin Vulgate (Traditional) still held its own against Jerome's Vulgate.
1300	Jesuits translate the Vulgate into Italian.
1400	Jesuits translate the Vulgate into French.
1450	Printing is invented.

1453	End of Dark Ages
1453	Constantinople falls; thousands of MSS [Greek] taken to Europe.
1510-1514	Erasmus teaches at Cambridge.
	Tyndale studies Greek with him.
1516	Erasmus' Greek New Testament printed
	Erasmus' Greek New Testament is first in 1,000 years.
1521	Loyola wounded at the siege of Pampeluna.
1522	Erasmus' third edition is printed: foundation for Textus Receptus.
1525	Tyndale's New Testament is published.
1530	Tyndale's Pentateuch is published.
1633	Erasmus rejects a number of selected readings from Codex B.
1534	Tyndale's amended edition of New Testament is printed.
1536	On August 6, Tyndale is burned.
1537	Olivetan's French Bible
1545-1563	Council of Trent
1546	Council decrees that apocryphal books plus unwritten tradition are on equal ground with the Word of God.
1550	Stephen's Greek N.T. printed
1557	The Geneva N.T. in English
1558-1642	The Elizabethan period: generally regarded as most important era in English literature
1560	The Geneva Bible in English
1563	Council of Trent closes.
1568-1638	Dates of Cyril Lucar
1582	Jesuit Bible is printed in English at Rheims, France " *to shake out of the deceived people's hand, the false heretical translations of a sect called Waldenses.*" "*In the preface . . . they state that It was not translated into English because it was necessary that the Bible should be in the mother tongue, or that God had appointed the Scriptures to be read by all; . . .*"
1582	Jesuits dominate 287 colleges and universities in Europe.
1583	"[Jerome's Vulgate] *was full of errors almost innumerable*"-- monk of Casine.
1587	O.T. of the Vaticanus is printed; third edition is called "Sixtine," being published at Rome under Pope Sixtus V.
1588	Spanish Armada destroyed
1590	Date of Beza, associate of Calvin
1593	Jesuit University moves back to Douay from Rheims, France.
1598	Beza's Greek New Testament is printed.

1600	The *"Douay of 1600 and that of 1900 are not the same in many ways."*
1602	Cyril becomes patriarch of Alexandria.
1603	Queen Elizabeth dies.
1607	Diodati's Greek New Testament appears at Geneva.
1609-1610	Complete Jesuit Bible is published at Douay.
1611	King James Version is printed.
	Waldensian influence
	Opportune condition of English Language
	Vast store of manuscripts available
	Triumph of the King James Version
	Same problems and evidence as those of 1881
	Abilities of the translators
1620	Puritans leave England with the KJV.
1620	*Mayflower* Lands in Plymouth in Dec.
1624	Elzevir's Greek New Testament printed
1627	Alexandrinus Manuscript arrives in London.
	Cyril starts his Confession of Faith.
1628	Alexandrinus is presented to King Charles I.
1629	Cyril's Confession of Faith is printed at Geneva.
1638	Cyril Lucar dies by Jesuits.
1655	Terrible massacres of Waldenses
1657	Date of Walton
1669	Leger publishes *General History of the Evangelical Churches of the Piedmontese Valleys.*
1675	Date of Fell
1707	Date of Mill
1754	Melanchthon's Latin grammar ran for fifty-one editions until this date.
1734	Date of Bengel
1745-1812	Dates of Griesbach
1749-1752	Douay's revisions by Bishop Challoner
1751	Date of Wetstein
1773	European nations demand that the pope suppress Jesuits order.
1789	French Revolution
1793-1851	Dates of Lachmann
1796-1838	Dates of Molder
1812	Napoleon is taken prisoner.
1813	John William Burgon is born August 21.
1813-1875	Dates of Tregelles
1814	Jesuits motored by the pope

1815-1874 Dates of Tischendorf
1823 Gilly's sad findings at Cambridge
1825 Leger's book is called "scarce."
1825-1901 Dates of Westcott
1825-1892 Dates of Hort
1832 Great crowds assemble to hear Edward Irving.
1833 The issue: Premillenarianism or Liberalism (literalism or allegorism)
1833-1883 Years of terrific Romanizing campaigns
1841 Burgon matriculates at Oxford.
1844 Sinaiticus deposited in a wastepaper basket.
1845 Tregelles goes to Rome to see Vaticanus.
1847 Westcott writes to fiancee about Pieta.
1847 Westcott writes of the possibility of his being called a "heretic."
1848 Burgon receives his M.A. from Oxford.
1848 On July 6, Hort writes, *The pure Romish view seems to be nearer, and more likely to lead to the truth than the Evangelical.*
1849 Bishop Kenrick publishes an English translation of the Catholic Bible.
1850 Newman is considered the most distinguished Roman Catholic theologian.
1851 Hort writes: *Think of that vile Textus Receptus.*
1853 Westcott and Hort start their Greek Text.
1854 Pantheism is strong, even among key Protestants.
1856-1930 Dates of Robert Dick Wilson
1856 In May, the Earl of Shaftesbury states: "[With all the versions, you must] *go to some learned pundit in whom you reposed confidence, and ask him which version he recommended; and when you had taken his version, you must be bound by his opinion.*"
1857 First efforts to secure a revision
1857-1872 Tregelles' edition of the Greek N.T.
1858 On Oct. 21, Hort writes: *Evangelicals seem to me perverted rather than untrue.*
1859 Tischendorf's seventh edition of his Greek N.T.
1859 Tischendorf's discovery of Sinaiticus on February 4
1859 Darwin's *Origin of Species* is published.
1860 Burgon examines Codex B.
1860 On April 3, Hort writes: *The book which has most engaged*

	me is Darwin. . . . It is a book that one is proud to be contemporary with."
1860	On Oct. 15, Hort writes to Westcott: *"The popular doctrine of substitution is an immoral and material counterfeit."*
1862	Burgon examines the treasures of St. Catherine's Convent on Mt. Sinai.
1862	In Oct., Tischendorf publishes his edition of the Sinaitic Manuscript.
1864	Privy Council of England permits seven Church of England clergymen, who had attacked inspiration of the Bible, to retain their position.
1864	Dr. Scrivener publishes *A Full Collation of the Codex Sinaiticus.*
1864	On Sept. 23, Hort writes to Westcott: *"Protestantism is only parenthetical and temporary."*
1864-1938	Dates of Herman C. Hoskier
1865	On Good Friday, Westcott writes: *"[I] regard the Christian as in Christ--absolutely one with Him, and he does what Christ has done."*
1863	On Oct. 17, Hort writes to Westcott: *"Mary-worship and 'Jesus'-worship have very much in common."*
1865	On Nov. 17, Westcott writes: *"I wish I could see to what forgotten truth Mariolatry bears witness."*
1867	Tischendorf studies the Vatican Codex for 42 hours.
1867	On Oct. 26, Hort writes to Lightfoot: *"But you know I am a staunch sacerdotalist."*
1870	Oxford Movement is powerful in England.
1870	Papal declaration of infallibility
1870	Westcott and Hort print a tentative edition of their Greek New Testament.
1870	On Feb. 10, resolution appears which expresses the desirability of revision of the KJV.
1870	On May 28, Westcott writes to Hort: *"I feel that as 'we three' are together it would be wrong not to 'make the best of it' as Lightfoot says."*
1870	On June 4, Westcott writes to Lightfoot: *"Ought we not to have a conference before the first meeting for Revision?"*
1870	Committee is established to produce a Revised
1870	On June 22, Vance Smith, Unitarian, receives Holy Communion but does not recite Nicene Creed.
1870	Vatican and Sinaitic Manuscripts become king.

1870-1881	Dates of Revision
1871	Burgon writes *The last Twelve Verses of Mark.*
1871	On May 24, Westcott writes: *"We have had hard fighting during these last two days."*
1871	On July 25, Hort writes: *"I felt how impossible it would be for me to absent myself."*
1872	Tischendorf publishes his eighth edition for the first time on Vaticanus and Sinaiticus.
1875	On Jan. 27. Westcott writes: *"Our work yesterday was positively distressing."*
1876	R. D. Wilson graduates from Princeton.
1881	Dr. Ellicott submits the Revised Version to the Southern Convocation.
1881	In May, the Revised Version is published.
1881	On May 20, the Revised Version is published in America; it has immediate success in both England and America.
1881	On May 22, the Chicago *Tribune* and the Chicago *Times* published the entire New Testament.
1881	Westcott-Hort theory is hailed as final.
1881	Burgon writes three articles in the *Quarterly Review* against the Revised Version.
1881	Popularity of RV doesn't spread to the masses.
1881	MSS of RV had been abandoned since 500 A.D.
1881	Revisers of RV disagree basically with KJV scholars.
1883	Burgon publishes *The Revision Revised.*
1885	On June 7, Dr. George Sayles Bishop preaches a discourse concerning *"the new version and just in what direction it tends."*
1886	On March 22, Westcott writes: *"[Textual criticism] is a little gift which from school days seemed to be committed to me."*
1887	In June, John Fulton writes: *"It was not the design of the Divine Author to use classical Greek as the medium of His revelation."*
1888	On August 4, Burgon dies.
1890	On March 4,. Westcott writes, *"No one now, I suppose, holds that the first three chapters of Genesis, for example, give a literal history--I could never understand how any one reading them with open eyes could think they did."*
1893	Chicago World's Fair
1896	E. Miller, using fragments of Burgon's, publishes *The Traditional Text of the Holy Gospels* and *The Causes of the*

	Corruption of the Traditional Text.
1901	American Revised Version is published.
1903	Westcott's son comments in defense of his father.
1908	Date of Harris
1908	"Conscious agreement with [Westcott-Hort theory] or conscious disagreement and qualification mark all work in this field since 1881."
1910	Date of Conybeare
1910	Ferrar Fenton publishes his translation.
1914	Hoskier writes: "[Burgon] *maintained that Aleph and B had been tampered with and revised.*"
1914-1918	World War I
1920	In Dec., in one week the front page of one of great New York dailies has scarcely space free for anything except reports of murders, burglaries, and other crimes.
1921	On Dec. 22, the *United Presbyterian* gives a description of its *"Shorter Bible."*
1924	On July 16, the *Herald and Presbyter* state: *"The Revisers had a wonderful opportunity. They might have made a few changes and removed a few archaic expressions, and made the A.V. the most acceptable and beautiful and wonderful book of all time to come."*
1928	Article entitled *"Who Killed Goliath?"*
1929	On Dec. 29, it is reported: *"Every seminary of standing in this country has been teaching. . . almost everything contained in the new Commentary."*
1929	Article entitled: *"The dispute about Goliath."*
1929	Liberalism takes over Princeton.
1930	Robert Dick Wilson dies.
1930	Our *Authorized Bible Vindicated* is published by Dr. Benjamin G. Wilkinson.
1941	Date of Lake
1948	War of Liberation (Israel)
1951	Alfred Martin's dissertation for his Doctor of theology is titled: *"A Critical Examination of the Westcott-Hort Textual Theory."*

XXIX. Important Events in English and European Bible Translation History

1. Early Versions

Unger's Bible Dictionary says, *"There were portions of the Bible, and possibly the entire work, rendered into the English vernacular very early in the history of the language. Gildas states that 'When the English martyrs gave up their lives in the 4th century, all the copies of the Holy Scriptures which could be found were burned in the street.'"*

Now, in view of what we have seen above, that English was not spoken on the island of Britain until the arrival of the Germanic tribes in the mid-5th century, these Bibles most certainly were copies of the Old Latin in the hands of the Celts.

With this assessment Bruce agrees,

"Christianity was planted in Britain by the beginning of the 4th century at the latest. In A.D. 314, we have the record of three British bishops (those of York, London and Lincoln) attending the Council of Arles. The earliest British writer was one of the outstanding figures in early Christian literature--Pelagius (c. 370-450), who in the first decade of the 5th century produced at Rome commentaries on the thirteen epistles of Paul. About the end of the 4th century Ninjan, appointed bishop of the district now known as Galloway and Dumfries, evangelized the southern Picts, and established a monastery at Whithorn (Ad Candidam Casam) from which the Gospel was carried farther afield, in particular to Northern Ireland."

But there is no evidence of Bible translation having been carried out at this time in the languages of Britain and Ireland. Pelagius wrote in Latin, as did all the other churchmen of Western Europe. And even if the Bible had been translated into the native languages in those days, such translations would have had no place in the history of the English Bible. That history has as its starting point the arrival in Britain of the Germanic-speaking Angles and Saxons and Jutes in the course of the 5th century and their evangelization in the 6th and 7th centuries.

The following are the earliest known portions of the Scripture in the Anglo-Saxon vernacular (from Unger).

1)   Caedmon's versifications (689).
2)   Cuthbert's *Evangelistarium* (689). A portion of the Latin Vulgate with an interlinear English translation.

3)   Aldhelm's translation of the Psalms (early 8th century).

4)   Eadfurth's translation of the Gospels (720).

5)   The Venerable Bede's translation of John (735).

6)   King Alfred's translation of the Psalms (901).

7)   Archbishop Aelfric and others endeavored to provide translations which could be read in churches (late 10th century).

The Rushworth Gospels - eighth century, with tenth-century Interlinear Gloss

Rushworth Gospels--eighth century, with tenth century Interlinear Gloss
This interlinear English is based on Cuthbert's version.

Each of the above translations were apparently based on the Latin Vulgate.

The Venerable Bede spoke of the heavenly endowment granted to the herdsman Caedman in the latter part of the 7th century, which enabled him to sing in English verse the substance and themes of Scripture.

"He sang the creation of the world, the origin of man, and all the history of Genesis, and made many verses on the departure of the

children of Israel out of Egypt, and their entering into the promised land, with many other histories from Holy Writ; the Incarnation, Passion and Resurrection of our Lord, and His ascending into heaven; the coming of the Holy Ghost, and the preaching of the apostles; also the terror of judgement to come, the horror of the pains of hell, and the joys of heaven." (Bruce)

Of the venerable Bede himself, Terrence Brown records,
In A.D. 735, Bede labored at Jarrow on his translation of the Gospel. A letter written by one of his pupils describes, how the aged scholar pressed on with his work of translating the Scriptures up to, the last moment of his life. Early in the morning of *"Ascension Day"* in A.D. 735, he summoned his helpers to continue with the task and dictated to them the translation of John's Gospel from the words, *"What are they among so many?"* As the sun was setting, one of the scribes told him there was only one more chapter, but it seemed hard for Bede to speak. He replied, *"Nay, it is easy, take up thy pen and write quickly."* The young scribe wrote on until he could tell his master that only one sentence was wanting. When Bede dictated it the young man exclaimed, *"It is finished, master!"* Bede replied, *"Aye, it is finished! Lift me up and place me by the window where I have so often prayed to God."* Then with the Name of the Father, Son and Holy Spirit upon his lips, he passed into the presence of the Lord.

2.   Wycliffe's Bible

The next four hundred years were an important period in the development of the English language. It is not possible to give precise dates but from A.D. 1066 to about 1150 Saxon and Norman French were in use side by side. From about 1150 the gradual fusion of the two peoples caused their languages to mingle and merge with one another, producing what has been described as *"semi-Saxon."* The old Saxon and the Norman French fell into disuse, and from about 1250 *"English emerges to pass through a century or more of development before being used as the vehicle of Wycliffe's English Bible of A.D. 1382"* (Brown).

Leading up to Wycliffe, about 1300 a metrical version of the Psalms was made. It was followed by several prose translations, one of which was by Richard Rolle. Portions of the New Testament were also translated (*New Bible Dictionary*).

The crowning achievement of the latter part of the Middle English period was the translation associated with John Wycliffe. (See also above in the section dealing with the Latin Vulgate.)

John Wycliffe is justly styled the "Morning Star of the Reformation." In Roman Catholic England, he spoke out forcibly on the use of Scripture. He constantly appealed to Holy Scripture as the primary and absolute authority in matters of faith and morals, and maintained the desirability of its being made generally accessible to Christians. The idea that Wycliffe himself translated the Bible into English rests on a statement of his great Czech disciple, Jan Hus; it is certain, at any rate, that the Wycliffite versions are rightly so called, whether he actually did much translation himself or not, as the work was carried out under his influence and in accordance with his policy. Whatever be the final verdict on the subject, Wycliffe's Biblical scholarship cannot be gainsaid.

There are two Wycliffite versions of the Bible which must be distinguished from each other. One of these was the work of Nicholas of Hereford, a follower of Wycliffe, so far as the Old testament as far as Baruch 3:20 is concerned (thus unfortunately it had the Apocrypha). Purvey's prologue to his version is interesting and part of it is worth quoting:

'A simple creature hath translated the Bible out of Latin into English. First this simple creature had much travail, with divers fellows and helpers, to gather many old Bibles, and other doctors, and common glosses, and to make one Latin Bible some deal true. . .

A translator hath great need to study well the sense both before and after, and then also he hath need to live a clean life and be full devout in prayers, and have not his wit occupied about worldly things, that the Holy Spirit, Author of all wisdom and cunning and truth, dress him for his work and suffer him not to err.

God grant to us all grace to know well and to keep well Holy Writ, and to suffer joyfully some pain for it at the last.' (Bruce)

The following will give you an idea, of the late Middle English of Wycliffe's Bible. The portion is John 11.

> *"The disciplis scien to hum, Maister now the Jewis soughten for to stoone thee, and est goist thou thidir? Jheus answered whether ther ben not twelve ouris of the dai? If any man wandre in the night he stomblish, for light is not in him. He saith these thingis and aftir these thingis he seith to hem Lazarus oure freend slepith but Y go to reise hym fro sleep therfor hise disciplis seiden: Lord if he slepith he schal be saaf."*

Miller's Church History gives us a challenging summary of Wycliffe and his great work,

Without following more minutely the general labors of Wycliffe, or the plottings of his enemies to interrupt him, we will not notice that which was the great work of his useful life--the complete English Version of the Holy Scriptures. We have seen him boldly and fearlessly assailing and exposing the countless abuses of Popery, unfolding the truth to the students, and zealously preaching the Gospel to the poor; but he is now engaged in a work which will a thousand times more enrich his own world. He is yet more exclusively engaged with the Sacred Writings. It was not until he became more fully acquainted with the Bible that he rejected the false doctrines of the Church of Rome. It is one thing to see the outward abuses of the hierarchy, it is quite another to see the mind of God in the doctrines of His Word.

The Later Wycliffite Bible--early fifteenth century
British Museum
(Actual size 15 in. x 10¼ in.)

The Latter Wycliffite Bible--early fifteenth century, British Museum
(Actual size 15 in. x 10.25 in.)

As soon as the translation of a portion was finished, the labor of the copyists began, and the Bible was ere long widely circulated either wholly or in parts. The effect of thus bring home the Word of God to the unlearned--to citizens, soldiers, and the lower classes--is beyond human power to estimate.

Minds were enlightened, souls were saved, and God was glorified. *"Wycliffe,"* said one of his adversaries, *"has made the Gospel common, and more open to laymen and to women who can read than it is wont to* be to clerks well learned and of good understanding; so that the pearl of the Gospel is scattered and is trodden under foot of swine." In the year 1380 the English Bible was complete. In 1390 the bishops attempted to get the version condemned by Parliament, lest it should become an occasion of heresies; but John of Gaunt declared that the English would not submit to the degradation of being denied a vernacular Bible. *"The Word of God is the faith of His people,"* it was said, *"and though the Pope and all his clerks should disappear from the face of the earth, our faith would not fail, for it is founded on Jesus alone, our Master and our God."* The attempt at prohibition having failed, the English Bible spread far and wide, being diffused chiefly through the exertions of the *"poor priests,"* like *"the poor men of Lyons"* at an earlier period.

The Christian reader will not fail to trace the hand of the Lord in this great work. The grand, the Divine, instrument was now ready and in the hands of the people, by means of which the Reformation in the sixteenth century was to be accomplished. The Word of God which liveth and abideth for ever is rescued from the dark mysteries of scholasticism, from the dust-covered shelves of the cloister, from the obscurity of ages, and given to the English people in their own mother-tongue. Who can estimate the blessing? Let the ten thousand times ten thousand tongues which shall praise the Lord for ever give the answer. But, oh! The wickedness--the soul-murdering wickedness--of the Romish priesthood in keeping the Word of Life from the laity! Is the glorious truth of God's love to the world in the light of His Son-of the efficacy of the blood of Christ to cleanse from all sin--to be concealed from the perishing multitude, and seen only by a privileged few? There is no refinement in cruelty on the face of the whole earth to compare with this. It is the ruin of both soul and body in Hell forever.

Having received many warnings, many threatenings, and experienced some narrow escapes from the loathsome dungeon and the burning pile, Wycliffe was allowed to close his days in peace, in the midst of his flock and his pastoral labors at Lutterworth. After a forty-eight hours' illness from a stroke of paralysis, he died on the last day of the year 1384.

The humble Christian, the bold witness, the faithful preacher, the able professor, and the great reformer has passed off the scene. He has gone to his rest and his reward is on high. But the doctrines which he propagated with so much zeal can never die. His name in his followers continued formidable to the false priests of Rome. *"Every second man you meet in the way,"* said a bitter adversary, *"is a Wycliffite."* He was used of God to give an impulse to Christian inquiry which was felt in the most distant corners of Europe.

3. The Invention of Printing

About twenty years after Wycliffe's death, a boy named Gensfeisch ("Gooseflesh") was amusing himself cutting out the letters of his name from a piece of bark. He dropped one of these accidentally in a pot of hot dye, snatched it out and dropped it on a piece of white skin on a bench near the fire and was intrigued to see the pattern of the letter was impressed on the skin. It is possible that this experience lingered in his mind and suggested the idea of printing. Thirty years afterwards he set up his famous press at Menz under the name of Gutenberg, his mother's family name. This was an epoch-making invention and was to contribute greatly towards the rapid reproduction of the Scriptures and the establishment of the Reformation in Europe (Brown).

Again to quote the stirring words of Andrew Miller:

Just at this period the Lord was making *"all things work together for good"* in a most remarkable way. Two silent agents of immense influence and power were ordained to precede the living voices of His Gospel preachers--the invention of printing and the manufacture of paper. These harmonious inventions were brought to great perfection during the latter half of the 15th century, for which we can lift up our hearts in praise and thanksgiving to God.

We have now reached a turning point in our history: and not only in the history of the Church, but of civilization, of the social condition of the European states, and of the human family. It is well to pause on such an eminence and look around us for a moment. We see a Divine hand for the good of all gathering things together, though apparently unconnected. The falling of an empire, the flight of a few Greeks, with their literary treasures, the awakening of the long dormant mind of the western world, the invention of printing from movable types, and the discovery of making fine white paper from linen rags. Incongruous as *"linen rags"* may sound with the literature of the Greeks and the skill of Gutenberg, both would have proved of little avail without the improved paper. Means, the most insignificant in man's account, when used of God, are all sufficient. By miraculous power, a dry rod in the hand of Moses shakes Egypt from center to circumference, divides the Red Sea, and gives living water from the flinty rock; a smooth pebble from the brook, or an empty ram's horn accomplishes great deliverances in Israel. The power is of God; faith looks only to Him.

It is a deeply interesting fact to the Christian, that the first complete book which Gutenberg printed with his cut metal types was a folio edition of the Bible in the Latin Vulgate, consisting of six hundred and forty-one leaves. Hallam, in his *Literary History* beautifully observes: *"It is a very striking circumstance, that the high-minded investors of the great art tried at the very outset so bold a flight as the printing of an entire Bible, and executed it with great success. . . . We may see in imagination this venerable and splendid volume leading up the crowded myriads of its followers, and imploring, as it were, a blessing on the new art, by dedicating its firstfruits to the service of heaven."*

From an early period the mode of printing from blocks of wood had been practiced.   Sometimes the engravings, or impressions, were accompanied by a few lines of letters cut in the block. Gradually these were extended to a few leaves and called block-books. An ingenious blacksmith, it is said, invented in the 11th century separate letters made of wood. The celebrated John Gutenberg, who was born at a village near Mentz, in the year 1397, substituted metal for the wooden letters; his associate, Schoeffer, cut the characters in a matrix, after which the types were cast, and thus completed the art of printing as it now remains.

Parchment, preparations of straw, the bark of trees, papyrus, and cotton had sufficed for the printer and transcriber till the 14th century. But these preparations would have been utterly inadequate to supply the demand of the new process. Happily, however, the discovery of making paper from rags coincided with the discovery of letterpress printing. The first paper-mill in England was erected at Dartmouth, by a German named Spielmann, in 1588.

(1) The First Printed Bible

All historians seem to agree, that Gutenberg, having spent nearly ten years in bringing his experiments to perfection, had so impoverished himself that he found it necessary to invite some capitalist to join him. John Faust, the wealthy goldsmith of Mentz, to whom he made known his secret, agreed to go into partnership with him, and to supply the means for carrying out the design. But it does not appear that Gutenberg and his associates, Schoeffer and Faust, were actuated by any loftier motive in executing this glorious work, than that of realizing a large sum of money by the enterprise. The letters were such an exact imitation of the best copyists, that they intended to pass them off as fine manuscript copies, and thus to obtain the usual high prices. Those employed in the work were bound to the strictest secrecy. The first edition appears to have been sold at manuscript prices without the secret having transpired. A second edition was brought out about 1462, when John Faust went to Paris with a number of copies. He sold one to the king for seven hundred crowns and another to the archbishop for four hundred crowns. The prelate, delighted with such a beautiful copy at so low a price, showed it to the king. His majesty-produced his, for which he had paid nearly double the money; but what was their astonishment on finding they were identical even in the most minute strokes and dots. They became alarmed, and concluded they must be produced by magic, and the capital letters being in red ink, they supposed that it was blood, and no longer doubted that he was in league with the Devil and assisted by him in his magical art.

Information was forthwith given to the police against John Faust. His lodgings were searched, and his Bibles seized. Other copies which he had sold were collected and compared; and finding they were all precisely alike, he was pronounced a magician. The king ordered him to be thrown into prison, and he would soon have been thrown into the flames, but he saved himself by confessing to the deceit, and by making a full revelation of the secret of his art. The mystery was now revealed, the workmen were no longer bound to secrecy, printers were dispersed abroad, carrying the secret of their art wherever they found a welcome, and the sounds of printing presses were soon heard in many lands. About 1474, the art was introduced into England by William Caxton; and in 1508 it was introduced into Scotland by Walter Chepman.

Before the days of printing, many valuable books existed in manuscript, and seminaries of learning flourished in all civilized countries, but knowledge was necessarily confined to a comparatively small number of people. The manuscripts were so scarce and dear that they could only be purchased by kings and nobles, by collegiate and ecclesiastical establishments. *"A copy of the Bible cost from forty to fifty pounds for the writing only, for it took an expert copyist about ten months' labor to make one."* Although several other books issued from the new presses, the Latin Bible was the favorite book with all the printers. They usually commence operations, wherever they went, by issuing an edition of the Latin Bible. It was most in demand, and brought high prices. In this way Latin Bibles multiplied rapidly. Translators now began their work; and by individual reformers in different countries, the Word of God was translated into various languages in the course of a few years. *"Thus an Italian version appeared in 1474, a Bohemian in 1475, a Dutch in 1477, a French in 1477, and a Spanish in 1478; as if heralding the approach of the coming Reformation."*

(2)   Rome's Opposition to the Rapidly Spreading Word

But, as usual, the great enemies of truth and light and liberty took the alarm. The Archbishop of Mentz placed the printers of the city under strict censorship. Pope Alexander VI issued a Bill prohibiting the printers of Mentz, Cologne, Treves, and Magdeburg from publishing any books without the express licence of their archbishops. Finding that the reading of the Bible was extending, the priests began to preach against it from their pulpits. *"They had found out,"* said a French monk, *"a new language called Greek: we must carefully guard ourselves against it. That language will be the mother of all sorts of heresies. I see in the hands of a great number of persons a book written in this language called, 'The New Testament'; it is a book full of brambles, with vipers in them. As to the Hebrew, whoever learns that becomes a Jew at once."* Bibles and Testaments were seized wherever found, and burnt; but more Bibles and Testaments seemed to rise as if by magic from their ashes. The printers also were seized and burnt. *"We must root out printing, or printing will root out us,"* said the Vicar of Croydon in a sermon preached at Paul's Cross. And the university of Paris, panic-stricken, declared before the Parliament: *"There is an end of religion if the study of Greek and Hebrew is permitted."*

The great success of the new translations spread alarm throughout the Romish Church. She trembled for the supremacy of her own favorite Vulgate. The fears of the priests and monks were increased when they saw the people reading the Scriptures in their own mother tongue, and observed a growing disposition to call in question the value of attending mass, and the authority of the priesthood. Instead of saying their prayers through the priests in Latin, they began to pray to God direct in their native tongue. The clergy, finding their revenues diminishing, appealed to the Sorbonne, the most renowned theological school in Europe. The Sorbonne called upon Parliament to interfere with a strong hand. War was immediately proclaimed against books, and the printers of them. Printers who were convicted of having printed Bibles were burnt. In the year 1534, about twenty men and one woman were burnt alive in Paris. In 1535 the Sorbonne obtained an ordinance from the King for the suppression of printing. *"But it was too late,"* as an able writer observes; *"the art was now full born, and could no more be suppressed than light, or air, or life. Books had become a public necessity, and supplied a great public want; and every year saw them multiplying more abundantly."*

While Rome was thus thundering her awful prohibitions against the liberty of thought, and lengthening her arm to persecute wherever the

Bible had penetrated and found followers, at least all over France, God was hastening by means of His own Word and the printing press, that mighty revolution which was so soon to change the destinies of both Church and State.

The darkness of the middle ages is rapidly passing away. The rising sun of the Reformation will ere long dispel the gloom of Jezebel's long reign of a thousand years.

4.   The Received Text Is Printed

(1)   The Man Erasmus

Referring to Miller:

"Reuchlin and Erasmus--these famous names--may be conveniently and appropriately introduced here.   Although not reformers, they contributed much to the success of the Reformation.   They were called "Humanists"--men eminent for human learning.   The revival of literature, but especially the critical study of the languages in which the Holy Scriptures were written--Hebrew, Greek and Latin--rendered the highest service to the first reformers.   As in the days of Josiah, Ezra and Nehemiah, the great Reformation was an immediate connection with the recovery and study of the written Word of God.   The Bible, which had lain so long silent in manuscript beneath the dust of old libraries, was now printed, and laid before the people in their own tongue.   This was light from God, and that which armed the reformers with invincible power.   Down to the days of Reuchlin and Erasmus the Vulgate was the received text.   Greek and Hebrew were almost unknown in the West."

Reuchlin studied at the University of Paris.   Happily for him, the celebrated Wesselus was then teaching Hebrew at that renowned school of theology.   There he received, not only the first rudiments of the language, but a knowledge of the Gospel of the grace of God.   He also studied Greek, and learned to speak Latin with great purity.   At the early age of twenty he began to teach philosophy, Greek and Latin at Basle; *"and,"* says D'Aubigne, *"what then passed for a miracle, a German was heard speaking Greek."*   He afterwards settled at Wittenberg--the cradle of the Reformation--instructed the young Melanchthon in Hebrew and prepared for publication the first Hebrew and German grammar and lexicon.   Who can estimate all that the Reformation owes to Reuchlin, though he remained in the communion of the Romish Church!

Erasmus, who was about twelve years younger than Reuchlin, pursued the same line of study, but with still higher powers and greater celebrity. From about 1500 to 1518, when Luther rose into notice, Erasmus was the most distinguished literary person in Christendom. He was born at Rotterdam, in 1465; was left an orphan at the age of thirteen; was robbed by his guardians, who, to cover their dishonesty, persuaded him to enter a monastery. In 1492, he was ordained a priest, but he always entertained the greatest dislike for a monastic life, and embraced the first opportunity to regain his liberty. After leaving the Augustinian convent at Stein, he went to pursue his favorite studies at the University of Paris.

With the most indefatigable industry he devoted himself entirely to literature, and soon acquired a great reputation among the learned. The society of the poor student was courted by the varied talent of the time. Lord Mountjoy, whom he met as a Pupil at Paris, invited him to England. His first visit to this country, in 1498, was followed by several others, down to the year 1515, during which he became acquainted with many eminent men, received many honors, formed some warm friendships, and spent most of his brightest days. He resided at both the Universities and, during his third and longest visit, was professor of Greek at Cambridge. All acknowledged his supremacy in the world of letters, and for a long time he reigned without a rival. But our object at present is rather to inquire, *"What was his influence on the Reformation?"*

Under the gracious, guiding hand of Him who sees the end from the beginning, Erasmus bent all his great mental powers, and all his laborious studies to the preparation of a critical edition of the Greek Testament. This work appeared at Basle in 1516, one year before the Reformation, accompanied by a Latin translation, in which he corrected the errors of the Vulgate. This was daring work in those days. There was a great outcry from many quarters against this dangerous novelty. *"His New Testament was attacked,"* says Robertson; *"why should the language of the schismatic Greeks interfere with the sacred and traditional Latin? How could any improvement be made on the Vulgate translation? There was a college at Cambridge, especially proud of its theological character, which would not admit a copy within its gates. But the editor was able to shelter himself under the name of Pope Leo, who had accepted the dedication of the volume."*

To question the fidelity of the Vulgate, was a crime of the greatest magnitude in the eyes of the Roman Catholic Church. The Vulgate could no longer be of absolute exclusive authority; the Greek was its superior not only in antiquity, but yet more as the original text. At this time Erasmus stood at the head of scholars and men of letters. He was patronized by the Pope, many prelates, and by the chief princes of

Europe. Sheltered behind such an ample shield, he was perfectly secure and, knowing this, fearlessly went on with his great work.

To give the reader some idea of the popularity of this singularly great, yet in some respects weak man, we may just notice that his book, entitled *Praise of Folly*, went through twenty-seven editions during his lifetime; and his *Colloquies* were so eagerly received that in one year, twenty-four thousand copies were sold. In these books, he assailed with great power, and the most bitter satire, the inconsistencies of the monks--their intrusiveness and rapacity in connection with deathbeds, wills, and funerals--and thus indirectly served the cause of the Reformation.

Erasmus had many tempting offers as to pensions and promotion, but his love for his learned labors led him to prefer comparative poverty with perfect liberty. In 1516, he took up his abode at Basle, where his works were printed by Froben, and he diligently labored in correcting proofs, and otherwise assisting that learned printer with his fine editions of classical works.

But the great work for which he seems to have been specially fitted by God was his Greek New Testament. *"Erasmus,"* says D'Aubigne, *"thus did for the New Testament what Reuchlin had done for the Old. Henceforward divines were able to read the Word of God in the original languages, and at a later period to recognize the purity of the reformed doctrines. Reuchlin and Erasmus gave the Bible to the learned; Luther gave it to the people."*

The chain of witnesses was now complete. Wesselus, Reuchlin, Erasmus, and Luther were linked together.

We allow Wilkinson to describe further this man God used at this most important epoch.

The Revival of Learning produced that giant intellect and scholar, Erasmus. It is a common proverb that *"Erasmus laid the egg and Luther hatched it."* The streams of Grecian learning were again flowing into the European plains, and a man of caliber was needed to draw from their best and bestow it upon the needy nations of the West. Endowed by nature with a mind that could do ten hours' work in one, Erasmus, during his mature years in the earlier part of the 16th century, was the intellectual giant of Europe. He was ever at work, visiting libraries, searching in every nook and corner for the profitable. He was ever collecting comparing, writing and publishing. Europe was rocked from end to end by his books which exposed the ignorance of the monks, the superstitions of the priesthood, the bigotry and the childish and coarse religion of the day. He classified the Greek Manuscripts and read the Fathers.

It is customary even today with those who are bitter against the pure teachings of the Received Text, to sneer at Erasmus. No perversion of facts is too great to belittle his work. Yet while he lived, Europe was at his feet. Several times the King of England offered him any position in the kingdom, at his own price; the Emperor of Germany did the same. The Pope offered to make him a cardinal. This he steadfastly refused, as he would not compromise his conscience. In fact, had he been so minded, he perhaps could have made himself Pope. France and Spain sought him to become a dweller in their realm; while Holland prepared to claim him as her most distinguished citizen.

Erasmus' New Testament--1516 (Actual size as reproduced, 9.5 in. x 6.5 in.)

Book after book came from his hand. Faster and faster came the demands for his publications. But his crowning work was the New Testament in Greek. At last after one thousand years, the New Testament was printed (1516 A.D.) in the original tongue. Astonished and confounded, the world, deluged by superstitions, coarse traditions, and monkeries, read the pure story of the Gospels. The effect was marvelous. At once, all recognized the great value of this work which for over four hundred years (1516 to 1931) was to hold the dominant place in an era of Bibles. Translation after translation has been taken from it, such as the German and the English and others. Critics have tried to belittle the Greek manuscripts he used, but the enemies of Erasmus, or rather the enemies of the Received Text, have found insuperable difficulties withstanding their attacks. Writing to Peter Baberius August 13, 1521, Erasmus says:

> *"I did my best with the New Testament, but it provoked endless quarrels. Edward Lee pretended to have discovered 300 errors. They appointed a commission, which professed to have found bushels of them. Every dinner table rang with the blunders of Erasmus. I required particulars, and could not have them."*

There were hundreds of manuscripts for Erasmus to examine, and he did; but he used only a few. What matters? The vast bulk of manuscripts in Greek are practically all the Received Text. If the few Erasmus used were typical, that is, after he had thoroughly balanced the evidence of many and used a few which displayed that balance, did he not, with all the problems before him, arrive at practically the same result which only could be arrived at today by a fair and comprehensive investigation?

Moreover, the text he chose had such an outstanding history in the Greek, the Syrian, and the Waldensian Churches, that it constituted an irresistible argument for and proof of God's providence. God did not write a hundred Bibles; there is only one Bible, the others at best are only approximations. In other words the Greek New Testament of Erasmus, known as the Received Text, is none other than the Greek New Testament which successfully met the rage of its pagan and papal enemies.

We are told that testimony from the ranks of our enemies constitutes the highest kind of evidence. The following statement which I now submit, is taken from the defense of their doings by two members of that body so hostile to the Greek New Testament of Erasmus--the Revisers of 1870-1881. This quotation shows that the manuscripts of Erasmus coincide with the great bulk of manuscripts.

> *"The manuscripts which Erasmus used, differ, for the most part, only in small and insignificant details from the bulk of the cursive manuscripts. The general character of their text is the same. By this observation the pedigree of the Received Text is carried up beyond the individual manuscripts used by Erasmus to a great body of*

manuscripts of which the earliest are assigned to the 9th century."
(Hort)

Then after quoting Doctor Hort, they draw this conclusion on his statement: *"This remarkable statement completes the pedigree of the Received Text. That pedigree stretches back to a remote antiquity. The first ancestor of the Received Text was, as Dr. Hort is careful to remind us, at least contemporary with the oldest of our extant manuscripts, if not older than any one of them."*

(2)   Particulars of The Greek Text Edited by Erasmus

Strouse states that Erasmus primarily used the following five MSS in the first edition (1516):

11th century	MS of the Gospels, Acts, and Epistles
15th century	MS of the Gospels
12th-14th cent	MS of Acts and Epistles
15th century	MS of Acts and Epistles
12th century	MS of Revelation

Erasmus had translated the Greek into a Latin Version in 1505-1506 and presumably had other MSS than these five.

These are the manuscripts to which F. J .A. Hort referred when he wrote to a friend, *"Think of that vile Textus Receptus leaning entirely on late MSS."*   But as shown above, Erasmus knew that they were representative of the overwhelming majority of MSS.   Subsequent investigation since has shown that Erasmus' judgement was correct. The Bible believer resting on the promises of Christ to preserve His Word can see the guiding hand of God in the choice of these MSS.

Erasmus produced five editions in which there were a number of refinements and corrections.

1516	Dedicated to Pope Leo X. (Remember all of Europe was still under Catholicism. Luther posted his Ninety-five Theses on 31 October 1517. Erasmus welcomed it and sent copies to his friends in England.)
1519	Revision of Greek and Latin
1522	Includes I John 5:7
1527	Three columns (Greek, Vulgate, Erasmus' Latin)
1535	Omitted Vulgate

(3)   The Analysis by Edward F. Hills

Possibly the most penetrating analysis ever written on the early publication of the Received Text is the following by Edward F. Hills.

One of the leading principles of the Protestant Reformation was the sole and absolute authority of the holy Scriptures. The New Testament text in which early Protestants placed such implicit confidence was the Textus Receptus (Received Text) which was first printed in 1516 under the editorship of Erasmus and only slightly modified in subsequent editions during the 16th and 17th centuries. The more important of these later editions of the Textus Receptus include the second edition of Erasmus (1519), which formed the basis of Luther's German Version, the third edition of Stephanus (1550), which is that form of the Textus Receptus generally preferred by English scholars, the fifth edition of Beza (1598), on which the King James Version was mainly based, and the second Elzevir edition (1633), which was generally adopted on the European Continent and in which the term Textus Receptus first appeared.

The Textus Receptus is virtually identical with the Traditional text found in the majority of the Greek New Testament manuscripts. Kirsopp Lake and his associates (1928) demonstrated this fact in their intensive researches in the Traditional (Byzantine) text. Using their collations, they came to the conclusion that in the eleventh chapter of Mark *"the most popular text in manuscripts of the 10th to 14th century"* differed from the Textus Receptus only four times. This small number of differences seems almost negligible in view of the fact that in this same chapter Aleph, B, and D differ from the Textus Receptus 69, 71, and 95 times respectively. Also add to this the fact that in this same chapter B differs from Aleph 34 times and from D 102 times and that Aleph differs from D 100 times.

(a) The Received Text and the Providence of God

The Textus Receptus, then, is that form of the Greek New Testament text which God in His providence provided for His people during the days of the Protestant Reformation and which still remains, in spite of the detractions of naturalistic critics, the best printed text of the Greek New Testament that has yet been produced. Back of the labors of Erasmus and the other early editors who brought the Textus Receptus into being stood the guiding providence of God. The more we consider the factors involved in this process, the more we see that this is so.

1. The Greek Manuscripts Used by Erasmus

When Erasmus came to Basle in July, 1515, to begin work on the first edition of his printed Greek New Testament, he found five Greek New Testament manuscripts ready for his use. These are now designated by the following numbers: 1 (an 11th century manuscript of the Gospels, Acts and Epistles); 2 (a 15th century manuscript of the Gospels); 2ap (a 12-14th century manuscript of Acts and the Epistles); 4ap (a 15th century manuscript of Acts and the Epistles); and 1r (a 12th century manuscript of Revelation). Of these manuscripts Erasmus used 1 and 4ap only occasionally. In the Gospels, Acts and Epistles, his main reliance was on 2 and 2ap.

The fact that the Textus Receptus was based only on the few late manuscripts which Erasmus found at Basle is usually held against it. In the opinion of naturalistic critics this was just an unhappy accident. *"Erasmus used only a handful of manuscripts, which happened to be at Basle."* So Kenyon (1937) observes. But those that take this attitude do not reckon sufficiently with the providence of God. When we view this circumstance in its proper perspective, we see the divine plan behind it all. The text which Erasmus published was not his own but was taken, virtually without change, from the few manuscripts which God, working providentially, had placed at his disposal. These manuscripts were of the Traditional type, and thus in the providence of God it came about that during the Protestant Reformation and ever since God's people have been provided with the Traditional (true) New Testament text found in the vast majority of the New Testament manuscripts.

2. The Human Aspects of the Received Text

God works providentially through sinful and fallible human beings, and therefore His providential guidance has its human as well as its divine side. And these human elements were very evident in the first edition (1516) of the Textus Receptus. For one thing, the work was performed so hastily that the text was disfigured with a great number of typographical errors. These misprints, however, were soon eliminated by Erasmus himself in his later editions and by other early editors and hence are not a factor which need be taken into account in any estimation of the abiding value of the Textus Receptus.

But the thing for which Erasmus has been most severely criticized is his handling of the book of Revelation. His manuscript of Revelation (1r) had been mutilated at the end with the consequent loss of verses 16-21 of chapter 22, and its text in other places was sometimes hard to distinguish from the commentary of Andreas of Caesarea in which it was embedded. Erasmus endeavored to supply these deficiencies in his manuscript by retranslating the Latin Vulgate into Greek. In his fourth edition of his Greek New Testament (1527), Erasmus corrected much of this translation Greek on the basis of a comparison with the *Complutensian Polyglot* (1522), but he overlooked some of it, and this still remains in the Textus Receptus. [Did Stephanus or Beza make changes here?]

It is customary for naturalistic critics to make the most of these and to sneer at it as a mean and almost sordid thing. These critics picture the Textus Receptus merely as a money-making venture on the part of Froben the publisher. Froben, they say, heard that the Spanish Cardinal Ximenes was about to publish a printed Greek New Testament as part of his great *Complutensian Polyglot* Bible. In order, therefore, to get something on the market first, it is said, Froben hired Erasmus, at a good salary, as his editor and rushed a Greek New Testament through his press in less than a year's time. But those who concentrate in this way on the human factors involved in the production of the Textus Receptus are utterly unmindful of the providence of God. God had a deadline to meet as well as Froben. For in the very next year the Reformation was to break out in Wittenberg, and it was important that the Greek New Testament should be published first in one of the future strongholds of Protestantism rather than in Spain, the land of the Inquisition.

3. *Latin Vulgate Readings in the Received Text*

The God who brought the New Testament text safely through the ancient and medieval manuscript period did not fumble when it came time to transfer this text to the modern printed page. This is the conviction which guides the believing Bible student as he considers the relationship of the printed Textus Receptus to the Traditional New Testament text found in the majority of the Greek manuscripts. As has been stated, these two texts are virtually identical. There are a few places, however, in which they differ, though not seriously. The most important of these differences are due to the fact that Erasmus, influenced by the usage of the Latin-speaking Church in which he was reared, sometimes followed the Latin Vulgate rather than the Traditional Greek text that lay before him.

Are the readings which Erasmus thus introduced into the Textus Receptus necessarily erroneous? To the believing Bible student this is a most unlikely supposition. It is hardly possible that the divine providence which had preserved the New Testament text during the long ages of the manuscript period would blunder when at last this text was committed to the printing press. Surely it is much more probable that the Textus Receptus was a further step in God's providential preservation of the New Testament text and that these few Latin Vulgate readings which were incorporated into the Textus Receptus were genuine readings which had been preserved in the usage of the Latin-speaking Church. Erasmus, we may well believe, was guided providentially by the usage of the Latin Church to include these readings in this printed Greek New Testament text. In the Textus Receptus God corrected the few mistakes of any consequence which yet remained in the Traditional New Testament text of the majority of the Greek manuscripts.

Hence, we may conclude, it was in the special providence of God that the text of the Greek New Testament was first printed and published not in the East but in Western Europe where the influence of the Latin usage and of the Latin Vulgate was very strong. Through the influence of the usage of the Latin-speaking Church Erasmus was providentially guided to follow the Latin Vulgate here and there in those few places in which the Latin Church usage rather than the Greek Church usage had preserved the genuine reading. Thus the Textus Receptus was not a blunder or a set-back but a further step in the providential preservation of the New Testament text. In it the few errors of any consequence which yet remained in the Traditional Greek text were corrected by the providence of God operating through the usage of the Latin-speaking Church of Western Europe.

The following are the most familiar and important of those relatively few Latin Vulgate readings which, though not part of the Traditional Greek text, seem to have been placed in the Textus Receptus by the direction of God's special providence and therefore are to be retained. The reader will note that these Latin Vulgate readings are also found in other ancient witnesses, namely, old Greek manuscripts, versions and Fathers.

Matt. 10:8.   *raise the dead* is omitted by the majority of the Greek manuscripts. This reading is present, however, in B, Aleph. C, D. 1, the Latin Vulgate, and the Textus Receptus.

Matt. 27:35   *that it might be fulfilled which was spoken by the prophet, They parted my garments among them, and upon my vesture did they cast lots*: present in Eusebius (c. 325), 1 and other "Caesarean" manuscripts, the Harclean Syriac, the Old Latin, the Vulgate, and the Textus Receptus; omitted by the majority of the Greek manuscripts.

John 3:25   *Then there arose a questioning between some of John's disciples and the Jews about purifying*: Papyrus 66, Aleph, 1 and the other "Caesarean" manuscripts, the Old Latin, the Vulgate, and the Textus Receptus read *the Jews*, Papyrus 75, B, the Peshitta, and the majority of the Greek manuscripts read *a Jew*.

Acts 8:37   *And Philip said, If thou believest with all thine heart, thou mayest. And he answered and said, I believe that Jesus Christ is the Son of God.* This reading is absent from the majority of the Greek manuscripts, but it is present in some of them. including E (6th or 7th century). It is cited by Irenaeus (c. 180) and Cyprian (c. 250) and is found in the Old Latin and the Vulgate. In his notes Erasmus says that he took this reading from the margin of 4ap and incorporated it into the Textus Receptus.

Act 9:5   *It is hard for thee to kick against the pricks*: This reading is absent here from the Greek manuscripts but present in Old Latin manuscripts and in the Latin Vulgate known to Erasmus. It is present also at the end of Acts 9:4 in E, 431, the Peshitta, and certain manuscripts of the Latin Vulgate. In Acts 26:14, however, this reading is present in all the Greek manuscripts. In his notes Erasmus indicates that he took this reading from Acts 26:14 and inserted it here.

Acts 9:6   *And he trembling and astonished said, Lord, what wilt Thou have me to do? and the Lord said unto him*: This reading is found in the Latin Vulgate and in other ancient witnesses. It is absent, however, from the Greek manuscripts, due, according to Lake and Cadbury (1933), *"to the paucity of Western Greek texts and the absence of D at this point."* In his notes Erasmus indicates that this reading is a translation made by him from the Vulgate into Greek.

Acts 20:28   *Church of God*: Here the majority of the manuscripts read, Church of the Lord and God. The Latin Vulgate, however, and the Textus Receptus read, Church of God, which is also the reading of B, Aleph, and other ancient witnesses.

Rom. 16:25-27 In the majority of the manuscripts this doxology is placed at the end of chapter 14. In the Latin Vulgate and the Textus Receptus it is placed at the end of chapter 16, and this is also the position it occupies in B, Aleph, C, and D.

(b) Should I John 5:7 be in our Bible?

In the Textus Receptus I John 5:7-8 reads as follows:

7 *For there are three that bear witness IN HEAVEN, THE FATHER, THE WORD, AND THE HOLY SPIRIT; AND THESE THREE ARE ONE.*
8 *AND THERE ARE THREE THAT BEAR WITNESS IN EARTH, the spirit, and the water, and the blood: and these three agree in one.*

The words printed in capital letters constitute the so-called Johannine Comma, the best known of the Latin Vulgate readings of the Textus Receptus, a reading which, on believing principles, must also be regarded as possibly genuine. This comma has been the occasion of much controversy and is still an object of interest to textual critics. One of the more recent discussions of it is found in *Windisch's Katholischen Briefe* (revised by Preisker, 1951); a more accessible treatment of it in English is that provided by A. E. Brooke (1912) in the International Critical Commentary. Metzger (1964) also deals with this passage in his handbook, but briefly.

1. How I John 5:7 Entered the Received Text

As has been observed above, the Textus Receptus has both its human aspect and its divine aspect, like the Protestant Reformation itself or any other work of God's providence. And when we consider the manner in which the Johannine comma entered the Textus Receptus, we see this human element at work. Erasmus omitted the Johannine comma from the first edition (1516) of his printed Greek New Testament on the ground that it occurred only in the Latin version and not in any Greek manuscript. To quiet the outcry which arose, he agreed to restore it if but one Greek manuscript could be found which contained it. When one such manuscript was discovered soon afterwards, bound by his promise, he included the disputed reading in his third edition (1522), and thus it gained a permanent place in the Textus Receptus. The manuscript which forced Erasmus to reverse his stand seems to have been 61, a 15th or 16th century manuscript now kept at Trinity College, Dublin. Many critics believe that this manuscript was written at Oxford about 1520 for the special purpose of refuting Erasmus, and this is what Erasmus himself suggested in his notes.

The Johannine Comma is also found in Codex Ravianus, in the margin of 88, and in 629. The evidence of these three manuscripts, however, is not regarded as very weighty, since the first two are thought to have taken this disputed reading from early printed Greek texts and the latter (like 61) from the Vulgate. [Since Hills wrote this, the latest United Bible Society Greek Testament lists six Greek cursive MSS which contain it--61, 88 mg, 429 mg, 629, 636 mg, 918. Moreover Dr. D. A. Waite cites evidence of some fourteen others containing it. Tom Strouse, from whom this information is taken was able to confirm in addition to the above--634 mg, omega 110, 221 and 2318; along with two lectionaries--60, 173; and four Fathers--Tertullian, Cyprian, Augustine and Jerome.]

But whatever may have been the immediate cause, still, in the last analysis, it was not trickery which was responsible for the inclusion of the Johannine Comma in the Textus Receptus but the usage of the Latin-speaking Church. It was this usage which made men feel that this reading ought to be included in the Greek text and eager to keep it there after its inclusion had been accomplished. Back of this usage, we may well believe, was the guiding providence of God, and therefore the Johannine Comma ought to be retained as genuine.

2. The Early Existence of I John 5:7

Evidence for the early existence of the Johannine Comma is found in the Latin versions and in the writings of the Latin Church Fathers. For example, it seems to have been quoted at Carthage by Cyprian (c. 250), who writes as follows: *"And again concerning the Father and the Son and the Holy Spirit it is written: and the Three are One."* It is true that Facundus, a 6th century African bishop, interpreted Cyprian as referring to the following verse, but, as Scrivener (1883) remarks, it is *"surely safer and more candid"* to admit that Cyprian read the Johannine Comma in his New Testament manuscript *"than to resort to the explanation of Facundus."*

The first undisputed citations of the Johannine comma occur in the writings of two 4th century Spanish bishops, Priscillian, who in 385 was beheaded by the Emperor Maximus on the charge of sorcery and heresy, and Idacius Clarus, Priscillian's principal adversary and accuser. In the 5th century the Johannine comma was quoted by several orthodox African writers to defend the doctrine of the Trinity against the gainsaying of the Vandals, who ruled North Africa from 439 to 534 and were fanatically attached to the Arian heresy. And about the same time it was cited by Cassiodorus (480-570) in Italy. The comma is also found in an Old Latin manuscript of the 5th or 6th century, and in the *Speculum*, a treatise which contains an Old Latin text. It was not included in Jerome's original edition of the Latin Vulgate, but around the year 800 it was taken into the text of the Vulgate from the Old Latin manuscripts. It was found in the great mass of the later Vulgate manuscripts and in the Clementine edition of the Vulgate, the official Bible of the Roman Catholic Church.

3. Is I John 5:7 an Interpolation?

Thus on the basis of the external evidence it is at least possible that the Johannine comma is a reading that somehow dropped out of the Greek New Testament text but was preserved in the Latin text through the usage of the Latin-speaking Church, and this possibility grows more and more toward probability as we consider the internal evidence.

In the first place, how did the Johannine comma originate if it be not genuine, and how did it come to be interpolated into the Latin New Testament text? To this question modern scholars have a ready answer. It arose, they say, as a trinitarian interpretation of I John 5:8, which originally read as follows: For there are three that bear witness, the spirit, and the water, and the blood: and these three agree in one. Augustine was one of those who interpreted I John 5:8 as referring to the Trinity. *"If we wish to inquire about these things, what they signify, not absurdly does the Trinity suggest Itself, who is the one, only, true, and highest God, Father, Son, and Holy Spirit, concerning whom it could most truly be said, Three are Witnesses, and the Three are One. By the word spirit we consider God the Father to be signified, concerning the worship of whom the Lord spoke, when He said, God is a spirit. By the word blood the Son is signified, because the Word was made flesh. And by the word water we understand the Holy Spirit. For when Jesus spoke concerning the water*

which He was about to give the thirsty, the evangelist says, This He spoke
concerning the Spirit, whom those that believed in Him would receive."

Thus, according to the critical theory, there grew up in the Latin-
speaking regions of ancient Christendom a trinitarian interpretation of the
spirit, the water, and the blood mentioned in 1 John 5:8, the spirit
signifying the Father, the blood the Son, and the water the Holy Spirit.
And out of this trinitarian interpretation of I John 5:8 developed the
Johannine Comma, which contrasts the witness of the Holy Trinity in
heaven with the witness of the spirit, the water, and the blood on earth.

But just at this point the critical theory encounters a serious
difficulty. If the comma originated in a trinitarian interpretation of 1 John
5:8, why does it not contain the usual trinitarian formula the Father, the
Son, and the Holy Spirit? Why does it exhibit the singular combination,
never met with elsewhere, the Father, The Word, and the Holy Spirit?
According to some critics, this unusual phraseology was due to the efforts
of the interpolator who first inserted the Johannine comma into the New
Testament Text. In a mistaken attempt to imitate the style of the Apostle
John he changed the term Son to the term Word. But this is to attribute to
the interpolator a craftiness which thwarted his own purpose in making
this interpolation, which was surely to uphold the doctrine of the Trinity,
including the eternal generation of the Son. With this as his main concern
it is very unlikely that he would abandon the time-honored formula,
Father, Son and Holy Spirit, and devise an altogether new one, Father,
Word, and Holy Spirit.

In the second place, the omission of the Johannine comma seems to
leave the passage incomplete. For it is a common scriptural usage to
present solemn truths or warnings in groups of three and four; for
example, the repeated thee things, yea four of Proverbs 30, and the
constantly recurring refrain, for three transgressions and for four, of the
prophet Amos. In Genesis 40 the butler saw three branches, and the
baker saw three baskets. And in Matthew 12:40 Jesus says, As Jonas was
three days and three nights in the whale's belly; so shall the Son of man
be three days and three nights in the heart of the earth. It is in accord
with biblical usage, therefore, to expect that in I John 5:7-8 the formula,
there are three that bear witness, will be repeated at least twice. When the
Johannine comma is included the formula is repeated twice. When the
comma is omitted, the formula is repeated only once, which seems very
strange.

In the third place, the omission of the Johannine comma involves a
grammatical difficulty. The words spirit, water, and blood are neuter in
gender, but in I John 5:8 the spirit, the water, and the blood are

personalized and that this is the reason for the adoption of the masculine gender. But it is hard to see how such personalization would involve the change from the neuter to the masculine. For in verse 6 the word Spirit plainly refers to the Holy Spirit, the Third Person of the Trinity. Surely in this verse the word Spirit is "personalized," and yet the neuter gender is used. Therefore, since personalization did not bring about a change of gender in verse 6, it cannot fairly be pleaded as the reason for such a change in verse 8. If, however, the Johannine comma is retained, a reason for placing the neuter nouns spirit, water, and blood in the masculine gender becomes readily apparent. It was due to the influence of the nouns Father and Word, which are masculine. Thus the hypothesis that the Johannine comma is an interpolation is full of difficulties.

4. Reasons for the Possible Omission of I John 5:7

For the absence of the Johannine comma from all New Testament documents save those of the Latin-speaking West the following explanations are possible:

In the first place, it must be remembered that the comma could easily have been omitted accidentally through a common type of error which is called homoioteleuton (similar ending). A scribe copying I John 5:7-8 under distracting conditions might have begun to write down these words of verse 7, there are three that bear witness, but have been forced to look up before his pen had completed this task. When he resumed his work, his eye fell by mistake on the identical expression in verse 8. This error would cause him to omit all of the Johannine comma except the words *in earth*, and these might easily have been dropped later in the copying of this faulty copy. Such an accidental omission might even have occurred several times, and in this way there might have grown up a considerable number of Greek manuscripts which did not contain this reading.

In the second place, it must be remembered that during the second and third centuries (between 220 and 270, according to Harnack) the heresy which orthodox Christians were called upon to combat was not Arianism (since this error had not yet arisen) but Sabellianism (so named after Sabellius, one of its principal promoters), according to which the Father, the Son, and the Holy Spirit were one in the sense that they were identical. Those that advocated this heretical view were called Patripassians (Father-sufferers), because they believed that God the Father, being identical with Christ, suffered and died upon the cross, and Monarchians, because they claimed to uphold the Monarchy (sole-government) of God.

It is possible, therefore, that the Sabellian heresy brought the Johannine comma into disfavor with orthodox Christians. The statement, these three are one, no doubt seemed to them to teach the Sabellian view that the Father, the Son, and the Holy Spirit were identical. And if during the course of the controversy manuscripts were discovered which had lost this reading in the accidental manner described above, it is easy to see how the orthodox party would consider these mutilated manuscripts to represent the true text and regard the Johannine comma as a heretical addition. In the Greek-speaking East especially the comma would be unanimously rejected, for here the struggle against Sabellianism was particularly severe.

Thus it is not impossible that during the 3rd century, amid the stress and strain of the Sabellian controversy, the Johannine comma lost its place in the Greek text but was preserved in the Latin texts of Africa and Spain, where the influence of Sabellianism was probably not so great. To suppose this, at any rate, is strictly in accord with the principles of believing Bible study. For although, the Greek New Testament text was the special object of God's providential care, nevertheless, this care also extended, in lesser degree, to the ancient versions and to the usage not only of Greek-speaking Christians but also of the other branches of the Christian Church. Hence, although the Traditional text found in the vast majority of the Greek manuscripts is a fully trustworthy reproduction of the divinely inspired original text, still it is possible that the text of the Latin Vulgate, which really represents the long-established usage of the Latin Church, preserves a few genuine readings not found in the Greek manuscripts. And hence, also, it is possible that the Johannine comma is one of these exceptional readings which, we may well believe, were included in the Textus Receptus under the direction of God's special providence.

(4)   Erasmus Rejected the Readings of Vaticanus and Similar

As we have seen Vaticanus is the primary pillar of our modern versions. This is the manuscript that is supposed to be so much better and ancient that those used by Erasmus. However, according to Wilkinson, Erasmus, through a certain Professor Paulus Bombasius at Rome, had access to, and received from him *"such variant readings as he wished."* And in 1533 a correspondent of Erasmus sent him *"a number of selected readings from Codex B as proof of its superiority to the Received Greek Text."* Erasmus, however, rejected these varying readings because he considered from the massive evidence of his day that the Received Text was correct. Therefore, modern Bibles are built upon a foundation that Erasmus rejected. And we can see the guiding hand of God in this rejection.

With the Received Text now in print, we come to the next major epoch in the history of the Bible.

5. Luther's German Bible

Continuing with Miller,

When peace was established he turned to his favorite object--the translation of the New Testament; and after it had undergone the more critical revision of Melanchthon, he published it in September of 1522. The appearance of such a work, and at a time when the minds of all men were in a most excited condition, produced, as might be supposed, the most extraordinary effects. As if carried on the wings of the wind, it spread from one end of Germany to the other, and to many other countries. *"It is written,"* according to D'Aubigne, *"in the very tone of the Holy Writings, in a language yet in its youthful vigor, and which for the first time displayed its great beauties; it interested, charmed, and moved the lowest as well as the highest ranks."* Even the Papal historian, Mainibourg, confesses that *"Luther's translation was remarkably elegant, and in general so much approved, that it was read by almost everybody throughout Germany. Women of the first distinction studied it with the most industrious and persevering attention, and obstinately defended the tenets of the Reformer against bishops, monks and Catholic doctors."* It was a national book. It was the book of the people--the Book of God. This work served more than all Luther's writings to the spread and consolidation of the reformed doctrines. The Reformation was now placed on its own proper foundation--the Word of God, which liveth and abideth forever.

The following statistics show the wonderful success of the work: *"A second edition appeared in the month of December; and by 1533 seventeen editions had been printed at Wittenberg, thirteen at Augsburg, twelve at Basle, one at Erfurt, one at Grimma, one at Leipsic, and thirteen at Strasburg."*

Meanwhile Luther proceeded in the accomplishment of his great work--the translation of the Old Testament. With the assistance of Melanchthon and other friends, the work was published in parts as they were finished, and wholly completed in the year 1530. Luther's great work was now done. Hitherto he had spoken, but now God Himself was to speak to the hearts and consciences of men. Vast, wonderful, mighty thought! The Divine testimonies of truth presented to a great nation, which had hitherto been *"perishing for lack of knowledge."* *"The Divine Word no longer to be concealed under an unknown tongue; the way of peace no longer to be obscured by the traditions of men; and the testimony of God Himself concerning Christ and salvation rescued from the superstitions of the Romish system."*

Hills states that Luther's version was based on Erasmus' second edition which appeared in 1519. It is with sadness though that we must inform the reader that Luther *"segregated Hebrews, James, Jude and Revelation at the end of his New Testament as books of lesser value."* (Kenyon)

We now come to the second mighty translation based upon the Received Text of Erasmus.

6. The English Bible of William Tyndale

Tyndale's New Testament-1525
(Not reduced; actual size of whole page 7¼ in. × 5¼ in.)

Tyndale's New Testament--1525 (Actual size of whole page 7.5 in. x 5.5 in.)

God, who foresaw the coming greatness of the English-speaking world, prepared in advance the agent who early would give direction to the course of its thinking. One man stands out silhouetted against the horizon above all others, as having stamped his genius upon English thought and upon the English language. That man was William Tyndale.

The Received Text in Greek, having through Erasmus reassumed its ascendancy in the West of Europe as it had always maintained it in the East, bequeathed its indispensable heritage to the English. It meant much that the right genius was engaged to clamp the English future within this heavenly mold. Providence never is wanting when the hour strikes. And the world at last is awakening fully to appreciate that William Tyndale is the true hero of the English Reformation.

The Spirit of God presided over Tyndale's calling and training. He early passed through Oxford and Cambridge Universities. He went from Oxford to Cambridge to learn Greek under Erasmus, who was teaching there from 1510 to 1514. Even after Erasmus returned to the Continent Tyndale kept informed on the revolutionizing productions which fell from that master's pen. Tyndale was not one of those students whose appetite for facts is omnivorous but who is unable to look down through a system. Knowledge to him was an organic whole in which, should discords come, created by illogical articulation, he would be able to detect quibblings at once. He had a natural aptitude for languages, but he did not shut himself into an airtight compartment with his results, to issue forth with some great conclusion which would chill the faith of the world. He had a soul. He felt everywhere the sweetness of the life of God, and he offered himself as a martyr, if only the Word of God might live.

Herman Buschius, a friend of Erasmus and one of the leaders in the revival of letters, spoke of Tyndale as *"so skilled in seven languages, Hebrew, Greek, Latin, Italian, Spanish, English, French, that whichever he spoke you would suppose it his native tongue." "Modern Catholic Versions are enormously indebted to Tyndale,"* says Dr. Jacobus. From the standpoint of English, not from the standpoint of doctrine, much work has been done to approximate the Douay to the King James.

When Tyndale left Cambridge, he accepted a position as tutor in the home of an influential landowner. Here his attacks upon the superstitions of Popery threw him into sharp discussions with a stagnant clergy, and brought down upon his head the wrath of the reactionaries. It was then, in disputing with a learned man who put the Pope's laws above God's laws, that he made his famous vow, *"If God spare my life, ere many years, I will cause a boy that driveth a plough shall know more of the Scripture than thou doest."*

From that moment until he was burnt at the stake, his life was one of continual sacrifice and persecution. The man who was to charm whole continents and bind them together as one in principle and purpose by his translation of God's Word, was compelled to build his masterpiece in a foreign land amid other tongues than his own. As Luther took the Greek New Testament of Erasmus and made the German language, so Tyndale took the same immortal gift of God and made the English language. Across the sea, he translated the New Testament and a large part of the Old Testament. Two-thirds of the Bible was translated into English by Tyndale, and what he did not translate was finished by those who worked with him and were under the spell of his genius. The Authorized Bible of the English language is Tyndale's after his work passed through two or three revisions (Wilkinson).

Terrence Brown gives the following fascinating account of Tyndale and his Bible.

Tyndale with the means of giving to English readers for the first time a New Testament translated directly from the Greek, the language in which it was first written. Like Wycliffe, Tyndale was accused of heresy, and was not allowed to pursue his studies in peace. He spent several years on the Continent and was eventually betrayed by a false friend, arrested, imprisoned and burned at the stake at Vilvorde in Belgium in 1536. The place is marked by a memorial erected by the Trinitarian Bible Society and the Belgian Bible Society and the inscriptions include Tyndale's dying prayer--*"Lord open the eyes of the King of England."* His prayer was answered when in 1538 King Henry VIII gave instructions that a large Bible should be placed in every parish church.

Tyndale published an edition of the New Testament in a conveniently small size and arranged for thousands of copies to be smuggled into England in barrels, bales of cloth, and even in flour sacks. By these means the New Testament was rapidly and widely distributed. Many copies were seized and burned at St. Paul's, as *"a burnt offering most pleasing to Almighty God"*--as Cardinal Campeggio wrote to Wolsey. Tyndale said that he was not surprised and would not be surprised if later they should burn him also.

The Bishop of London, who was anxious to obstruct the progress of the Reformation, consulted with Pakington a merchant with connections in Antwerp and asked his advice about buying up all the copies that could be obtained in Europe. He did not know that Pakington was a friend of Tyndale. *Halle's Chronicle* contains a quaint description of the incident. *"Gentle Master Pakington,"* said the Bishop, deeming that he had God by the toe, when in truth he had, as he after thought, the devil by the fist, *"do your diligence to get them for me, and I will gladly give you whatever they cost, for the books are naughty and I intend to destroy them all, and to burn them at Paul's Cross."* The bargain was made, and the story continues, *"The Bishop had the Books, Pakington had the thanks, and*

Tyndale had the money."

Tyndale was quite pleased with the arrangement, as the money relieved him of his debts, the burning of some of the Testaments had the effect of encouraging many people to support the work he was doing, and he now had resources to spend on an improved edition. Some time afterwards a man named Constantine was being tried before Sir Thomas Moore for heresy. He was promised leniency if he would tell where Tyndale and his helpers obtained the money to pay for their editions. Constantine replied *"It is the Bishop of London that hath holpen us, for he bestowed among us a great deal of money upon New Testaments to burn them, and that hath been our chief succour and comfort."*

The New Testament was based on the second and third editions of Erasmus' Text (1519 and 1522). The New Testament was finished in 1525-1526. A large part of the Old Testament was completed before his martyrdom in 1536 (*New Bible Dictionary*). Bruce says, *"The influence of Luther's work on Tyndale is obvious to anyone who compares the two versions, but Tyndale is far from being a mere echo of Luther."* The influence of the wording and structure of Tyndale's New Testament on the Authorized Version is immense, and the latter provides a continuing tribute to the simplicity, freshness, vitality and felicity of his work. (*NBD*).

The following gives a sample of Tyndale's version from Phil. 2.

"Let the same mynde be in you the which was in Christ Jesu. Which beynge in the shape of God, and thought yt not robbery to be equal with God. Nevertheless, he made hymsilfe of no reputacion, and toke on him the shape of a servaunte, and becam lyke unto men, and was founde in his apparell as a man. He humbled hym sylfe and becam obedient unto the deeth, even the deeth of the crosse. Wherfore God hath exalted hym, and gyven hym a name above all names, that in the name of Jesus shulde every knee bowe, both of thingis in heven and thingis in erth and thingis under erth, and that all tonges shulde confesse that Jesus Christ is the lorde, unto the prayse of God the father. Wherfore, my dearly beloved: as ye have alwayes obeyed, not when I was present only, but nowe moche more in myne absence, even so performe youre owne health with feare and tremblynge. For yt is God which worketh in you, both the wyll and also the dede, even of good wyll."

7. Roman Catholic Editions of the 15th and Early 16th Centuries

(1) The Complutensian Polyglot--1522

Complutensian Polyglot--1522
(Actual size 12 in. x 9 in.)

Complutensian Polyglot--1522 (Actual size 12 in. x 9 in.)

In 1502 Cardinal Ximenes formed a plan for a printed Bible containing the Hebrew, Greek and Latin texts in parallel columns., Many years were spent in collecting and comparing MSS, with the assistance of several scholars. It was not until 1514 that the New Testament was printed, and the Old Testament was only completed in 1517. Even then various delays occurred, including the death of Ximenes himself. The actual publication did not take place until 1522 and by that time lost the honor of being the first printed Greek Bible. Only 600 copies were printed. Complutensian is Latin for Alcala, the town in Spain where it was printed (Kenyon).

(2) The Rheims-Douay English Version--1582 & 1610

The New Testament was published at Rheims, France in 1582 and the Old Testament in Douay in 1610. This first Roman Catholic English translation of the Scriptures was based on the Latin Vulgate with some reference to the Greek.

Benjamin Wilkinson describes the powers behind this Bible.

So instant and so powerful was the influence of Tyndale's gift upon England, that Catholicism, through those newly formed papal invincibles, called the Jesuits, sprang to its feet and brought forth, in the form of a Jesuit New Testament, the most effective instrument of learning the Papacy, up to that time, had produced in the English language. This newly invented rival version advanced to the attack, and we are now called to consider how a crisis in the world's history was met when the Jesuit Bible became a challenge to Tyndale's, translation.

(a) The Jesuits

The Catholic Church has 69 organizations of men, some of which have been in existence for over one thousand years. Of these we might name the Augustinians, the Benedictines, the Capuchins, the Dominicans, and so on. The Benedictines were founded about 540 A.D. Each order has many members, often reaching into the thousands and tens of thousands. The Augustinians, for example (to which order Martin Luther belonged), numbered 35,000 in his day. The men of these orders never marry but live in communities or large fraternity houses known as monasteries, which are for men what the convents are for women. Each organization exists for a distinct line of endeavor, and each, in turn, is directly under the order of the Pope. They overrun all countries and constitute the army militant of the Papacy. The monks are called the regular clergy, while the priests, bishops, and others who conduct churches are called the secular clergy. Let us see why the Jesuits stand predominantly above all these, so that the general of the Jesuits has great authority within all the vast ranks of the Catholic clergy, regular and secular.

Within thirty-five years after Luther had nailed his theses upon the door of the Cathedral of Wittenberg, and launched his attacks upon the errors and corrupt practices of Rome, the Protestant Reformation was thoroughly established. The great contributing factor to this spiritual upheaval was the translation by Luther of the Greek New Testament of Erasmus into German. The medieval Papacy awakened from its superstitious lethargy to see that in one-third of a century, the Reformation had carried away two-thirds of Europe. Germany, England, the Scandinavian countries, Holland, and Switzerland had become

Protestant. France, Poland, Bavaria, Austria, and Belgium were swinging that way.

In consternation, the Papacy looked around in every direction for help. If the Jesuits had not come forward and offered to save the situation, today there might not be a Catholic Church. What was the offer, and what were these weapons, the like of which man never before had forged?

The founder of the Jesuits was a Spaniard, Ignatius Loyola, whom the Catholic Church has canonized and made Saint Ignatius. He was a soldier in the war which King Ferdinand and Queen Isabella of Spain were waging to drive the Muhammadans out of Spain, about the time that Columbus discovered America.

Wounded at the siege of Pampeluna (1521 A.D.) so that his military career was over, Ignatius turned his thoughts to spiritual conquests and spiritual glory. Soon afterwards, he wrote the book called *Spiritual Exercises*, which did more than any other document to erect a new papal theocracy and to bring about the establishment of the infallibility of the Pope. In other words, Catholicism since the Reformation is a new Catholicism. It is more fanatical and more intolerant.

Ignatius Loyola came forward and must have said in substance to the Pope: *"Let the Augustinians continue to provide monasteries of retreat for contemplative minds; let the Benedictines give themselves up to the field of literary endeavor; let the Dominicans retain their responsibility for maintaining the Inquisition; but we, the Jesuits, will capture the colleges and the universities. We will gain control of Instruction in law, medicine, science, education, and so weed out from all books of instruction, anything injurious to Roman Catholicism. We will mold the thoughts and ideas of the youth. We will enroll ourselves as Protestant preachers and college professors in the different Protestant faiths. Sooner or later, we will undermine the authority of the Greek New Testament of Erasmus, and also of those Old Testament productions which have dared to raise their heads against tradition. And thus will we undermine the Protestant Reformation."*

How well the Jesuits have succeeded, let the following pages tell. Soon the brains of the Catholic Church were to be found in that order. About 1582, when the Jesuit Bible was launched to destroy Tyndale's English Version, the Jesuits dominated 287 colleges and universities in Europe. Their complete system of education and of drilling was likened, in the constitution of the order itself, to the reducing of all its members to the placidity of a corpse, whereby the whole could be turned and returned at the will of the superior. We quote from their constitution :

> *"As for holy obedience, this virtue must be perfect in every
> point--in execution, in will, in intellect--doing what is enjoined
> with all celerity, spiritual joy, and perseverance; persuading
> ourselves that everything is just; suppressing every repugnant
> thought and judgement of one's own, in a certain obedience;
> and let every one persuade himself that he who lives under
> obedience should be moved and directed, under Divine
> Providence, by his superior, just as if he were a* corpse
> (perinde ac si cadaver esset), *which allows itself to be moved
> and led in any direction."* (R. W. Thompson *Footsteps of the
> Jesuits*)

That which put an edge on the newly forged mentality was the
unparalleled system of education impressed upon the pick of Catholic
youth. The Pope, perforce, virtually threw open the ranks of the many
millions of Catholic young men and told the Jesuits to go in and select the
most intelligent. The initiation rites were such as to make a lifelong
impression on the candidate for admission. He never would forget the
first trial of his faith. Thus the youth are admitted under a test which
virtually binds forever the will, if it has not already been enslaved. What
matters to him? Eternal life is secure, and all is for the greater glory of
God.

Then follow the long years of intense mental training, interspersed
with periods of practice. They undergo the severest methods of quick and
accurate learning.

Dominant in the south of Europe, the great order soon went forth
conquering and to conquer. In spite of oceans and deserts, of hunger and
pestilence, of spies and penal laws, of dungeons and racks, of gibbets and
quartering blocks, Jesuits were to be found under every disguise, and in
every country; scholars, physicians, merchants, serving men; in the
hostile court of Sweden, in the old manor house of Cheshire, among the
hovels of Connaught; arguing, instructing, consoling, stealing away the
hearts of the young, animating the courage of the timid, holding up the
crucifix before the eyes of the dying.

Nor was it less their office to plot against the thrones and lives of
the apostate kings, to spread evil rumors, to raise tumults, to inflame civil
wars, to arm the hand of the assassin. Inflexible in nothing but in their
fidelity to the Church, they were equally ready to appeal in her cause to
the spirit of loyalty and to the spirit of freedom. Extreme doctrines of
obedience and extreme doctrines of liberty, the right of rulers to mis-
govern the people, the right of every one of the people to plunge his knife

in the heart of a bad ruler.

And again: If Protestantism, or the semblance of Protestantism, showed itself in any quarter, it was instantly met, not by petty, teasing persecution, but by persecution of that sort which bows down and crushes all but a very few select spirits. Whoever was suspected of heresy, whatever his rank, his learning, or his reputation, knew that he must purge himself to the satisfaction of a severe and vigilant tribunal, or die by fire. Heretical books were sought out and destroyed with similar rigor.

(b) The Council of Trent is Called to Defeat the Reformation (1545-1563)

The Council of Trent was dominated by the Jesuits. This we must bear in mind as we study that Council. It is the leading characteristic of that assembly. The great Convention was called by Paul III when he saw that such a council was imperative if the Reformation was to be checked. And when it did assemble, he so contrived the manipulation of the program and the attendance of the delegates, that the Jesuitical conception of a theocratic Papacy should be incorporated into the canons of the church.

So prominent had been the Reformers denunciations of the abuses of the church, against her exactions, and against her shocking immoralities, that we would naturally expect that this council, which marks so great a turning point in church history, would have promptly met the charges. But this it did not do. The very first propositions to be discussed at length and with intense interest were those relating to the Scriptures. This shows how fundamental to all reform, as well as to the great Reformation, is the determining power over Christian order and faith of the disputed readings and the disputed books of the Bible. Moreover, these propositions denounced by the Council, which we give below, the Council did not draw up itself. They were taken from the writings of Luther. We thus see how fundamental to the faith of Protestantism is their acceptance; while their rejection constitutes the keystone to the superstitions and to the tyrannical theology of the Papacy. These four propositions which first engaged the attention of the Council, and which the Council condemned, are:

They Condemned: 1 *"That Holy Scriptures contained all things necessary for salvation, and that it was impious to place apostolic tradition on a level with Scripture."*

They Condemned: 2 *"That certain books accepted as canonical in the*

Vulgate were apocryphal and not canonical."

They Condemned: 3   *"That Scripture must be studied in the original languages, and that there were errors in the Vulgate."*

They Condemned: 4   *"That the meaning of Scripture is plain, and that it can be understood without commentary with the help of Christ's Spirit."*

For eighteen long years, the Council deliberated. The papal scholars determined what was the Catholic faith. During these eighteen years, the Papacy gathered up to itself what survived of Catholic territory. The Church of Rome consolidated her remaining forces and took her stand solidly on the grounds that tradition was of equal value with the Scriptures; that the seven apocryphal books of the Vulgate were as much Scripture as the other books; that those readings of the Vulgate in the accepted books, which differed from the Greek, were not errors, as Luther and the Reformers had said, but were authentic, and finally, that lay members of the church had no right to interpret the Scriptures apart from the Clergy.

(c)   The Jesuit Bible of 1582

The opening decrees of the Council of Trent had set the pace for centuries to come. They pointed out the line of battle which the Catholic reaction would wage against the Reformation. First undermine the Bible, then destroy the Protestant teaching and doctrine.

If we include the time spent in studying these questions before the opening session of the Council in 1545 until the Jesuit Bible made it first appearance in 1582, fully forty years were passed in the preparation of the Jesuit students who were being drilled in these departments of learning. The first attack on the position of the Reformers regarding the Bible must soon come. It was clearly seen then, as it is now, that if confusion on the origin and authenticity of the Scriptures could be spread abroad in the world, the amazing certainty of the Reformers on these points, which had astonished and confounded the Papacy, could be broken down. In time the Reformation would be splintered to pieces, and driven as the chaff before the wind. The leadership in the battle for the Reformation was passing over from Germany to England. Here it advanced mightily, helped greatly by the new version of Tyndale. Therefore, Jesuitical scholarship, with at least forty years of training, must bring forth in English a Jesuit Version capable of superseding the

Bible of Tyndale. Could it be done?

Sixty years elapsed from the close of the Council of Trent (1563) to the landing of the Pilgrims in America. During those sixty years, England had been changing from a Catholic nation to a Bible-loving people. Since 1525, when Tyndale's Bible appeared, the Scriptures had obtained a wide circulation. As Tyndale foresaw, the influence of the Divine Word had weaned the people away from pomp and ceremony in religion. But this result had not been obtained without years of struggle. Spain, at that time, was not only the greatest nation in the world, but also was fanatically Catholic. All the new world belonged to Spain, she ruled the seas and dominated Europe. The Spanish sovereign and the Papacy united in their efforts to send into England bands of highly trained Jesuits. By these, plot after plot was hatched to place a Catholic ruler on England's throne.

At the same time, the Jesuits were acting to turn the English people from the Bible, back to Romanism. As a means to this end, they brought forth in English a Bible of their own. Let it always be borne in mind that the Bible adopted by Constantine was in Greek; that Jerome's Bible was in Latin; but that the Jesuit Bible was in English. If England could be retained in the Catholic column, Spain and England together would see to it that all America, north and south, would be Catholic. In fact, wherever the influence of the English-speaking race extended, Catholicism would reign. If this result were to be thwarted, it was necessary to meet the danger brought about by the Jesuit Version.

(d) The Great Stir Over This Edition

So powerful was the swing toward Protestantism during the reign of Queen Elizabeth, and so strong the love for Tyndale's Version, that there was neither place nor Catholic scholarship enough in England to bring forth a Catholic Bible in strength. Priests were in prison for their plotting, and many had fled to the Continent. There they founded schools to train English youth and send them back to England as priests. Two of these colleges alone sent over, in a few years, not less than three hundred priests.

The most prominent of these colleges, called seminaries, was at Rheims, France. Here the Jesuits assembled a company of learned scholars. From here they kept the Pope informed of the changes of the situation in England, and from here they directed the movements of Philip II of Spain as he prepared a great fleet to crush England and bring it back to the feet of the Pope.

The burning desire to give the common people the Holy Word of God was the reason why Tyndale had translated it into English. No such reason impelled the Jesuits at Rheims. In the preface of their Rheims New Testament, they state that it was not translated into English because it was necessary that the Bible should be in the mother tongue, or that God had appointed the Scriptures to be read by all; but from the special consideration of the state of their mother country. This translation was intended to do on the inside of England what the great navy of Philip II was to do on the outside. One was to be used as a moral attack, the other as a physical attack--both to reclaim England. The preface especially urged that those portions be committed to memory *"which made most against heretics."*

The principal object of the Rhemish translators was not only to circulate their doctrines through the country, but also to depreciate as much as possible the English translations.

The appearance of the Jesuit New Testament of 1582 produced consternation in England. It was understood at once to be a menace against the new English unity. It was to serve as a wedge between Protestants and Catholics. It was the product of unusual ability and years of learning. Immediately, the scholarship of England was astir. Queen Elizabeth sent forth the call for a David to meet this Goliath. Finding no one in her kingdom satisfactory to her, she sent to Geneva, where Calvin was building up his great work, and besought Beza, the co-worker of Calvin, to undertake the task of answering the objectionable matter contained in this Jesuit Version. In this department of learning, Beza was easily recognized as chief. To the astonishment of the Queen, Beza modestly replied that her majesty had within her own realm a scholar more able to undertake the task than he. He referred to Thomas Cartwright, the great Puritan divine. Beza said, *"The sun does not shine on a greater scholar than Cartwright."*

Cartwright was a Puritan, and Elizabeth disliked the Puritans as much as she did the Catholics. She wanted an Episcopalian or a Presbyterian to undertake the answer. Cartwright was ignored. But time was passing and English Protestantism wanted Cartwright. The universities of Cambridge and Oxford, Episcopalian though they were, sent to Cartwright a request signed by their outstanding scholars. Cartwright decided to undertake it. He reached out one arm and grasped all the power of the Latin manuscripts and testimony. He reached out his other arm and in it he embraced all the vast stores of Greek and Hebrew literature. With inescapable logic, he marshaled the facts of his vast learning and leveled blow after blow against, this latest and most dangerous product of Catholic theology.

Meanwhile, 136 great Spanish galleons, some armed with 50 cannons, were slowly sailing up the English Channel to make England Catholic. England had no ships. Elizabeth asked Parliament for 15 men-of-war--they voted 30. With these, assisted by harbor tugs under Drake, England sailed forth to meet the greatest fleet the world had ever seen. All England teemed with excitement. God helped: the Armada was crushed, and England became a great sea power.

The Rheims-Douay and the King James Version were published less than thirty years apart. Since then the King James has steadily held its own. The Rheims-Douay has been repeatedly changed to approximate the King James. The result is that the Douay of 1600 and that of 1900 are not the same in many ways.

The New Testament was published at Rheims in 1582. The university was moved back to Douay in 1593, where the Old Testament was published in 1609-1610. This completed what is known as the original Douay Bible. There are said to have been two revisions of the Douay Old Testament and eight of the Douay New Testament, representing such an extent of verbal alterations, and modernized spelling that a Roman Catholic authority says, *"The version now in use has been so seriously altered that it can be scarcely considered identical with that which first went by the name of the Douay Bible,"* and further that, *"it never had any episcopal imprimatur, much less any papal approbation."*

"Although the Bibles in use at the present day by the Catholics of England and Ireland are popularly styled the Douay Version, they are most improperly so called; they are founded, with more or less alteration, on a series of revisions undertaken by Bishop Challoner in 1749-1752. His object was to meet the practical want felt by the Catholics of his day of a Bible moderate in size and price, in readable English, and with notes more suitable to the time. The changes introduced by him were so considerable that, according to Cardinal Newman, they 'almost amounted to a new translation.' So also, Cardinal Wiseman wrote, "To call it any longer the Douay or Rhemish is an abuse of terms. It has been altered and modified until scarcely any verse remains as it was originally published. In nearly every case, Challoner's changes took the form approximating to the Authorized Version."

Note the above quotations. Because if you seek to compare the Douay with the American Revised Version, you will find that the older, or first Douay of 1582, is more like it in Catholic readings than those editions of today, inasmuch as the 1582 Version had been doctored and redoctored. Yet, even in the later editions, you will find many of those corruptions which the Reformers denounced and which reappear in the American Revised Version.

A thousand years had passed before time permitted the trial of strength between the Greek Bible and the Latin. They had fairly met in the struggles of 1582 and the thirty years following in their respective English translations. The Vulgate yielded before the Received Text. The Latin was vanquished before the Greek; the mutilated version before the pure Word. The Jesuits were obliged to shift their line of battle. They saw, that armed only with the Latin, they could fight no longer. They therefore resolved to enter the field of the Greek and become superb masters of the Greek; only that they might meet the influence of the Greek. They knew that manuscripts in Greek, of the type from which the Bible adopted by Constantine had been taken, were awaiting them--manuscripts, moreover, which involved the Old Testament as well as the New. To use them to overthrow the Received Text would demand great training and almost Herculean labors, for the Received Text was apparently invincible.

But still more. Before they could get under way, the English champions of the Greek had moved up and consolidated their gains. Flushed with their glorious victory over the Jesuit Bible of 1582, and over the Spanish Armada of 1588, every energy pulsating with certainty and hope. English Protestantism brought forth a perfect masterpiece. They gave to the world what has been considered by hosts of scholars, the greatest version ever produced in any language--The King James Bible, called *"The Miracle of English Prose."* This was not taken from the Latin in either the Old or the New Testament, but from the languages in which God originally wrote His Word, namely, from the Hebrew in the Old Testament and from the Greek in the New Testament.

The Jesuits had therefore before them a double task--both to supplant the authority of the Greek of the Received Text by another Greek New Testament, and then upon this mutilated foundation to bring forth a new English Version which might retire the King James into the background. In other words, they must, before they could again give standing to the Vulgate, bring Protestantism to accept a mutilated Greek text and an English version based upon it.

The manuscripts from which the New Version must be taken would be like the Greek manuscripts which Jerome used in producing the Vulgate. The opponents of the King James Version would even do more. They would enter the field of the Old Testament, namely, the Hebrew, and, from the translations of it into Greek in the early centuries, seize whatever advantages they could. In other words, the Jesuits had put forth one Bible in English, that of 1582; of course they could get out another!!

Thus Wilkinson is saying that there is a Jesuit influence in key areas of Bible revision since the days of the King James Version. And that this influence is not limited to the standard Roman Catholic editions. Certainly time and time again in preparing this paper, I have noted that many of the naturalistic scholars seem to be overly generous and friendly in their statements toward the Roman position. They certainly do not seem very forthright in defending the Protestant position. A number of key modern translations openly state that there has been Catholic participation in the project.

An example of this *"let's get friendly"* approach by a noted scholar can be seen in the following:

In his article, *"One Bible--Many Versions"* in the *Christian* of 9th October, 1964, Professor F. F. Bruce mentioned that in one group of teacher training college the Roman and non-Roman colleges set identical papers in Divinity, except that the Roman Catholic papers were based on the Douay Bible and the other colleges used the Revised Version and more recently the N.E.B. Soon after the change from the R.V. to the N.E.B. was made, news was released of progress on the Roman Catholic Edition of the Revised Standard Version. Professor Bruce expected the Roman colleges to adopt this version in due course, and expressed his regret that the non-Roman colleges did not also switch to the Revised Standard Version. This version is thus advocated as more or less equally acceptable to Romanists and Protestants.

The same writer declared that he did not share the desire expressed by some for an Evangelical version, but looked for a version *"Which is as truthful as human skill, aided by the divine grace, can make it,"* a version which would commend itself to Evangelicals and non-Evangelicals alike. Professor Bruce expressed the view that the Revised Standard Version, with certain improvements, would come very close to this ideal.

See *"Rome and the R.S.V."* prepared by the Trinitarian Bible Society, 217 Kingston Road, London, S.W.19.

(3)   The Sixtine and Clementine Latin Bibles 1590 & 1592

After the Polyglot of Ximenes (1522) no authoritative printed edition of the Latin appeared until Sixtus V became Pope in 1585. Immediately on his accession, he appointed a commission to revise the Vulgate, in which work he himself took an active part. Surprisingly, and much to his credit, the N.T. generally resembles and was evidently based on the Received Text Edition of Stephanus (see below).

But hardly had it issued from the press, and Sixtus declared his edition to be the *"sole authentic and authorized form of the Bible,"* that he died. One of the first acts of Clement VIII, his successor in 1592, was to call in all copies of the Sixtine Bible. The alleged reason was that the edition was full of errors. This charge has been shown to be baseless. It is believed, however, that Clement was incited to this by the Jesuits.

The Sixtine was altered in over 3000 readings and was published in late 1592 as the Clementine Bible. This is the authorized edition of the Latin Bible current in the-Catholic Church today. (Based on Kenyon.)

8. Greek Editions of the Received Text After Erasmus

(1)   Editions of Stephanus: 1546-1551

The great printer-editor, Robert Estienne, or Stephanus of Paris (sometimes anglicized as Stephens) issued four editions of the Greek New Testament based mainly on the later editions (1527 and 1535) of Erasmus.

The first two appeared in 1546 and 1549. The third published in 1550 was the first Greek Testament to contain a critical apparatus (i.e. a listing of variant readings) for which 15 MSS were used. One of these was Codex Bezae, but of this little use was made. It is this 1550 edition which since that time has been most frequently reprinted and has been the standard edition of the Received Text. It was known as the royal edition.

Shortly afterwards, Estienne was forced to retire to Geneva on account of his Protestantism and there issued in 1551 the first edition to contain the modern verse divisions. (Note that the texts of Erasmus and Tyndale do not have verses.) The chapter division was done by Stephen Langton in the 13th century (Kenyon). Except for the verse divisions, this was a reprint of the 1550 edition.

(2)   Editions of Beza: 1565-1611

Theodore Beza of Geneva edited ten editions of the Received Text, with the last one appearing after his death.

Four of these were editions of the Stephens Text with some changes and a Latin translation of his own in parallel. Textual notes were printed under the text. These folio editions appeared in 1565, 1582, 1588 and 1598. Beza produced several octavo editions in 1565, 1567, 1580, 1590 and 1604.

The King James Version was based primarily upon Beza's 1598

edition. This Greek edition is available from the Trinitarian Bible Society (Strouse and Brown). I would strongly recommend using this edition in our study of the Greek New Testament.

(3) Editions by the Elzevir Brothers: 1624-1678

They produced seven editions. In the preface of their second edition (1633) they wrote "*textum . . . nunc ab omnibus receptum*"--"*text . . .now received by all.*" This popularized the term "Received Text" as descriptive of the vast majority of Greek MSS which have been passed down through the centuries (Strouse).

9. Foreign Language Versions

Following Luther's version in 1522, was the French version of Oliveton (1535), the Spanish and Czech translations (both in 1602), and Diodati's Italian translation of 1607 (Bruce).

Wilkinson says more particularly,

Four Bibles produced under Waldensian influence touched the history of Calvin: namely, a Greek, a Waldensian vernacular, a French, and an Italian. Calvin himself was led to his great work by Olivetan, a Waldensian. Thus was the Reformation brought to Calvin, that brilliant student of the Paris University. Farel, also a Waldensian, besought him to come to Geneva and open up a work there. Calvin felt that he should labor in Paris. According to Leger, Calvin recognized a relationship to the Calvins of the Valley of St. Martin, one of the Waldensian Valleys.

Finally, persecution at Paris and the solicitation of Farel caused Calvin to settle at Geneva, where, with Beza, he brought out an edition of the Textus Receptus--the one the author now uses in his college class rooms, as edited by Scrivener. Of Beza, Dr. Edgar says that he "*astonished and confounded the world*" with the Greek manuscripts he unearthed. This later edition of the Received Text is in reality a Greek New Testament brought out under Waldensian influence. Unquestionably, the leaders of the Reformation--German, French and English--were convinced that the Received Text was the genuine New Testament, not only by its own irresistible history and internal evidence, but also because it matched with the Received Text which in Waldensian form came down from the days of the apostles.

The other three Bibles of Waldensian connection were due to three men who were at Geneva with Calvin, or when he died, with Beza, his successor, namely, Olivetan, Leger and Diodati. How readily the two streams of descent of the Received Text, through the Greek East and the Waldensian West, ran together, is illustrated by the meeting of the Olivetan Bible and the Received Text. Olivetan, one of the most illustrious pastors of the Waldensian Valleys, a relative of Calvin, according to Leger, and a splendid student, translated the New Testament into French. Leger bore testimony that the Olivetan Bible, which accorded with the Textus Receptus, was unlike the old manuscripts of the Papists, because they were full of falsification. Later, Calvin edited a second edition of the Olivetan Bible. The Olivetan in turn became the basis of the Geneva Bible in English which was the leading version in England in 1611 when the King James appeared.

Diodati, who succeeded Beza in the chair of Theology at Geneva, translated the Received Text into Italian. This version was adopted by the Waldenses, although there was in use at that time a Waldensian Bible in their own peculiar language. This we know because Sir Samuel Morland, under the protection of Oliver Cromwell, received from Leger the Waldensian New Testament which now lies in the Cambridge University library. After the devastating massacre of the Waldenses in 1655, Leger felt that he should collect and give into the hands of Sir Samuel Morland as many pieces of the ancient Waldensian literature as were available.

It is interesting to trace back the Waldensian Bible which Luther had before him when he translated the New Testament. Luther used the Tepl Bible, named from Tepl, Bohemia. This Tepl manuscript represented a translation of the Waldensian Bible into the German which was spoken before the days of the Reformation. Of this remarkable manuscript, Comba says :

"When the manuscript of Tepl appeared, the attention of the learned was aroused by the fact that the text it presents corresponds word for word with that of the first three editions of the ancient German Bible. Then Louis Keller, an original writer, with the decided opinions of a layman and versed in the history of the sects of the Middle Ages, declared the Tepl manuscript to be Waldensian. Another writer, Hermann Haupt, who belongs to the old Catholic party, supported his opinion vigorously."

From Comba we also learn that the Tepl manuscript has an origin different from the version adopted by the Church of Rome; that it seems to agree rather with the Latin versions anterior to Jerome, the author of the Vulgate; and that Luther followed it in his translation, which probably is the reason why the Catholic Church reproved Luther for following the Waldenses. Another peculiarity is its small size, which seems to single it out as one of those little books which the Waldensian evangelists carried with them hidden under their rough cloaks. We have, therefore, an indication of how much the Reformation under Luther as well as Luther's Bible owed to the Waldenses.

Waldensian influence, both from the Waldensian Bibles and from Waldensian relationships, entered into the King James translation of 1611. Referring to the King James translators, one author speaks thus of a Waldensian Bible they used: *"It is known that among modern versions they consulted was an Italian, and though no name is mentioned, there cannot be room for doubt that it was the elegant translation made with great ability from the original Scriptures by Giovanni Diodati, which had only recently (1607) appeared in Geneva."*

It is therefore evident that the translators of 1611 had before them four Bibles which had come under Waldensian influences: the Diodati in Italian, the Olivetan in French, the Lutheran in German, and the Genevan in English. We have every reason to believe that they had access to at least six Waldensian Bibles written in the old Waldensian vernacular, including Dublin MS A4. No 13, once the property of Archbishop Ussher, was presented by King Charles II of England to the University of Dublin.

Dr. Nolan, who had already acquired fame for his Greek and Latin scholarship and researches into Egyptian chronology, and was a lecturer of note, spent twenty-eight years to trace back the Received Text to its apostolic origin. He was powerfully impressed to examine the history of the Waldensian Bible. He felt certain that researches in this direction would demonstrate that the Italic New Testament, or the New Testament of those primitive Christians of northern Italy whose lineal descendants the Waldenses were, would turn out to be the Received Text. He says:

"The author perceived, without any labor of enquiry, that it derived its name from that diocese, which has been termed the Italick, as contradistinguished from the Roman. This is a supposition, which receives a sufficient confirmation from the fact--that the principal copies of that version have been preserved in that diocese, the metropolitan church of which was situated in Milan. The circumstance is at present mentioned, as the author thence formed a hope, that some remains of the primitive Italick version might be found in the early translations made by the Waldenses, who were the lineal descendants of the Italick church; and who have asserted their independence against the usurpations of the Church of Rome, and have ever enjoyed the free use of the Scriptures.

In the search to which these considerations have led the author, his fondest expectations have been fully realized. It has furnished him with abundant proof on that point to which his enquiry was chiefly directed; as it has supplied him with the unequivocal testimony of a truly apostolical branch of the primitive church, that the celebrated text of the heavenly witnesses was adopted in the version which prevailed in the Latin Church, previously to the introduction of the modern Vulgate. " (Fredrick Nolan, *Integrity of the Greek Vulgate*)

10. English Versions Between Tyndale and the K.J.V.

The following has been taken from Kenyon.

(1)   Coverdale's Bible: 1535

Tyndale was burnt; but he, with even greater right than Latimer, might say that he had lighted such a candle, by God's grace, in England, as should never be put out. His own New Testament had been rigorously excluded from England, so far as those in authority could exclude it; but the case for which he gave his life was won. Even before his death he might have heard that a Bible, partly founded on his own, had been issued in England under the protection of the highest authorities. In 1534 the Upper House of Convocation of Canterbury had petitioned the King to authorize a translation of the Bible into English, and it was probably at this time that Cranmer proposed a scheme for a joint translation by nine or ten of the most learned bishops and other scholars. Cranmer's scheme came to nothing; but Cromwell, now Secretary of State, incited Miles Coverdale to publish a work of translation on which he had been already engaged. Coverdale had known Tyndale abroad, and is said to have assisted him in his translation of the Pentateuch; but he was no Greek or Hebrew scholar, and his version, which was printed abroad in 1535 (probably, according to the latest expert view, at Marburg) and appeared in England in that year or the next, professed only to be translated from the Dutch (i.e. German) and Latin, Coverdale, a moderate, tolerant, earnest man, claimed no originality, and expressly looked forward to the Bible being more faithfully presented both *"by the ministration of other that begun it afore"* (Tyndale) and by the future scholars who should follow him; but his Bible has two important claims on our interest. Though not expressly authorized, it was undertaken at the wish of Cromwell, and a dedication to Henry VIII, printed apparently by Nycholson of Southwark, was inserted among the prefatory matter of the German-printed sheets, which were no doubt imported unbound. It is thus the first English Bible which circulated in England without let or hindrance from the higher powers. It is also the first complete English printed Bible, since Tyndale had not been able to finish the whole of the Old Testament. In the Old Testament Coverdale depended mainly on the Swiss-German version published by Zwingli and Leo Juda in 1524-1529, though in the Pentateuch he also made considerable use of Tyndale's translation. The New Testament is a careful revision of Tyndale by comparison with the German. It is to Coverdale therefore that our English versions of the poetical and prophetical books are primarily due, and in handling the work of others he showed great skill. Many of Coverdale's phrases have passed into the Authorized Version. In one respect he departed markedly from his predecessor--namely, in bringing back to the English Bible the ecclesiastical terms which Tyndale had banished.

Coverdale's Bible--1535 (Actual size 10.75 in. x 6.5 in.)

The demand for the Bible continued unabated, and a further step had been made in the direction of securing official authorization. Two revised editions were published in 1537, this time printed in England by Nycholson; and one of these, in quarto, bore the announcement that it was *"set forth with the king's most gracious license."* The bishops in Convocation might still discuss the expediency of allowing the Scriptures to circulate in English, but the question had been decided without them. The Bible circulated, and there could be no returning to the old ways.

(2)   Matthew's Bible: 1537

Fresh translations, or, to speak more accurately, fresh revisions, of the Bible now followed one another in quick succession. The first to follow Coverdale's was that which is known as Matthew's Bible, but which is in fact the completion of Tyndale's work. Tyndale had only published the Pentateuch, Jonah and the New Testament, but he had never abandoned his work on the Old Testament, and he had left behind him in manuscript a version of the books from Joshua to II Chronicles. The person into whose hands this version fell, and who was responsible for its publication, was John Rogers, a disciple of Tyndale and an earnest reformer; and whether Thomas Matthew, whose name stands at the foot of the dedication, was an assistant of Rogers, or was Rogers himself under another name, has never been clearly ascertained.

It has also been suggested that Matthew stands for Tyndale, to whom the greater part of the translation was really due. The appearance of Tyndale's name on the title-page would have made it impossible for Henry VIII to admit it into England without convicting himself of error in proscribing Tyndale's New Testament.

There is, however, no doubt that Rogers was the person responsible for it, and that 'Matthew' has no other known existence. The Bible which Rogers published in 1537, at the expense of two London merchants, consisted of Tyndale's version of Genesis to II Chronicles, Coverdale's for the rest of the Old Testament (including the Apocrypha), and Tyndale's New Testament according to his final edition in 1535; the whole being very slightly revised, and accompanied by introductions, summaries of chapters, wood-cuts and copious marginal comments of a somewhat contentious character. It was printed abroad, probably at Antwerp, was dedicated to Henry VIII, and was cordially welcomed and promoted by Cranmer. Cromwell himself, at Cranmer's request presented it to Henry and procured his permission for it to be sold publicly; and so it came about that Tyndale's translation, which Henry and all the heads of the Church had in 1525 proscribed, was in 1537 sold in England by leave of Henry and through the active support of the Secretary of State and the archbishop of Canterbury.

(3)   The Great Bible: 1539 1541

The English Bible had now been licensed, but it had not yet been commanded to be read in churches. That honor was reserved for a new revision which Cromwell (perhaps anxious lest the substantial identity of

Matthew's Bible with Tyndale's, and the controversial character of the notes, should come to the King's knowledge) employed Coverdale to make on the basis of Matthew's Bible. It was decided to print it in Paris, where better paper and more sumptuous printing were to be had. The French king's licence was obtained, and printing was begun in 1538. Before it was completed, however, friction arose between the English and French courts, and on the suggestion of the French ambassador in London the Inquisition was prompted to seize the sheets. Coverdale, however, rescued a great number of the sheets, conveyed printers, presses, and type to London, and there completed the work, of which Cromwell had already, in September 1538, ordered that a copy should be put up in some convenient place in every church. The Bible thus issued in the spring of 1539 is a splendidly printed volume of large size, from which characteristic its popular name was derived. Prefixed to it is a fine engraved title-page. it represents the Almighty at the top blessing Henry, who hands out copies of the Bible to Cranmer and Cromwell on his right and left. Below, the archbishop and the Secretary of State, distinguished by their coats of arms beneath them, are distributing copies to the clergy and laity respectively, while the bottom of the page is filled with a crowd of people exclaiming *Vivat Rex*! ('Long live the King!'). In contents, it is Matthew's Bible revised throughout, the Old Testament especially being considerably altered in accordance with Munster's Latin version, which was greatly superior to the Zurich Bible on which Coverdale had relied in preparing his first translation. The New Testament was also revised, with special reference to the Latin version of Erasmus. Coverdale's characteristic style of working was thus exhibited again in the formation of the Great Bible. He did not attempt to contribute independent work of his own, but took the best materials which were available at the time and combined them with the skill of a master of language.

In accordance with Cromwell's order, which was repeated by royal proclamation in 1541, copies of the Great Bible were set up in every church; and we have a curious picture of the eagerness with which people flocked to make acquaintance with the English Scriptures in the complaint of Bishop Bonner that *"diverse wilful and unlearned persons inconsiderately and indiscreetly read the same, especially and chiefly at the time of divine service, yea in the time of the sermon and declaration of the word of God."* One can picture to oneself the great length of Old St. Paul's (of which the bishop is speaking) with the preacher haranguing from the pulpit at one end, while elsewhere eager volunteers are reading from the six volumes of the English Bible which Bonner had put up in different parts of the cathedral, surrounded by crowds of listeners who, regardless of the order of divine service, are far more anxious to hear the Word of God itself than expositions of it by the preacher in the pulpit. Over all the land copies of the Bible spread and multiplied, so that a contemporary witness testifies that it had entirely superseded the old romances as the favorite reading of the people. Edition after edition was required from the press. The first had appeared in 1539; a second (in which the books of the Prophets had again been considerably revised by Coverdale) followed in April 1540, with a preface by Cranmer, and a third in July. In that month Cromwell was overthrown and executed, and his arms were excised from the title-page in subsequent editions; but the progress of the Bible was not checked. Another edition appeared in November, and on the title-page was the authorization of Bishop Tunstall. of London, who had thus lived to sanction a revised form of the very work which, as originally issued by Tyndale, he had formerly proscribed and burnt. Three more editions appeared in 1541, all substantially reproducing the revision of April 1540, though with some variations; and by this time the immediate demand for copies had been satisfied, and the work alike of printing and of revising the Bible came for the moment to a pause.

It is worth noting that the Great Bible, in spite of its size, was not confined to use as a lectern Bible in churches. There is good evidence that it was also bought for private study. A manuscript in the British Museum (Harl. MS. 590, f.77) contains the narrative of one W. Maldon of Newington, who states that he was about fifteen years of age when the order for the placing of the Bible in churches was issued: *"and immediately after divers poor men in the town of Chelmsford in the county of Essex bought the New Testament of Jesus Christ, and on Sundays did sit reading it in the lower end of the Church, and many would flock about them to hear their reading."* He describes how his father took him away from listening to these readings: *"then thought I, I will learn to read English, and then will I have the New Testament and read thereon myself. The Maytide following, I and my father's prentice, Thomas Jeffery, laid our money together and bought the New Testament in English, and hid it in our bedstraw";* for which, on discovery by his father, he was soundly thrashed.

It is from the time of the Great Bible that we may fairly date the origin of the love and knowledge of the Bible which has characterized, and which it may be hoped will always characterize, the English nation. The successive issues of Tyndale's translation had been largely wasted in providing fuel for the opponents of the Reformation; but every copy of the seven editions of the Great Bible found, not merely a single reader, but a congregation of readers. The Bible took hold of the people, superseding, as we have seen, the most popular romances; and through the rest of the sixteenth and the seventeenth centuries the extent to which it had sunk into their hearts is seen in their speech, their writings, and even in the daily strife of politics. And one portion of the Great Bible has had a deeper and more enduring influence still. When the first Prayer Book of Edward VI was drawn up, directions were given in it for the use of the Psalms from the Great Bible; and from that day to this the Psalter of the Great Bible has held its place in our *Book of Common Prayer*.

The Great Bible--1539 (Actual size 13.5 in. x 9.5 in.)

(4)   Taverner's Bible: 1539

One other translation should be noticed in this place for completeness's sake, although it had no effect on the subsequent history of the English Bible. This was the Bible of R. Taverner, an Oxford scholar, who undertook an independent revision of Matthew's Bible at the same time as Coverdale was preparing the first edition of the Great Bible under Cromwell's auspices. Taverner was a good Greek scholar, but not a Hebraist; consequently the best part of his work is the revision of the New Testament, in which he introduces not a few changes for the better. The Old Testament is more slightly revised, chiefly with reference to the Vulgate. Taverner's Bible appeared in 1539, and was once reprinted; but it was entirely superseded for general use by the authorized Great Bible, and exercised no influence upon later translations.

(5) The Geneva Bible: 1557-1560

The Geneva Bible

The Geneva Bible

The closing years of Henry's reign were marked by a reaction against the principles of the Reformation. Although he had thrown off the supremacy of the Pope, he was by no means favorably disposed towards the teachings and practices of the Protestant leaders, either at home or abroad; and after the fall of Cromwell his distrust of them took a more marked form. In 1543 all translations of the Bible bearing the name of Tyndale were ordered to be destroyed; all notes or comments in other Bibles were to be obliterated; and the common people were forbidden to read any part of the Bible either in public or in private. In 1546 Coverdale's New Testament was joined in the same condemnation with Tyndale's, and a great destruction of these earlier Testaments then took place. Thus, in spite of a resolution of Convocation, instructing certain of the bishops and others to take in hand a revision of the errors of the Great Bible, not only was the work of making fresh translations suspended for several years, but the continued existence of those which had been previously made seemed to be in danger.

The accession of Edward VI in 1547 removed this danger, and during his reign all the previous translations were frequently reprinted. It is said that some forty editions of the existing translations--Tyndale's, Coverdale's, Matthew's, the Great Bible, and even Taverner's were issued in the course of this short reign; but no new translation or revision made its appearance.

Under Mary it was not likely that the work of translation would make any progress. Two of the men most intimately associated with the previous versions, Cranmer and Rogers, were burnt at the stake, and Coverdale (who under Edward VI had become bishop of Exeter) escaped with difficulty. The public use of the English Bible was forbidden, and copies were removed from the churches; but beyond this no special destruction of the Bible was attempted.

Meanwhile the fugitives from the persecution of England were gathering beyond sea, and the more advanced and earnest among them were soon attracted by the influence of Calvin to a congenial home at Geneva. Here the interrupted task of perfecting the English Bible was resumed. The place was very favorable for the purpose. Geneva was the home, not only of Calvin, but of Beza, the most prominent Biblical scholar then living and no considerations of State policy or expediency need affect the translators. Since the last revision of the English translation much had been done, both by Beza and by others, to improve and elucidate the Bible text. A company of Frenchmen was already at work in Geneva on the production of a revised translation of the French Bible, which eventually became the standard version for the Protestants of that country. Amid such surroundings a body of English scholars took in hand the task of revising the Great Bible. The first-fruits of this activity was the New Testament of W. Whittingham, brother-in-law of Calvin's wife and a fellow of All Souls College, Oxford, which was printed in 1557, in a convenient small octavo form; but this was soon superseded by a more comprehensive and complete revision of the whole Bible by Whittingham himself and a group of other scholars. Taking for their basis the Great Bible in the Old Testament, and Tyndale's last revision in the New, they revised the whole with much care and scholarship. In the Old Testament the changes introduced are chiefly in the prophetical books. In the New Testament they took Beza's Latin translation and commentary as their guide, and by far the greater number of the changes in this part of the Bible are traceable to his influence. The whole Bible was accompanied by explanatory comments in the margin, of a somewhat Calvinistic character, but without any excessive violence or partisanship. The division of chapters into verses, which had been introduced by Whittingham from Stephanus' Graeco-Latin New Testament of 1551, was here for the first time adopted for the whole English Bible. In all previous translations the division had been into paragraphs, as in our present Revised Version. For the Old Testament, the verse division was that made by Rabbi Nathan in 1448, which was first printed in a Venice edition of 1524. Stephanus' Latin Bible of 1555, is the first to show the present division in both Testaments, and it was this that was followed in the Geneva Bible.

Next to Tyndale, the authors of the Geneva Bible have exercised the most marked influence of all the early translators on the Authorized Version. Their own scholarship, both in Hebrew and in Greek, seems to have been sound and sober; and Beza, their principal guide in the New Testament, was unsurpassed in his own day as an interpreter of the sacred text. Printed in legible Roman type and in a convenient quarto or smaller form, with a few illustrative wood-cuts, and accompanied by an intelligible and sensible commentary, the Geneva Bible (either as originally published in 1560, or with the New Testament further revised by Tomson, in fuller harmony with Beza's views, in 1576) became the Bible of the household, as the Great Bible was the Bible of the church. It was never authorized for use in churches, and Archbishop Parker, who was interested in its rival, described below, seems to have obstructed the printing of it in England; but there was nothing to prevent its importation from Geneva, and up to 1617 there was hardly a year which did not see one or more reprints of it. The bishops in general seem to have welcomed it, and it was powerfully supported by Walsingham; and until the final victory of King James's version it was by far the most popular Bible in England for private reading. Many of its improvements, in phrase or in interpretation, were adopted in the Authorized Version.

The Geneva Version was produced during a period when the Protestants were suffering violent persecution, and it is not surprising that the marginal notes very pungently exposed the errors of the Roman Church.

For example the comments on Rev. 9:3 where the *"locusts that came out of the bottomless pit"* are explained as meaning *"false teachers, heretics and worldly subtle prelates, with Monks, Friars, Cardinals, Patriarchs, Archbishops, Bishops, Doctors, Bachelors and Masters of Arts, which forsake Christ to maintain false doctrine."* No wonder it was disliked in episcopal and academic circles! (from *The Books and the Parchments* by Bruce)

(6)   The Bishops' Bible: 1568

With the accession of Elizabeth a new day dawned for the Bible in England. The public reading of it was naturally restored, and the clergy were required once more to have a copy of the Great Bible placed in their churches, which all might read with due order and reverence. But the publication of the Geneva Bible made it impossible for the Great Bible to maintain its position as the authorized form of the English Scripture. The superior correctness of the Geneva version threw discredit on the official Bible; and yet, being itself the Bible of one particular party in the Church, and reflecting in its commentary the views of that party, it could not properly be adopted as the universal Bible for public service. The necessity of a revision of the Great Bible was therefore obvious, and it happened that the archbishop of Canterbury, Matthew Parker, was himself a textual scholar, a collector of manuscripts, an editor of learned works, and consequently fitted to take up the task which lay ready to his hand. Accordingly, about the year 1563, he set on foot a scheme for the revision of the Bible by a number of scholars working separately. Portions of the Bible were assigned to each of the selected divines for revision., the archbishop reserving for himself the task of editing the whole and passing it through the press. A considerable number of the selected revisers were bishops, and hence the result of their labors obtained the name of the Bishops' Bible.

The Bishops' Bible was published in 1568, and it at once superseded the Great Bible for official use in churches. No edition of the earlier text was printed after 1569, and the mandate of Convocation for the provision of the new version in all churches and bishops' palaces, though not as imperative as the injunctions in the case of the Great Bible, must have eventually secured its general use in public services. Nevertheless, on the whole, the revision cannot be considered a success, and the Geneva Bible continued to be preferred as the Bible of the household and the individual. In the forty-three years which elapsed before the appearance of the Authorized Version, nearly 120 editions of the Geneva Bible issued from the press, as against twenty of the Bishops' Bible, and while the former are mostly of small compass, the latter are mainly the large volumes which would be used in churches. The method of revision did not conduce to uniformity of results. There was, apparently, no habitual consultation between the several revisers. Each carried out his own assigned portion of the task, subject only to the general supervision of the archbishop. The natural result is a considerable amount of unevenness. The historical books of the Old Testament were comparatively little altered; in the remaining books changes were much more frequent, but they are not always happy or even correct. The New Testament portion was better done, Greek being apparently better known by the revisers than Hebrew. Like almost all its predecessors, the Bishops' Bible was provided with a marginal commentary, on a rather smaller scale than that in the Geneva Bible.

11. Questions Raised by the Inclusion of the Apocrypha in These Versions

The following is from Kenyon and Brown:
One important characteristic of our English Bible makes its first appearance in Coverdale's Bible of 1535. This is the segregation of the books which we call the Apocrypha. These books formed and integral part of the Greek Old Testament, being intermixed among the books which we know as canonical. They were, however, rejected from the Hebrew Canon. Many of the early Fathers concurred in this rejection. The Syrian version omitted them; in the Canon of Athanasius they were placed in a class apart; and Jerome refused to include them in his Vulgate. They had, however, been included in the Old Latin version, which was translated from the *Septuagint*; and the Roman Church was reluctant to abandon them. The Provincial Council of Carthage in 397, under the influence of Augustine, expressly included them in the Canon; and in the Latin Bible they remained, the Old Latin translation of them being incorporated in Jerome's Vulgate. When the Reformation came, however, Luther reverted to the Hebrew Canon, and placed these books apart under the title of 'Apocrypha.'

Tyndale did not translate these books completely, but his revised edition of his New Testament included the *"Epistles from the Old Testament according to the use of Salisbury."* This service book, one of the forerunners of the Book of Common Prayer, included a list of

"Gospels and Epistles" to be read on certain days. Some of the "Epistles" were passages from the Apocryphal books, and Tyndale included six of these lessons in his translation. This part of Tyndale's work was apparently not followed by either Coverdale or Rogers, and their version of the Apocrypha is quite independent.

It was Coverdale though who actually bound eleven Apocryphal books in the back of the Old Testament. The Bible believer is naturally sorry that this was done but is thankful that they are separated and not interspersed as had previously been the case.

In his preface to the Apocrypha, Coverdale wrote,

"Apocripha, the bokes and treatises which amonge the fathers of olde are not rekened to be of like authorite with the other bokes of the byble, neither are they founde in the Canon of the Hebrue."

This was the basic example to be followed in the subsequent English Versions of this time. Unfortunately, Thomas Cranmer in the Great Bible places these books under the title "Hagiographa" (Holy Writings), thus confusing them with the "Writings," the third section of the Hebrew O.T., which also is called Hagiographa.

The Geneva Bible contains the Apocrypha preceded by and article entitled *"The Argument"* asserting that these books were not received by a common consent to be read and expounded publicly in the church, and that they could not be used to confirm a matter of doctrine excepting in instances where they are in agreement with the canonical Scriptures. Some copies of the 1599 edition of the Geneva Bible were issued without the Apocrypha, but the gap in the page numbers shows that the type-setting included the Apocrypha and that the binder made up some copies without these books.

The Roman Church, on the other hand, at the Council of Trent in 1546, adopted by a majority the opinion that all the books of the larger Canon should be received as of equal authority, making this for the first time a dogma of the Church, and enforcing it by anathema.

In the Bishops' Bible, it appears at the end of the Old Testament without any preface to describe its uninspired character (though an edition dated 1575 appeared without the Apocrypha).

When the time arrived for work to commence on the revision which was to become so widely known as the Authorized Version the Apocrypha had an established, if unwarranted, place in the printed English Bible and a committee of six scholars, among them Samuel Ward, Downes, and Boys, labored at Cambridge on this part of the undertaking. They didn't seem to have their heart in it though. Scrivener wrote, *"It is well known to Biblical scholars that the Apocrypha received very inadequate attention from the revisers of 1611 and their predecessors, so that whole passages remain unaltered from the racy, spirited, rhythmical, but hasty, loose and most inaccurate version made by Coverdale for the Bible of 1536."*

According to Rivington's *Records of the Stationers Co.* quoted by Scrivener in *The Authorized Edition of the English Bible of 1611*, Archbishop Abbot in 1615 forbade anyone to issue a Bible without the Apocrypha on pain of one year's imprisonment. Nevertheless, Norton and Bill, *"Printers to the King's most excellent Majesty"* published in 1629 a small quarto edition without the Apocrypha, but this had "APO" after the tailpiece at the end of Malachi--indicating that the inclusion of the books was intended. The following year Robert Barker issued a reprint of this Bible with the Apocrypha between the Testaments. The very fact that exclusion was forbidden in 1615, indicates that there must have been a number of printings where the Apocrypha had been excluded.

In 1644 the Long Parliament forbade the reading of lessons from it in public; but the lectionary of the English Church has always included lessons from it. John Canne, a leader of the English "Brownists," fled to Amsterdam after the Restoration of Charles II and issued there in 1664 an octavo edition of the Authorized Version without the Apocrypha.

The first edition printed in America in 1782 is without it. In 1826, the British and Foreign Bible Society, which has been one of the principal agents in the circulation of the Scriptures throughout the world, resolved never in future to print or circulate copies containing the Apocrypha.

This clear exclusion of the Apocrypha held its place in the rules of the Society for 140 years until in 1967 a change in the Society's constitution made it possible for the Apocrypha to be included at the discretion of the Committee in any version circulated by the Society. During that long period, more Bibles were circulated than in the first eighteen centuries of the Christian era--and they all went forth without the Apocrypha. The present decade has seen the birth of the *"Common Bible"* concept and *"interconfessional co-operation on Bible translations."* The national Bible Societies are inviting Roman Catholic and Greek Orthodox scholars to join hands with liberal and evangelical "Protestant" scholars with the object of producing Bibles which Protestants and Roman Catholics will use without distinction. Such a plan makes the inclusion of the Apocrypha, at least in some editions, quite inevitable. Hence the recent change in the rules.

Thus, fear of Rome was the reason for the inclusion of the Apocrypha.

XXX. The Crowning Jewel, The Authorized Version of 1611

1. The Authorized Version Was the Capstone of a Long Period of Spiritual and Textual Preparation

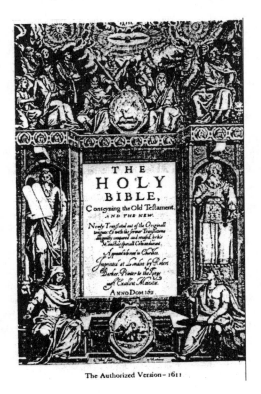

The Authorized Version--1611

Referring now to Wilkinson: the hour had arrived, and from the human point of view, conditions were perfect for God to bring forth a translation of the Bible which would sum up in itself the best of the ages. The Heavenly Father foresaw the opportunity of giving His Word to the inhabitants of earth by the coming of the British Empire with its dominions scattered throughout the world, and by the great American Republic, both speaking the English language.

Not only was the English language by 1611 in a more opportune condition than it had ever been before or ever would be again, but the Hebrew and the Greek likewise had been brought up with the accumulated treasures of their materials to a splendid working point. The age was not distracted by the rush of mechanical and industrial achievements. Moreover linguistic scholarship was at its peak. Men of giant minds, supported by excellent physical health, had possessed in a splendid state of perfection a knowledge of the languages and literature necessary for the ripest Biblical scholarship.

One hundred and fifty years of printing had permitted the Jewish rabbis to place at the disposal of scholars all the treasures in the Hebrew tongue which they had been accumulating for over two thousand years. In the words of the learned Professor E .C. Bissell:

> *"There ought to be no doubt that, in the text which we inherit from the Masoretes, and they from the Talmudists, and they in turn from a period when versions and paraphrases of the Scriptures in other languages now accessible to us were in common use--the same text being transmitted to this period from the time of Ezra under the peculiarly sacred seal of the Jewish canon--we have a correct copy of the original documents, and one worthy of all confidence."*

We are told that the revival of Masoretic studies in more recent times was the result of the vast learning and energy of Buxtorf of Basle. He had given the benefits of his Hebrew accomplishments in time to be used by the translators of the King James Version. And we have the word of a leading Revisionist, highly recommended by Bishop Ellicott, that it is not to the credit of Christian scholarship that so little has been done in Hebrew researches during the past 300 years.

What is true of the Hebrew is equally true of the Greek.

The five editions of Erasmus, the four of Stephanus, the nine of Beza provided the translators with a refined text, representative of that which was in the majority of the MSS.

As the above material shows the translation of the King James Version was the culmination of one hundred years of spiritual, textual and translational preparation.

2. The Better Condition of the English Language in 1611

We are now come, however, to a very striking situation which is little observed and rarely mentioned by those who discuss the merits of the King James Bible. The English language in 1611 was in the very best condition to receive into its bosom the Old and New Testaments. The past forty years had been years of extraordinary growth in English literature. Prose writers and poets Spenser, Sidney, Hooker, Marlowe, Shakespeare, to name only the greatest had combined to spread abroad a sense of literary style and to raise the standard of literary taste. Under the influence, conscious or unconscious, of masters such as these, the revisers wrought out the fine material left to them by Tyndale and his successors into the splendid monument of Elizabethan prose which the Authorized Version is universally admitted to be (Kenyon). Each word of the language was broad, simple and generic. That is to say, words were capable of containing in themselves not only their central thoughts, but also all the different shades of meaning, which were attached to that central thought.

Since then, words have lost that living, pliable breadth. Vast additions have been made to the English vocabulary during the past 300 years, so that several words are now necessary to convey the same meaning which formerly was conveyed by one. It will then be readily seen that while the English vocabulary has increased in quantity, nevertheless, single words have become fixed, capable of only one meaning, and therefore less adaptable to receiving into English the thoughts of the Hebrew which likewise is a simple, broad, generic language. New Testament Greek, is, in this report, like the Hebrew.

Further, the authors of the New Testament did not always use that tense of the Greek verb, called the aorist, in the same rigid, specific sense in which the Revisers claimed they had done. Undoubtedly, in a general way, the sacred writers understood the meaning of the aorist as distinguished from the perfect and imperfect; but they did not always use it so specifically as the Revisers claim. Thus, a translator needs spiritual enlightenment as well as grammatical skill.

3. The Steps Leading up to, and the Plan to Be Followed in the New Translation

After the life and death struggles with Spain, and the hard-fought battle to save the English people from the Jesuit Bible of 1582, victorious

Protestantism took stock of its situation and organized for the new era which had evidently dawned. A thousand ministers, it is said, sent a petition, called the Millenary Petition, to King James who had now succeeded Elizabeth as sovereign. One author describes the petition as follows:

"The petition craved reformation of sundry abuses in the worship, ministry, revenues, and discipline of the national Church. Among other of their demands, Dr. Reynolds, who was the chief speaker in their behalf, requested that there might be a new translation of the Bible, without note or comment."

The strictest element of Protestantism, the Puritan, we conclude was at the bottom of this request for a new and accurate translation; and the Puritan element on the committee appointed was strong.

The language of the Jesuit Bible had stung the sensibilities and the scholarship of Protestants. In the preface of that book it had criticized and belittled the Bible of the Protestants. The Puritans felt that the corrupted version of the Rheimists was spreading poison among the people, even as formerly by withholding the Bible, Rome had starved the people.

Referring now to Kenyon,

The attempt of Archbishop Parker and the Elizabethan bishops to provide a universally satisfactory Bible had failed. The Bishops' Bible had replaced the Great Bible for use in churches, and that was all. It had not superseded the Geneva Bible in private use; and faults and inequalities in it were visible to all scholars. For the remaining years of Elizabeth's reign it held its own; but in the settlement of religion which followed the accession of James I, the provision of a new Bible held a prominent place. At the Hampton Court Conference in 1604, to which bishops and Puritan clergy were alike invited by James in order to confer on the subject of religious toleration, Dr. Reynolds, president of Corpus Christi College, Oxford, raised the subject of the imperfection of the current Bibles. Bancroft, bishop of London, supported him; and although the conference itself arrived at no conclusion on this or any other subject, the king had become interested in the matter, and a scheme was formulated shortly afterwards for carrying the revision into effect. It appears to have been James himself who suggested the leading features of the scheme--namely, that the revision should be executed mainly by the universities; that it should be approved by the bishops and most learned of the Church, by the Privy Council, and by the king himself, so that all the Church should be concerned in it; and that it should have no marginal commentary, which might render it the Bible of a party only. To James were also submitted the names of the revisers; and it is no more than justice to a king whose political misconceptions and mismanagements have left him with a very indifferent character among English students of history, to allow that the good sense on which he prided himself seems to have been conspicuously manifested in respect of the preparation of the Authorized Version, which, by reason of its after effects, may fairly be considered the most important event of his reign.

It was in 1604 that the scheme of the revision was drawn up, and some of the revisers may have begun work upon it privately at this time; but it was not until 1607 that the task was formally taken in hand. The body of revisers was a strong one. It included the professors of Hebrew and Greek at both universities, with practically all the leading scholars and divines of the day. There is a slight uncertainty about some of the names, and some changes in the list may have been caused by death or retirement, but the total number of revisers was from forth-eight to fifty. These were *divided into six groups*, of which two sat at Westminster, two at Oxford and two at Cambridge. In the first instance each group worked separately, having a special part of the Bible assigned to it. The two Westminster groups revised Genesis - II Kings, and Romans - Jude; the Oxford groups Isaiah - Malachi, and the Gospels, Acts and Apocalypse; while those at Cambridge undertook I Chronicles - Ecclesiastes and the Apocrypha. Elaborate instructions were drawn up for their guidance, probably by Bancroft. The basis of the revision was to be the Bishop's Bible, though the earlier translations were to be consulted; the old ecclesiastical terms (about which Tyndale and More had so vehemently disagreed) were to be retained; no marginal notes were to be affixed, except necessary explanations of Hebrew and Greek words; *when any company had finished the revision of a book, it was to be sent to all the rest for their criticism and suggestions,* ultimate differences of opinion to be settled at a general meeting of the chief members of each company; learned men outside the board of revisers were to be invited to give their opinions, especially in cases of particular difficulty.

With these regulations to secure careful and repeated revision, the work was earnestly taken in hand. It occupied two years and nine months of strenuous toil, the last nine months being taken up by a final revision by a committee consisting of two members from each center. (Nothing, it may be observed, is heard of revision by the bishops, the Privy Council, or the king.) It was seen through the press by Dr. Miles Smith and Bishop Bilson, the former of whom is believed to have been the author of the valuable Preface of the Translators to the Reader; and in the year 1611 the result of the revisers' labors issued from the press. It was at once attacked by Dr. Hugh Broughton, a Biblical scholar of great eminence and erudition, who had been omitted from the list of revisers on account of his violent and impracticable disposition. His disappointment vented itself in a very hostile criticism of the new version; but this had very little effect, and the general reception of the revised Bible seems to have been eminently favorable. Though there is no record whatever of any decree ordaining its use, by either king, Parliament or Convocation, the words *"Appointed to be read in Churches"* appear on its title-page; and there can be no doubt that it at once superseded the Bishops' Bible (which, except for some half-dozen reprints of the New Testament, was not reprinted after 1606) as the official version of the Scriptures for public service. Against the Geneva Bible it had a sharper struggle, and for nearly half a century the two versions existed side by side in private use. From the first, however, the version of 1611 seems to have been received into popular favor, and the reprints of it far outnumber those of its rival. Three folio editions and at least fourteen in quarto or octavo appeared in the years 1611-1614, as against six of the Geneva Bible. Between 1611 and 1644, the Historical Catalogue of the British and Foreign Bible Society enumerates fifteen editions of the Geneva and 182 of the Authorized. After 1616, however, English-printed editions of the Geneva cease almost entirely, and this may be due to pressure from above. Nevertheless, it would be untrue to say that the version of 1611 owed its success to official backing from the authorities of Church or State, for its victory became complete just at the time when Church and State were overthrown, and when the Puritan party was dominant. It was its superior merit and its total freedom from party or sectarian spirit that secured the triumph of the Authorized Version, which from the middle of the seventeenth century took its place as the undisputed Bible of the English nation.

Into the details of the revision it is hardly necessary to go far. Tyndale no doubt fixed the general tone of the version more than any other translator, through the transmission of his influence down to the Bishops' Bible, which formed the basis of the revision; but many improvements in interpretation were taken from the Geneva Bible, and not a few phrases and single words from that of Rheims. Indeed, no source of information seems to have been left untried; and the result was a version at once more faithful to the original than any translation that had preceded it, and finer as a work of literary art than any translation either before or since. In the Old Testament the Hebrew tone and manner have been admirably reproduced, and have passed with the Authorized

Version into much of our literature. And in the New Testament, in particular, it is the simple truth that the English version is a far greater literary work than the original Greek. The Greek of the New Testament is a language which had passed its prime and had lost its natural grace and infinite adaptability. The English of the Authorized Version is the finest specimen of our prose literature at a time when English prose wore its stateliest and most majestic form.

4. The Influence and Excellence of the Authorized Version

The influence of the Authorized Version, alike on our religion and our literature, can never be exaggerated. Not only in the great works of our theologians, the resonant prose of the seventeenth-century Fathers of the English Church, but in the writings of nearly every author, whether of prose or verse, the stamp of its language is to be seen. Milton is full of it; naturally, perhaps, from the nature of his subjects, but still his practice shows his sense of the artistic value of its style. So deeply has its language entered into our common tongue, that one probably could not take up a newspaper or read a single book in which some phrase was not borrowed, consciously or unconsciously, from King James's version.

But great as has been the literary value of the Authorized Version, its religious significance has been greater still. For three centuries it has been the Bible, not merely of public use, not merely, of one sect or party, not even of a single country, but of the whole nation and of every English-speaking country on the face of the globe. It has been the literature of millions who have read little else, it has been the guide of conduct to men and women of every class in life and of every rank in learning and education. No small part of the attachment of the English people to their national Church is due to the common love borne by every party and well-nigh every individual for the English Bible. It was a national work in its creation, and it has been a national treasure since its completion. It was the work, not of one man, nor of one age, but of many laborers, of diverse and even opposing views, over a period of ninety years. It was watered with the blood of martyrs, and its slow growth gave time for the casting off of imperfections and for the full accomplishment of its destiny as the Bible of the English nation.

The common people found its language appealed to them with a greater charm and dignity than that of the Genevan version, to which they had been accustomed. As time went on the Authorized Version acquired the prescriptive right of age; its rhythms became familiar to the ears of all classes; its language entered into our literature; and Englishmen became prouder of their Bible than of any of the creative works of their own literature.

The above is taken from a man whose scholarship we are bound to respect but who unfortunately embraces the naturalistic position. Yet Kenyon is an example that all who take a deep objective look at this version, realize that something very unique in the history of Bible translating took place in 1611. The believer who holds to Psalms 12:6-7, 119:89; Isaiah 40:8; Matthew 5:18, 24:35; 1 Peter 1:23-25 sees here nothing less than the superintending hand of God.

5. The Difference Between the Translators of That Day and This

No one can study the lives of those men who gave us the King James Bible without being impressed with their profound and varied learning.

"It is confidently expected," says McClure, *"that the reader of these pages will yield to the conviction that all the colleges of Great Britain and America, even in this proud day of boastings, could not bring together the same number of divines equally qualified by learning and piety for the great undertaking. Few indeed are the living names worthy to be enrolled with those mighty men. It would be impossible to convene out of any one Christian denomination, or out of all, a body of translators on whom the whole Christ-community would bestow such confidence as is reposed upon that illustrious company or who would prove themselves as deserving of such confidence. Very many self-styled "improved versions" of the Bible, or parts of it, have been paraded before the world, but the religious public has doomed them all without exception to utter neglect."*

The translators of the King James, moreover, had something beyond great scholarship and unusual skill. They had gone through a period of great suffering. They had offered their lives that the truths which they loved might live.

This is especially true of the earlier translators who labored in the reigns of Henry VIII and Mary. The King James translators built upon a foundation well and truly laid by the martyrs of the previous century.

Dr. Cheyne, in giving his history of the founders of higher criticism, while extolling highly the mental brilliancy of the celebrated Hebrew scholar, Gesenius, expresses his regrets for the frivolity of that scholar. No such weakness was manifested in the scholarship of the Reformers.

*"Reverence, "*says Doctor Chambers, *"it is this more than any other one trait that gave to Luther and Tyndale their matchless skill and enduring preeminence as translators of the Bible. "*

It is difficult for us in this present prosperous age to understand how heavily the heroes of Protestantism in those days were forced to lean upon the arm of God. We find them speaking and exhorting one another by the promises of the Lord, that He would appear in judgement against their enemies. For that reason they gave full credit to the doctrine of the Second Coming of Christ as taught in the Holy Scriptures. Passages of notable value which refer to this glorious hope were not wrenched from their forceful setting as we find them in the Revised Versions and some modern Bibles, but were set forth with a fullness of clearness and hope.

Something other than an acquaintanceship, more or less, with a crushing mass of intricate details in the Hebrew and the Greek is necessary to be a successful translator of God's Holy Word. God's Holy Spirit must assist.

6.   The Power of the Authorized Version

The consistent Christian's course of action is quite clear. It is the course followed by Wycliffe, Tyndale, Luther, Cranmer, Latimer, Ridley, Huss, Erasmus, Stephanus, Elzevir, Hoskier, Miller, Burgon, Moody, Sunday, Spurgeon, Goforth, Taylor, Mueller, Scrivener, and Hills--*"And take the helmet of salvation, and the sword of the Spirit, which is the word of God. . . and having done all . . . stand therefore!"* (Eph. 6:17, 13, 14).

Gird your sword on your thigh and prepare for action.

As David said of Goliath's weapon, *"Give it me . . . there is none like that!"* Don't go into the last half of the last century of the Church Age, armed with butter-knives, plastic pen-knives, toothpicks, fingernail files, and hair pins! (RV, ASV, RSV, etc.)

Take out the old *"sword of the Spirit"* that makes hippies blush when it appears on a street corner, that makes College professors nervous when it is brought into a classroom, that disturbed Westcott and Hort so badly they devoted a lifetime to getting rid of it; get that old battered Book that was corrupted by Origen, hated by Eusebius, despised by Constantine, ignored by Augustine, that was ridiculed by the ASV and RSV committees; that razor-sharp blade which pierced Mel Trotter, Adoniram Judson, Dwight L. Moody, and B. H. Carroll to the soul and made Christians out of them, which pierced Charles Darwin, Huxley, Hobbes, Hume and Bernard Shaw to the soul and infuriated them, that word which was preached to the heathen in every corner of the earth, that word which has been used by the Spirit of God for 19 centuries to make fools out of scientists, educators and philosophers, to overthrow Popes and Kingdoms, to inspire men to die at the stake and in the arena; that infallible, everlasting BOOK which Angels desire to look into, and before which Devils tremble when they read their future; and if you don't know, by now, what Book this is we are talking about, you never will.

It is NOT any English translation published since 1800.

XXXI. Three Hundred and Fifty Years of Attack upon the Authorized Version

1.   The Strange Gathering Storm

"Wherever the so-called Counter-Reformation, started by the Jesuits, gained hold of the people, the vernacular was suppressed and the Bible kept from the laity.   So eager were the Jesuits to destroy the authority of the Bible--the paper pope of the Protestants, as they contemptuously called it--that they even did not refrain from criticizing its genuineness and historical value."

The opponents of the noble work of 1611 like to tell the story of how the great printing plants which publish the King James Bible have been obliged to go over it repeatedly to eliminate flaws of printing, to eliminate words which in time have changed in their meaning, or errors which have crept in through the years because of careless editing by different printing houses. They offer this as evidence of the fallibility of the Authorized Version.

They seem to overlook the fact that this labor of necessity is an argument for, rather than against, the dependability of the translations. Had each word of the Bible been set in a cement cast, incapable of the slightest flexibility and been kept so throughout the ages, there could have been no adaptability to the ever-changing structure of human language.   The artificiality of such a plan would have eliminated the living action of the Holy Spirit and would accuse both man and the Holy Spirit of being without an intelligent care for the Divine treasure.

On this point, the scholars of the Reformation made their position clear under three different aspects.   First, they claimed that the Holy Scriptures had come down to them unimpaired throughout the centuries ("Semler," *McClintock and Strong Encyclopedia*).

Second, they recognized that to reform any manifest oversight was not placing human hands on a Divine work and was not contrary to the mind of the Lord.

And lastly, they contended that the Received Text, both in Hebrew and in Greek, as they had it in their day would so continue unto the end of time (Brooke, Cartwright, pp. 274, 275).

In fact, a testimony no less can be drawn from the opponents of the Received Text. The higher critics, who have constructed such elaborate scaffolding, and who have built such great engines of war as their apparatus criticus, are obliged to describe the greatness and strength of the walls they are attacking in order to justify their war machine.

Of the Greek New Testament, Dr. Hort, who was an opponent of the Received Text and who dominated the English New Testament Revision Committee, says: *"An overwhelming proportion of the text in all known cursive manuscripts except a few is, as a matter of fact, identical."*

Thus strong testimonies can be given not only to the Received Text, but also to the phenomenal ability of the manuscript scribes writing in different countries and in different ages to preserve an identical Bible in the overwhelming mass of manuscripts.

The large number of conflicting readings which higher critics have gathered must come from only a few manuscripts, since the overwhelming mass of manuscripts is identical.

The phenomenon presented by this situation is so striking that we are pressed in spirit to inquire, Who are these who are so interested in urging on the world the finds of their criticism?

The King James Bible had hardly begun its career before the enemies commenced to fall upon it. Though it has been with us for three hundred years in splendid leadership--a striking phenomenon-- nevertheless, as the years increase, the attacks become more furious. If the Book were a dangerous document, a source of corrupting influence and a nuisance, we would wonder why it has been necessary to assail it since it would naturally die of its own weakness. But when it is a Divine blessing of great worth, a faultless power of transforming influence, who can they be who are so stirred up as to deliver against it one assault after another?

Great theological seminaries, in many lands, led by accepted teachers of learning, are laboring constantly to tear it to pieces. Point us out anywhere, any similar situation concerning the sacred books of any other religion, or even of Shakespeare, or of any other work of literature. Especially since 1814, when the Jesuits were restored by the order of the Pope--if they needed restoration--have the attacks on the Bible, by Catholic scholars and by other scholars who are Protestants in name, become bitter.

For it must be said that the Roman Catholic or the Jesuitical system of argument--the work of the Jesuits from the 16th century to the present day--evinces an amount of learning and dexterity, a subtlety of reasoning, a sophistry, a plausibility combined, of which ordinary Christians have but little idea.

As time went on, this wave of higher criticism mounted higher and higher until it became an ocean surge inundating France, Germany, England, Scotland, the Scandinavian nations, and even Russia. *"When the Privy Council of England handed down in 1864 its decision, breathlessly awaited everywhere, permitting those seven Church of England clergymen to retain their positions, who had ruthlessly attacked the inspiration of the Bible, a cry of horror went up from Protestant England; but 'the whole Catholic Church,'* said Dean Stanley, *'is, as we have seen, with the Privy Council and against the modern dogmatists'* (Stanley, *Essays, p. 140*). *By modern dogmatists, he meant those who believe the Bible, and the Bible only."*

The tide of higher criticism was soon seen to change its appearance and to menace the whole framework of fundamentalist thinking. The demand for revision became the order of the day. The crest was seen about 1870 in France, Germany, England, and the Scandinavian countries. Time-honored Bibles in these countries were radically overhauled and a new meaning was read into words of Inspiration.

Three lines of results are strongly discernible as features of the movement. First, "collation" became the watchword. Manuscripts were laid alongside of manuscripts to detect various readings and to justify that reading which the critic chose as the right one. With the majority of workers, especially those whose ideas have stamped the revision, it was astonishing to see how they tuned away from the overwhelming mass of manuscripts and invested with tyrannical superiority a certain few documents, some of them of a questionable character. Second, this wave of revision was soon seen to be hostile to the Reformation. There is something startlingly in common to be found in the modernist who denies the element of the miraculous in the Scriptures, and the Catholic Church which invests tradition with an inspiration equal to the Bible. As a result, it seems a desperately hard task to get justice done to the Reformers or their product. As Dr. Deniaus says:

"For many of the facts of Tyndale's life have been disputed or distorted, through prejudice, and through the malice of that school of writers in whose eyes the Reformation was a mistake, if not a crime, and who conceive it to be their mission to revive all the old calumnies that have

ever been circulated against the Reformers, supplementing them by new accusations of their own invention. "

A third result of this tide of revision is that when our time-honored Bibles are revised, the changes are generally in favor of Rome. We are told that Bible revision is a step forward; that new manuscripts have been made available and advance has been made in archaeology, philology, geography and the apparatus of criticism. How does it come then that we have been revised back into the arms of Rome? If my conclusion is true, this so-called Bible revision has become one of the deadliest of weapons in the hands of those who glorify the Dark Ages and who seek to bring Western nations back to the theological thinking which prevailed before the Reformation.

Some of the earliest critics in the field of collecting variant readings of the New Testament in Greek, were Mill and Bengel. We have Dr. Kenrick, Catholic Bishop of Philadelphia in 1849, as authority that they and others had examined these manuscripts recently exalted as superior, such as the Vaticanus, Alexandrinus, Beza, and Ephraem, and had pronounced in favor of the Vulgate, the Catholic Bible.

Simon, Astruc, and Geddes, with those German critics, Eichhorn, Semler, and DeWette, who carried their work on further and deeper, stand forth as leaders and representatives in the period which stretches from the date of the King James (1611) to the outbreak of the French Revolution (1789). Simon and Eichhorn were co-authors of a Hebrew Dictionary. These outstanding six--two French, one Scottish, and three German--with others of perhaps not equal prominence, began the work of discrediting the Received Text, both in the Hebrew and in the Greek, and of calling in question the generally accepted beliefs respecting the Bible which had prevailed in Protestant countries since the birth of the Reformation.

There was not much to do in France, since it was not a Protestant country; and the majority had not far to go to change their belief. There was not much done in England or Scotland because there a contrary mentality prevailed. The greatest inroads were made in Germany. Thus matters stood when in 1773 European nations arose and demanded that the Pope suppress the order of the Jesuits. It was too late, however, to smother the fury which sixteen years later broke forth in the French Revolution.

The upheaval which followed engaged the attention of all mankind for a quarter of a century. It was the period of indignation foreseen, as some scholars thought, by the prophet Daniel. As the armies of the Revolution and of Napoleon marched and counter-marched over the territories of Continental Europe, the foundations of the ancient regime were broken up. Even from the Vatican the cry arose, *"Religion is destroyed."* And when in 1812 Napoleon was taken prisoner, and the deluge had passed, men looked out upon a changed Europe. England had escaped invasion, although she had taken a leading part in the overthrow of Napoleon. France restored her Catholic monarchs--the Bourbons who *"never learned anything and never forgot anything."* In 1814 the Pope promptly restored the Jesuits.

Then followed in the Protestant world two outstanding currents of thought first, on the part of many, a stronger expression of faith in the Holy Scriptures, especially in the great prophecies which seemed to be on the eve of fulfillment where they predict the coming of a new dispensation. The other current took the form of a reaction, a growing disbelief in the leadership, of accepted Bible doctrines whose uselessness seemed proved by their apparent impotence in not preventing the French Revolution. And, as in the days before that outbreak, Germany, which had suffered the most, seemed to be fertile soil for a strong and rapid growth of higher criticism.

2.   Griesbach and Mohler

Among the foremost of those who tore the Received Text to pieces in the Old Testament stand the Hollander Kuenen, and the German scholars, Ewald and Wellhausen. Their findings, however, were confined to scholarly circles. The public were not moved by them, as their work appeared to be only negative. The two German critics who brought the hour of revision much nearer were the Protestant Griesbach and the Catholic Mohler. Mohler (1796-1838) did not spend his efforts on the text as did Griesbach, but he handled the points of difference in doctrine between the Protestants and the Catholics in such a way as to win over the Catholic mind to higher criticism and to throw open the door for Protestants who either loved higher criticism, or who, being disturbed by it, found in Catholicism a haven of refuge. Of him Hagenbach says: *"Whatever vigorous vitality is possessed by the most recent Catholic theological science is due to the labors of this man."*

Kurtz states: *"He sent rays of his spirit deep into the hearts and minds of hundreds of his enthusiastic pupils by his writings, addresses, and by his intercourses with them; and what the Roman Catholic Church of the present possesses of living scientific impulse and feeling was implanted, or at least revived and excited by him . . . In fact, long as was the opposition which existed between both churches, no work from the camp of the Roman Catholics produced as much agitation and excitement in the camp of the Protestants as this."*

Or, as Maurice writes concerning Ward, one of the powerful leaders of the Oxford Movement: *"Ward's notion of Lutheranism is taken, I feel pretty sure, from Mohler's very gross misrepresentations."*

Griesbach (1745-1812) attacked the Received Text of the New Testament in a new way. He did not stop at bringing to light and emphasizing the variant readings of the Greek manuscripts; he classified readings into three groups, and put all manuscripts under these groupings, giving them the names of "Constantinopolitan," or those of the Received Text, the "Alexandrian," and the "Western." While Griesbach used the Received Text as his measuring rod, nevertheless, the new Greek New Testament he brought forth by this measuring rod followed the Alexandrian manuscripts; that is, it followed Origen. His classification of the manuscripts was so novel and the result of such prodigious labors, that the critics everywhere hailed his Greek New Testament as the final word. It was not long, however, before other scholars took Griesbach's own theory of classification and proved him wrong.

3. The Gnosticism of German Theology Invades England

By 1833 the issue was becoming clearly defined. It was Premillenarianism, that is, belief in the return of Christ before the millennium, or Liberalism; it was with regard to the Scriptures either literalism or allegorism. As Cadman says of the Evangelicals of that day:

"Their fatalism inclined many of them to Premillenarianism as a refuge from the approaching catastrophes of the present dispensation . . . Famous divines strengthened and adorned the wider ranks of Evangelicalism, but few such were found within the pale of the Establishment. Robert Hall, John Foster, William Jay of Bath, and in Scotland, Thomas Chalmers, represented the vigor and fearlessness of an earlier day and maintained the excellence of Evangelical preaching."

Here was a faith in the Second Coming of Christ, at once Protestant and evangelical, which would resist any effort so to revise the Scriptures as to render them colorless, giving to them nothing more than a literary endorsement of plans of betterment, merely social or political. This faith was soon to be called upon to face a theology of an entirely different spirit. German religious thinking at that moment was taking on an aggressive attitude. Schleiermacher had captured the imagination of the age and would soon mold the theology of Oxford and Cambridge. Though he openly confessed himself a Protestant, nevertheless, like

Origen of old, he sat at the feet of Clement, the old Alexandrian teacher of 190 A.D.

Clement's passion for allegorizing Scripture offered an easy escape from those obligations imposed upon the soul by a plain message of the Bible. Schleiermacher modernized Clement's philosophy and made it beautiful to the parlor philosophers of the day by imaginary analysis of the realm of spirit. It was the old Gnosticism revived, and would surely dissolve Protestantism wherever accepted and would introduce such terms into the Bible, if revision could be secured, as to rob the trumpet of a certain sound. The great prophecies of the Bible would become mere literary addresses to the people of bygone days, and unless counter-checked by the noble Scriptures of the Reformers, the result would be either atheism or papal infallibility.

If Schleiermacher did more to captivate and enthrall the religious thinking of the 19th century than any other one scholar, Coleridge, his contemporary, did as much to give aggressive motion to the thinking of England's youth of his day, who, hardly without exception, drank enthusiastically of his teachings. He had been to Germany and returned a fervent devotee of its theology and textual criticism. At Cambridge University he became the star around which grouped a constellation of leaders in thought. Thirwall, Westcott, Hort, Moulton, and Milligan--who were all later members of the English Revision Committees and whose writings betray the voice of the master--felt the impact of his doctrines.

"His influence upon his own age, and especially upon its younger men of genius, was greater than that of any other Englishman. . . . Coleridgeans may be found now among every class of English divines, from the Broad Church to the Highest Puseyites," says *McClintock and Strong's Encyclopedia.*

The same article speaks of Coleridge as "Unitarian," "Metaphysical," a "Theologian," "Pantheistic," and says that *"he identifies reason with the divine Logos,"* and that he holds *"views of inspiration as low as the rationalists,"* and also holds views of the Trinity *"no better than a refined, Plantonized Sebellianism."*

4. Lachmann, Tischendorf, and Tregelles

It can be shown that Lachmann, Tischendorf, and Tregelles fell under the influence of Cardinal Wiseman's theories. There are more recent scholars of textual criticism who pass over these three and leap from Griesbach to Westcott and Hort, claiming that the two latter simply carried out the beginnings of classification made by the former. Nevertheless, since many writers bid us over and over again to look to Lachmann, Tischendorf, and Tregelles--until we hear of them morning, noon, and night--we would seek to give these laborious scholars all the praise justly due them, while we remember that there is a limit to all good things.

Lachmann's (1793-1851) bold determination to throw aside the Received Text and to construct a new Greek Testament from such manuscripts as he endorsed according to his own rules, has been the thing which endeared him to all who give no weight to the tremendous testimony of 1500 years of use of the Received Text. Yet Lachmann's cannon of criticism has been deserted by both Bishop Ellicott and Dr. Hort. Ellicott says, *"Lachmann's text is really one based on little more than four manuscripts, and so is really more of a critical recension than a critical text."* And again he calls it, *"A text composed on the narrowest and most exclusive principles."* While Dr. Hort says:

"Not again, in dealing with so various and complex a body of documentary attestation, is there any real advantage in attempting, with Lachmann, to allow the distributions of a very small number of the most ancient existing documents to construct for themselves a provisional text."

Tischendorf's (1815-1874) outstanding claim upon history is his discovery of the Sinaitic Manuscript in the convent at the foot of Mt. Sinai. Mankind is indebted to this prodigious worker for having published manuscripts not accessible to the average reader. Nevertheless, his discovery of Codex Aleph toppled over his judgement. Previous to that he had brought out seven different Greek New Testaments, declaring that the seventh was perfect and could not be superseded. Then, to the scandal of textual criticism, after he had found the Sinaitic Manuscript, he brought out his eighth Greek New Testament, which was different from his seventh in 3572 places! Moreover, he demonstrated how textual critics can artificially bring out Greek New Testaments when, at the request of a French publishing house, Firmin Didot, he edited an edition of the Greek Testament for Catholics, conforming it to the Latin Vulgate.

Tregelles (1813-1875) followed Lachmann's principles by going back to what he considered the ancient manuscripts and, like him, he ignored the Received Text and the great mass of cursive manuscripts. Of him, Ellicott says, *"His critical principles, especially his general principles of estimating and regarding modern manuscripts, are now, perhaps justly, called in question by many competent scholars,"* and that his text *"is rigid and mechanical, and sometimes fails to disclose that critical instinct and peculiar scholarly sagacity which is so much needed in the great and responsible work of constructing a critical text of the Greek Testament."*

Such were the antecedent conditions preparing the way to draw England into entangling alliances, to de-Protestantize her national church and to advocate at a dangerous hour the necessity of revising the King James Bible. The Earl of Shaftesbury, foreseeing the dark future of such an attempt, said in May, 1856:

"When you are confused or perplexed by a variety of versions, you would be obliged to go to some learned pundit in whom you reposed confidence, and ask him which version he recommended; and when you had taken his version, you must be bound by his opinion. I hold this to be the greatest danger that now threatens us. It is a danger pressed upon us from Germany, and pressed upon us by the neological spirit of the age. I hold it to be far more dangerous than Tractarianism, or Popery."

The campaigns of nearly three centuries against the Received Text did their work. The Greek New Testament of the Reformation was dethroned and with it the versions translated from it, whether English, German, French, or of any other language. It has been predicted that if the Revised Version were not of sufficient merit to be authorized and so displace the King James, confusion and division would be multiplied by a crop of unauthorized translations. The large output of heterogeneous Bibles verify the prediction. No competitor has yet appeared able to create a standard comparable to the text which has held sway for 1800 years in the original tongue, and for 300 years in its English translation, the King James Version.

5.   Westcott and Hort

Though a number of men laid the groundwork the chief architects of the critical theory which resulted in a revised Greek Testament were Brooke Foss Westcott (1825-1901), and Fenton J. A. Hort (1828-1892), two renowned Anglican scholars at Cambridge University.

(1)   Their Animosity Toward the Received Text

Referring to *INTT*,
Although Brooke Foss Westcott identified himself fully with the project and the results, it is generally understood that it was mainly

Fenton John Anthony Hort who developed the theory and composed the Introduction in their two-volume work. In the following discussion, I consider the W-H theory to be Hort's creation.

B. F. Westcott (1825-1901)   F. J. A. Hort (1828-1892)

At the age of 23, in late 1851, Hort wrote to a friend:

"I had no idea till the last few weeks of the importance of texts, having read so little Greek Testament, and dragged on with the villainous Textus Receptus. Think of that vile Textus Receptus leaning entirely on late MSS; it is a blessing there are such early ones."

Scarcely more than a year later, *"the plan of a joint [with B. F. Westcott] revision of the text of the Greek Testament was first definitely agreed upon."* And within that year (1853) Hort wrote to a friend that he hoped to have the new text out *"in little more than a year."* That it actually took twenty-eight years does not obscure the circumstance that though uninformed, by his own admission, Hort conceived a personal animosity for the Textus Receptus, and only because it was based entirely, as he thought, on late manuscripts. It appears Hort did not arrive at this theory through unprejudiced intercourse with the facts. Rather, he deliberately set out to construct a theory that would vindicate his preconceived animosity for the Received Text.

Colwell has made the same observation: *"Hort organized his entire argument to depose the Textus Receptus."*

(2) Their Plan of Attack

These are briefly listed below. Previously, we showed the fallacy of several of the more important principles of their theory. [See *INTT* for a complete refutation.]

1)   In textual criticism the N.T. is to be treated like any other book.

2)   There are no signs of deliberate falsification of the text.

3)   The numerical preponderance of the Received Text can be explained through genealogy. Basically this means frequent copying of the same kind of "defective" manuscripts.

4)   Despite its numerical advantage, the Received Text is merely one of several competing text types.

5)   The fact that the Received Text is fuller is because it is a conflated text. It was combined with the shorter readings of the other competing text types. This conflation was done with the official sanction of the Byzantine church during the 4th century.

6)   There are no distinctive Received Text readings in the writings of the Church Fathers before 350 A D.

7)   Where there are several variant readings, the right one can be determined by two kinds of internal evidence. The first is *"intrinsic probability,"* i.e. which reading best fits the context and conforms to the author's style and purpose? The second is *"transcriptional probability."* Whereas the first has to do with the author, the second concerns the copyist. What kind of error did he make deliberately or through carelessness? Under transcriptional probability, two basic norms were established. One : the shorter reading is to be preferred (on the assumption that a scribe would be more likely to add material). Two : the harder reading is to be preferred (on the assumption that the scribe has attempted to simplify).

8)   The primary basis for a Greek Text is to be found in Vaticanus and Sinaiticus.

9)   Harmonization. Parallel passages in the N.T. were made to say the same thing.

Most of the above points have been, I feel, satisfactorily answered in this paper. One that has not, deals with *"the shorter reading is to be preferred."* This is Hort's response to the fact that the TR is longer and fuller (in addition to conflation).

Referring to *INTT*,

Perhaps the canon most widely used against the "Byzantine" text is *brevior lectio potior*--the shorter reading is to be preferred. As Hort stated the alleged basis for the canon, *"In the New Testament, as in almost all prose writings which have been much copied, corruptions by interpolation are many times more numerous than corruptions by omission."* Accordingly it has been customary since Hort to tax the Received Text as being full and interpolated and to regard B and Aleph as prime examples of non-interpolated texts.

But is it really true that interpolations *"are many times more numerous"* than omissions in the transmission of the New Testament?

Pickering then marshals strong evidence against this conclusion. One quotation will have to suffice here.

The whole question of interpolations in ancient MSS has been set in an entirely new light by the researches of Mr. A. C. Clark, Corpus Professor of Latin at Oxford. In the *Descent of Manuscripts*, an investigation of the manuscript tradition of the Greek and Latin Classics, he proves conclusively that the error to which scribes were most prone was not interpolation but accidental omission. Hitherto the *maxim brevior lectio potior* has been assumed as a postulate of scientific criticism. Clark has shown that, so far as classical texts are concerned, the facts point entirely the other way.

(3) The Strange Response of Textual Scholars to the Westcott and Hort Theory

It is strange because the naturalistic critics themselves have shown each of the principles listed above to be defective, and yet in a greater or lesser way they still embrace them. Under no circumstance will they return to the Received Text! We see the same thing regarding the theory of evolution. Science has disproved it at each point but would not dare return to Biblical Creationism. What spirit does the reader see at work here ?

After going through the WH theory, Pickering says, *"And that completes our review of the WH critical theory. It is evidently erroneous at every point."*

He then quotes naturalistic critics who have come to the same basic conclusion:

Epp confesses that *"we simply do not have a theory of the text."* K. W. Clark says of the WH text: Again *"The textual history postulated for the textus receptus which we now trust has been exploded."* Also, *"The textual history that the Westcott-Hort text represents is no longer tenable in the light of newer discoveries and fuller textual analysis. In the effort to construct a congruent history, our failure suggests that we have lost the way, that we have reached a dead end, and that only a new and different insight will enable us to break through."*

But then Pickering adds,

The practical effect of the WH theory was a complete rejection of the "Syrian" text and an almost exclusive reference for the "Neutral" text (B and Aleph). Subsequent scholarship has generally rejected the notion of a "Neutral" text but sustained the rejection of the "Syrian" text.

Curiously, there seems to be a determination not to reconsider the status of the "Syrian" text even though each of the arguments Hort used in relegating it to oblivion has been challenged. Thus J. N. Birdsall, after referring to the work of Lake, Lagrange, Colwell, and Streeter, as well as his own, declares: *"It is evident that all presuppositions concerning the Byzantine text--or texts--except its inferiority to other types, must be doubted and investigated."* [But doesn't the supposed inferiority depend on those presuppositions?]

Colwell expresses it as well as anyone:

"The dead hand of Fenton John Anthony Hort lies heavy upon us. In the early years of this century Kirsopp Lake described Hort's work as a failure, though a glorious one. But Hort did not fail to reach his major goal. He dethroned the Textus Receptus. After Hort, the late medieval Greek Vulgate was not used by serious students, and the text supported by earlier witnesses became the standard text. This was a sensational achievement, an impressive success. Hort's success in this task and the cogency of his tightly reasoned theory shaped--and still shapes--the thinking of those who approach the textual criticism of the N.T. through the English language."

(4) A Brief Survey of the Views of Westcott and Hort

From Wilkinson,

It is interesting at this juncture to take a glance at Doctors Westcott and Hort, the dominating mentalities of the scheme of Revision, principally in that period of their lives before they sat on the Revision Committee. They were working together twenty years before Revision began, and swept the Revision Committee along with them after work commenced. Mainly from their own letters, partly from the comments of their respective sons, who collected and published their lives and letters, we shall here state the principles which affected their deeper lives.

(a) Their Higher Criticism

Westcott writes to his fiancee, Advent Sunday, 1847:
"All stigmatize him [Dr. Hampden] *as a 'heretic.' . . . If he be condemned, what will become of me! . . . The battle of the Inspiration of Scripture has yet to be fought, and how earnestly I could pray that I might aid the truth in that."*

Hort writes to Rev. Rowland Williams, October 21, 1858: *"Further I agree with them [authors of Essays and Reviews] in condemning many leading specific doctrines of the popular theology. . . . Evangelicals seem to me perverted rather than untrue. There are, I fear, still more serious differences between us on the subject of authority, and especially the authority of the Bible."*

(b) Their Leanings Toward Rome

Westcott writes from France to his fiancee, 1847:
"After leaving the monastery, we shaped our course to a little oratory which we discovered on the summit of a neighboring hill. . . . Fortunately we found the door open. It is very small, with one kneeling-place; and behind a screen was a 'Pieta' the size of life [i.e. a Virgin and dead Christ] . . . Had I been alone I could have knelt there for hours."

Hort writes to Westcott, October 17, 1865: *"I have been persuaded for many years that Mary-worship and 'Jesus'-worship have very much in common in their causes and their results."*

Hort writes to Westcott, September 23, 1864: *"I believe Coleridge was quite right in saying that Christianity without a substantial church is vanity and disillusion; and I remember shocking you and Lightfoot not so long ago by expressing a belief that 'Protestantism' is only parenthetical and temporary." "Perfect Catholicity has been nowhere since the Reformation."*

(c) Their Tendency Toward Evolution

Hort writes to Rev. John Ellerton, April 3, 1860: *"But the book which has most engaged me is Darwin. Whatever may be thought of it, it is a book that one is proud to be contemporary with . . . My feeling is strong that the theory is unanswerable. If so, it opens up a new period."*

Westcott writes to the Archbishop of Canterbury on Old Testament criticism, March 4, 1890: *"No one now, I suppose, holds that the first three chapters of Genesis, for example, give a literal history--I could never understand how any one reading them with open eyes could think they did."*

Hort writes to Mr. John Ellerton: *"I am inclined to think that no such state as 'Eden' (I mean the popular notion) ever existed, and that Adam's fall in no degree differed from the fall of each of his descendants, as Coleridge justly argues."*

(d) Their Views of the Death of Christ

Westcott writes to his wife, Good Friday, 1865: *"This morning I went to hear the Hulsean Lecturer. He preached on the Atonement. All he said was very good, but then he did not enter into the great difficulties of the notion of sacrifice and vicarious punishment. To me it is always most satisfactory to regard the Christian as in Christ--absolutely one with Him, and he does what Christ has done: Christ's actions become his, and Christ's life and death in some sense his life and death."*

Both rejected the atonement of the substitution of Christ for the sinner, or vicarious atonement; both denied that the death of Christ counted for anything as an atoning factor. They emphasized atonement through the Incarnation. This is the Catholic doctrine. It helps defend the Mass.

Hort writes to Westcott, October 15, 1860: *"Today's post brought also your letter. I entirely agree--correcting one word--with what you there say on the Atonement, having for many years believed that 'the absolute union of the Christian (or rather, of man) with Christ Himself' is the spiritual truth of which the popular doctrine of substitution is an immoral and material counterfeit . . . Certainly nothing could be more unscriptural than the modern limiting of Christ's bearing our sins and sufferings to his death; but indeed that is only one aspect of an almost universal heresy."*

A much fuller treatment of the views of Westcott and Hort is given in *"Dr. Stewart Custer answered on the T.R. and K.J.V."* by Dr. D.A. Waite.

Two manuscripts, one in the Pope's library, the other in a wastepaper bin in a Catholic monastery; and two Anglican clergymen-- are the reason why the late 20th century Church is awash with modern versions.

6. Revision at Last

(1) The Steps Taken

The following is from Benjamin Wilkinson,

By the year 1870, so powerful had become the influence of the Oxford Movement, that a theological bias in favour of Rome was affecting men in high authority. Many of the most sacred institutions of Protestant England had been assailed and some of them had been completely changed. The attack on the Thirty-nine Articles by Tract 90, and the subversion of fundamental Protestant doctrines within the Church of England had been so bold and thorough, that an attempt to substitute a version which would theologically and legally discredit our common Protestant Version would not be a surprise.

The first demands for revision were made with moderation of language. *"Nor can it be too distinctly or too emphatically affirmed that the reluctance of the public could never have been overcome but for the studious moderation and apparently rigid conservatism which the advocates of revision were careful to adopt"* (Hemphill, *History of the Revised Version*). Of course, the Tractarians were conscious of the strong hostility to their ritualism and said little in public about revision in order not to multiply the strength of their enemies.

The friends and devotees of the King James Bible naturally wished that certain retouches might be given the book which would replace words counted obsolete, bring about conformity to more modern rules of spelling and grammar, so that its bitter opponents, who made use of these minor disadvantages to discredit the whole, might be answered. Nevertheless, universal fear and distrust of revision pervaded the public mind, who recognized in it, as Archbishop Trench said, *"A question affecting . . . profoundly the whole moral and spiritual life of the English people,"* and the *"vast and solemn issues depending on it."* Moreover, the composition of the Authorized Version was recognized by scholars as the miracle of English prose, unsurpassed in clearness, precision, and vigor. The English of the King James Bible was the most perfect, if not the only, example of a lost art. It may be said truthfully that literary men as well as theologians frowned on the revision enterprise.

For years there had been a determined and aggressive campaign to take extensive liberties with the Received Text; and the Romanizing Movement in the universities of Oxford and Cambridge, both ritualistic and critical, had made it easy for hostile investigators to speak out with impunity. Lachmann had led the way by ignoring the great mass of manuscripts which favored the printed text and built his Greek New Testament, as Salmon says, *"of scanty material."* Tregelles, though English, *"was an isolated worker, and failed to gain any large number of adherents. Tischendorf, who had brought to light many new manuscripts and had done considerable collating, secured more authority as an editor than he deserved, and in spite of his vacillations in successive editions, became notorious in removing from the Sacred Text several passages hallowed by the veneration of centuries."*

The public would not have accepted the extreme, or, as some called it, "progressive" conclusions of these three. The names of Westcott and Hort were not prominently familiar at this time although they were Cambridge professors. Nevertheless, what was known of them was not such as to arouse distrust and apprehension. It was not until the work of revision was all over, that the world awoke to realize that Westcott and Hort had outdistanced Lachmann, Tischendorf, and Tregelles. As Salmon says, *"Westcott and Hort's Greek Testament has been described as an epoch-making book; and quite as correctly as the same phrase has been applied to the work done by Darwin."*

The first efforts to secure revision were cautiously made in 1857 by five clergymen (three of whom, Ellicott, Moberly and Humphrey, later were members of the New Testament Revision Committee) who put out a Revised Version of John's Gospel. Bishop Ellicott, who in the future was to be chairman of the New Testament Revision Committee, believed that there were clear tokens of corruptions in the Authorised Version.

The triumvirate who constantly worked to bring things to a head, and who later sat on the Revision Committee, were Ellicott, Lightfoot and Moulton. They found it difficult to get the project on foot. Twice they had appealed to the Government in hopes that, as in the case of the King James in 1611, Queen Victoria would appoint a royal commission. They were refused.

There was sufficient aggression in the Southern Convocation, which represented the Southern half of the Church of England, to vote Revision. But they lacked a leader. There was no outstanding name which would suffice in the public eye as a guarantee against the possible dangers. This difficulty, however, was at last overcome when Bishop Ellicott won over that most versatile and picturesque personality in the English Church, Samuel Wilberforce, the silver-tongued Bishop of Oxford. When Ellicott captured the persuasive Wilberforce, he captured Convocation, and revision suddenly came within the sphere of practical politics.

First came the resolution, February 10, 1870, which expressed the desirability of revision of the Authorised Version of the New Testament:

"Whether by marginal notes or otherwise, in all those passages where plain and clear errors, whether in the Hebrew or Greek text originally adopted by the translators, or in translation made from the same, shall, on due investigation, be found to exist" (W. F. Moulton, *The English Bible*).

An amendment was passed to include the Old Testament. Then a committee of sixteen--eight from the Upper and eight from the Lower House--was appointed. This committee solicited the participation of the Northern Convocation, but they declined to cooperate, saying that *"the time was not favorable for Revision, and that the risk was greater than the probable gain."*

Later the Southern Convocation adopted the rules which ordered that Revision should touch the Greek text only where found necessary; should alter the language only where, in the judgement of most competent scholars, such changes are absolutely necessary; the style of the King James should be followed; and also, that Convocation should nominate a committee of its own members who would be at liberty to invite the cooperation of other scholars in the work of Revision. This committee when elected consisted of eighteen members. It divided into two bodies, one to represent the Old Testament and the other to represent the New. As the majority of the most vital questions which concern us involve New Testament Revision, we will follow the fortunes of that body in the main.

The seven members of this English New Testament Revision Committee sent out invitations which were accepted by eighteen others, bringing the full membership of the English New Testament Committee to the number of twenty-five.

W. F. Moulton, a member of the committee who had spent some years in translating *Winer's Greek Grammar* from German into English, exercised a large influence in the selection of members. Dr. Moulton favored those modern rules appearing in Winer's work which, if followed in translating the Greek, would produce results different from that of the King James. How much Dr. Moulton was a devotee of the Vulgate may be seen in the following words from him:

"The Latin translation, being derived from manuscripts more ancient than any we now possess, is frequently a witness of the highest value in regard to the Greek text which was current in the earliest times, and . . . its testimony is in many cases confirmed by Greek manuscripts which have been discovered or examined since the 16th century."

From this it is evident that Dr. Moulton looked upon the Vulgate as a witness superior to the King James, and upon the Greek manuscripts which formed the base of the Vulgate as superior to the Greek manuscripts which formed the base of the King James. Furthermore, he said, speaking of the Jesuit New Testament of 1582, *"The Rhemish Testament agrees with the best critical editions of the present day."* Dr. Moulton, therefore, not only believed the manuscripts which were recently discovered to be similar to the Greek manuscripts from which the Vulgate was translated, but he also looked upon the Greek New Testaments of Lachmann, Tischendorf and Tregelles, built largely upon the same few manuscripts, *as "the best critical editions."* Since he exercised so large an influence in selecting the other members of the Committee, we can divine at the outset the attitude of mind which would likely prevail in the Revision Committee.

The Old Testament Committee also elected into its body other members which made the number in that company twenty-seven. Steps were now taken to secure cooperation from scholars in America. The whole matter was practically put in the hands of Dr. Philip Schaff of the Union Theological Seminary in New York City. Of Dr. Schaff's revolutionary influence on American theology through his bold Romanizing policy; of his trial for heresy; of his leadership in the American Oxford Movement, we will speak later. An appeal was made to the American Episcopal Church to take part in the Revision, but that body declined.

Through the activities of Dr. Schaff, two American Committees were formed, the Old Testament Company having fourteen members, and the New Testament with thirteen. These worked under the disadvantage of being chosen upon the basis that they should live near New York City in order that meetings of the committee might be convenient. The American Committee had no deciding vote on points of revision. As soon as portions of the Holy Book were revised by the English committees, they were sent to the American committees for confirmation or amendment. If the suggestions returned by the American committees were acceptable to their English co-workers, they were adopted; otherwise they had no independent claim for insertion. In other words, the American committees were simply reviewing bodies. In the long run, their differences were not many. The work then went on continuously in both countries, the English Companies revising, and the American Committees reviewing what was revised, and returning their suggestions. When this list is fully considered, the general reader will, we think, be surprised to find that the differences are really of such little moment, and in very many cases will probably wonder that the American divines thought it worth while thus to formally record their dissent.

Dr. Schaff, who was to America what Newman was to England, was president of both American Committees.

The story of the English New Testament Revision Committee is a stormy one, because it was the battleground of the whole problem. That Committee finished its work three years before the Old Testament Company, and this latter body had three years to profit by the staggering onslaught which assailed the product of the New Testament Committee. Moreover, the American Revised Bible did not appear until twenty years after the work of the English New Testament Committee, so that the American Revisers had twenty years to understand the fate which would await their volume.

When the English New Testament Committee met, it was immediately apparent what was going to happen. Though for ten long years the iron rule of silence kept the public ignorant of what was going on behind closed doors, the story is now known. The first meeting of the Committee found itself a divided body, the majority being determined to incorporate into the proposed revision the latest and most extreme higher criticism. This majority was dominated and carried along by a triumvirate consisting of Hort, Westcott and Lightfoot. The dominating mentality of this triumvirate was Dr. Hort. Before the Committee met, Westcott had written to Hort, *"The rules though liberal are vague, and the interpretation of them will depend upon decided action at first."* They were determined at the outset to be greater than the rules, and to manipulate them

The new members who had been elected into the body, and who had taken no part in drawing up the rules, threw these rules completely aside by interpreting them with the widest latitude. Moreover, Westcott and Hort, who had worked together before this for twenty years in bringing out a Greek New Testament constructed on principles which deviated the furthest ever yet known from the Received Text, came prepared to effect a systematic change in the Protestant Bible. On this point Westcott wrote to Hort concerning Dr. Ellicott, the chairman: *"The Bishop of Gloucester seems to me to be quite capable of accepting heartily and adopting personally a thorough scheme."*

And as we have previously seen, as early as 1851, before Westcott and Hort began their twenty years' labor on their Greek text, Hort wrote, *"Think of that vile Textus Receptus."* In 1851, when he knew little of the Greek New Testament, or of texts, he was dominated with the idea that the Received Text was "vile" and "villainous." The Received Text suffered fatal treatment at the hands of this master in debate.

We have spoken of Bishop Ellicott as the chairman. The first chairman was Bishop Wilberforce. One meeting, however, was sufficient for him. He wrote to an intimate friend, *"What can be done in this most miserable business?"* Unable to bear the situation, he absented himself and never took part in the proceedings. His tragic death occurred three years later. One factor had disturbed him considerably--the presence of Dr. G. Vance Smith, the Unitarian scholar. In this, however, he shared the feelings of the people of England, who were scandalized at the sight of a Unitarian, who denied the Divinity of Christ, participating in a communion service held at the suggestion of Bishop Westcott in Westminster Abbey, immediately preceding their first meeting.

The minority in the Committee was represented principally by Dr. Scrivener, probably the foremost scholar of the day in the manuscripts of the Greek New Testament and the history of the Text. If we may believe the words of Chairman Ellicott, the countless divisions in the Committee over the Greek Text *"was often a kind of critical duel between Dr. Hort and Dr. Scrivener."* Dr. Scrivener was continuously and systematically out-voted.

"Nor is it difficult to understand," says Dr. Hemphill, *"that many of their less resolute and decided colleagues must often have been completely carried off their feet by the persuasiveness and resourcefulness, and zeal of Hort, backed by the great prestige of Lightfoot, the popular Canon of St. Paul's and the quiet determination of Westcott, who set his face as a flint. In fact, it can hardly be doubted that Hort's was the strongest will of the whole Company, and his adroitness in debate was only equaled by his pertinacity."*

The conflict was intense and ofttimes the result seemed dubious. Scrivener and his little band did their best to save the day. He might have resigned; but like Bishop Wilberforce, he neither wished to wreck the product of revision by a crushing public blow, nor did he wish to let it run wild by absenting himself. Dr. Hort wrote his wife as follows: *"July 15, 1871. We have had some stiff battles today in Revision, though without any ill feeling, and usually with good success. But I, more than ever, felt how impossible it would be for me to absent myself."*

Concerning the battles within the Committee, Dr. Westcott writes:

"May 24, 1871. We have had hard fighting during these last two days, and a battle-royal is announced for tomorrow."

"January 27, 1875. Our work yesterday was positively distressing . . . However, I shall try to keep heart today, and if we fail again I think that I shall fly, utterly despairing of the work."

Same date. *"Today our work has been a little better--only a little, but just enough to be endurable."*

The *"ill-conceived and mismanaged"* attempts of the Revision Committee of the Southern Convocation to bring in the contemplated radical changes violated the rules that had been laid down for its control. Citations from ten out of the sixteen members of the Committee (sixteen was the average number in attendance) show that eleven members were fully determined to act upon the principle of exact and literal translation, which would permit them to travel far beyond the instructions they had received.

The Committee being assembled, the passage for consideration was read. Dr. Scrivener offered the evidence favoring the Received Text, while Dr. Hort took the other side. Then a vote was taken. Settling the Greek Text occupied the largest portion of time both in England and in America. The new Greek Testament upon which Westcott and Hort had been working for twenty years was, portion by portion, secretly committed into the hands of the Revision Committee. Their Greek Text was strongly radical and revolutionary. The Revisers followed the guidance of the two Cambridge editors, Westcott and Hort, who were constantly at their elbow, and whose radical Greek New Testament, deviating the furthest possible from the Received Text, is to all intents and purposes the Greek New Testament followed by the Revision Committee. And this Greek text, in the main, follows the Vatican and Sinaiticus Manuscripts.

Hort's partiality for the Vatican Manuscript was practically absolute.

As the Sinaiticus was the brother of the Vaticanus, wherever pages in the latter were missing, Hort used the former. He and Westcott considered that when the consensus of opinion of these two manuscripts favored a reading, that reading should be accepted as apostolic. This attitude of mind involved thousands of changes in our time-honored Greek New Testament because a Greek Text formed upon the united opinion of Codex B and Codex Aleph would be different in thousands of places from the Received Text.

So the Revisers went on changing until they had altered the Greek Text in 5337 places" (Everts, *"The Westcott and Hort Text Under Fire,"* *Bibliotheca Sacra*, Jan., 1921). Dr. Scrivener, in the Committee sessions, constantly issued his warning of what would be the outcome if Hort's imaginary theories were accepted. In fact, nine-tenths of the countless divisions and textual struggles around that table in the Jerusalem

Chamber arose over Hort's determination to base the Greek New Testament of the Revision on the Vatican Manuscript.

Of course the minority members of the Revision Committee, and especially the world in general, did not know of the twenty years' effort of these two Cambridge professors to base their own Greek New Testament upon these two manuscripts. Hort's *"excursion into cloudland,"* as one authority describes his fourth century revisions, was apparent to Dr. Scrivener, who uttered his protest. Here is his description of Hort's theory as Scrivener later published it:

"There is little hope for the stability of their imposing structure, if its foundations have been laid on the sandy ground of ingenious conjecture: and since barely the smallest vestige of historical evidence has ever been alleged in support of the views of these accomplished editors, their teaching must either be received as intuitively true, or dismissed from our consideration as precarious, and even visionary."

As Westcott and Hort outnumbered Scrivener two to one, so their followers outnumbered the other side two to one; and Scrivener was systematically outvoted. As Professor Sanday writes: *"They were thus able to make their views heard in the council chamber, and to support them with all the weight of their personal authority, while as yet the outer public had but partial access to them."*

As a consequence, the Greek New Testament upon which the Revised Version is based, is practically the Greek New Testament of Westcott and Hort. Dr. Schaff says: *"The result is that in typographical accuracy the Greek Testament of Westcott and Hort is probably unsurpassed and that it harmonizes essentially with the text adopted by the Revisers."*

(2)　The Revisers Were Liberal and Yet Narrow

We meet the paradox in the Revisers, as they sit assembled at their task, of men possessing high reputation for liberalism of thought, yet acting for a decade with extreme narrowness. Stanley, Thirlwall, Vaughan, Hort, Westcott, Moberly--men of leading intellect--would naturally be expected to be so broad as to give most sacred documents fair consideration. Dean Stanley had glorified the Church of England because within her ranks both ritualists and higher critics could officiate as well as the regular churchmen. When Bishop Colenso, of Natal, was on trial, amid great excitement throughout all England, for his destructive criticism of the first five books of Moses, Dean Stanley stood up among his religious peers and placed himself alongside of Colenso he said:

"I might mention one who . . . has ventured to say that the Pentateuch is not the work of Moses; . . . who has ventured to say that the narratives of those historical incidents are colored not infrequently by the necessary infirmities which belong to the human instruments by which they were conveyed--and that individual is the one who now addresses you. If you pronounce against the Bishop of Natal on grounds such as these, you must remember that there is one close at hand whom . . . you will be obliged to condemn."

Bishop Thirlwall, of *"princely intellect,"* had a well-known reputation for liberalism in theology. He introduced both the new theology of Schleiermacher and higher criticism into England. In fact, when Convocation yielded to public indignation so far as essentially to ask Dr. Smith, the Unitarian scholar, to resign, Bishop Thirwall retired from the committee and refused to be placated until it was settled that Dr. Smith should remain. (Vance Smith received Holy Communion with his fellow-revisers in Westminster Abbey on June 22, 1870, and said afterwards that he did not join in reciting the Nicene Creed and did not compromise his principles as a Unitarian.)

Cardinal Newman believed that tradition and the Catholic Church were above the Bible. Westcott and Hort were great admirers of Newman. Dean Stanley believed that the Word of God did not dwell in the Bible alone, but that it dwelt in the sacred books of other religions as well. Dr. Schaff sat in the Parliament of Religions at the Chicago World's Fair, 1893, and was so happy among the Buddhists, Confucianists, Shintoists and other world religions, that he said he would be willing to die among them. The spirit of the Revisionists on both sides of the ocean was an effort to find the Word of God by the study of comparative religions.

Evidence might be given to show liberalism in other members. These men were honorably bound to do justice to thousands of manuscripts if they assumed to reconstruct a Greek Text. We are informed by Dr. Scrivener that there are 2864 cursive and uncial manuscripts of the New Testament in whole or in part. Price says there are 112 uncials and 3500 cursives. These represent many different countries and different periods of time. Yet astonishing to relate, the majority of the Revisers ignored these and pinned their admiration and confidence practically to two--the Vaticanus and Sinaiticus.

Doctor Moberly, Bishop of Salisbury, Bishop Westcott, and Dr. G. Vance Smith came to the Committee with past relationships that seriously compromised them. Bishop Moberly *"belonged to the Oxford*

Movement, and it is stated in Dean Church's Life and Letters that he wrote a most kind letter of approval to Mr. Newman as to the famous Tract 90." While with regard to Dr. Westcott, his share in making the Ritualistic Movement a success has been recognized.

Dr. Vaughan, another member of the Revision Committee, was a close friend of Westcott. The extreme liberalism of Dr. G. Vance Smith, the Unitarian member of the Committee, is well-known through his book on the Bible and Theology. This amounted practically to Christianized infidelity. Nevertheless, the worshipful attitude of these men, as well as that of Lightfoot, Kennedy, and Humphrey toward Codex B, was unparalleled in Biblical history. The year 1870 was marked by the Papal declaration of infallibility. It has been well said that the blind adherence of the Revisionists to the Vatican manuscript proclaimed *"the second infallible voice from the Vatican."*

(3)   The Ruthless Changes Which Resulted

Even the jots and tittles of the Bible are important. God has pronounced terrible woes upon the man who adds to or takes away from the volume of inspiration. The Revisers apparently felt no constraint on this point, for they made 36,000 changes in the English of the King James Version, and very nearly 6,000 in the Greek Text.

As Canon Cook says: *"By far the greatest number of innovations, including those which give the severest shocks to our minds, are adopted on the authority of two manuscripts, or even of one manuscript, against the distinct testimony of all other manuscripts, uncial and cursive. . . . The Vatican Codex . . . sometimes alone, generally in accord with the Sinaitic, is responsible for nine-tenths of the most striking innovations in the Revised Version."*

That fact that guidance of the Holy Spirit as well as a knowledge of the rules of grammar are necessary for the translator can be seen in the following:

The instruments of warfare which they brought to their task were new and untried rules for the discrimination of manuscripts; for attacking the verb; for attacking the article; for attacking the preposition, the pronoun, the intensive, Hebraisms, and parallelisms. The following quotations show that literal and critically exact quotations frequently fail to render properly the original meaning:

"The self-imposed rule of the Revisers," says the Forum, *"required them invariably to translate the aoristic forms by their closest English equivalents; but the vast number of cases in which they have forsaken*

their own rule shows that it could not be followed without in effect changing the meaning of the original; and we may add that to whatever extent that rule has been slavishly followed, to that extent the broad sense of the original has been marred."

One of the Revisers wrote, after the work was finished: *"With reference to the rendering of the article, similar remarks may be made. As a rule, it is too often expressed. This sometimes injures the idiom of the English, and in truth impairs or misrepresents the force of the original."*

The obsession of the Revisionists for rendering literally Hebraisms and parallelisms has often left us with a doctrine seriously, if not fatally, weakened by their theory.

(4) The Revisers' Greatest Crime and a Crime That has Been Perpetuated Down to Our Own Day

When God has taught us that *"all Scripture is given by inspiration"* of the Holy Spirit and that *"men spake as they were moved by the Holy Ghost,"* the Holy Spirit must be credited with ability to transmit and preserve inviolate the Sacred Deposit. We cannot admit for a moment that the Received Text which, by the admission of its enemies themselves, has led the true people of God for centuries, can be whipped into fragments and set aside for a manuscript found in an out-of-the-way monastery, and for another of the same family which has lain, for man knows not how long, upon a shelf in the library of the Pope's palace. Both these documents are of uncertain ancestry, of questionable history, and of suspicious character. The Received Text was put for centuries in its position of leadership by Divine Providence, just as truly as the Star of Bethlehem was set in the heavens to guide the wise men. Neither was it the product of certain technical rules of textual criticism which some men have chosen in the last few decades to exalt as divine principles.

The change of one word in the Constitution of the United States, at least the transposition of two, could vitally affect thousands of people, millions of dollars, and many millions of acres of land. It took centuries of training to place within that document a combination of words which cannot be tampered with, without catastrophic results. It represents the mentality of a great people, and to change it would bring chaos into their well-ordered life.

Not of one nation only, but of all great nations, both ancient and modern, is the Bible the basis of the Constitution. It foretold the fall of Babylon; and when that empire had disappeared, the Bible survived. It announced beforehand the creation of the empires of Greece and Rome, and lived to tell their faults and why they failed. It warned succeeding kingdoms. All ages and continents have their life wrought into the fabric of this Book. It is the handiwork of God through the centuries. Only those whose records are lifted high above suspicion can be accepted as qualified to touch it. Certainly no living being, or any number of, them, ever had authority to make such astounding changes as were made by those men who were directly or indirectly influenced by the Oxford Movement.

The history of the Protestant world is inseparable from the Received Text. A single nation could break loose and plunge into anarchy and license. The Received Text shone high in the heavens to stabilize surrounding peoples. Even many nations at one time might fall under the shadow of some great revolutionary wave. But there stood the Received Text to fill their inner self with its moral majesty and call them back to law and order.

On what meat had Dr. Hort fed, when he dared, being only twenty-three years old, to call the Received Text "villainous" and "vile"? By his own confession he had at that time read little of the Greek New Testament, and knew nothing of texts and certainly nothing of Hebrew. What can be the most charitable estimate we can put upon that company of men who submitted to his lead, and would assure us in gentle words that they had done nothing, that there was really no great difference between the King James Bible and the Revised, while in another breath they reject as "villainous" and "vile" the Greek New Testament upon which the King James Bible is built? Did they belong to a superior race of beings, which entitled them to cast aside, as a thing of naught, the work of centuries? They gave us a Version which speaks with faltering tones, whose music is discordant. The Received Text is harmonious. It agrees with itself, it is self-proving, and it creeps into the affections of the heart.

When a company of men set out faithfully to translate genuine manuscripts in order to convey what God said, it is one thing. When a committee sets itself to revise or translate with ideas and a "scheme," it is another. But it may be objected that the translators of the King James were biased by their pro-Protestant views. The reader must judge whose bias he will accept--that of the influence of the Protestant Reformation, as heading up in the Authorized Version; or that of the influence of Darwinism, higher criticism, incipient modern religious liberalism, and a reversion to Rome, as heading up in the Revised Version.

A great deal of space has been given to the revision of the English Bible that took place last century. But when properly weighed and pondered it will be seen to be Satan's most subtle and devastating attack upon the Word in all history. The version itself was not popular but it opened the floodgates to the countless versions dancing before our eyes today. It took away the standard, the benchmark of the English-speaking world. And it placed a new Greek Text in our Bible Institutes and Colleges. It struck at foundations and did more to undermine the authority of God's Word than any other event. But most tragic of all, it was and is embraced by those who call themselves *"fundamentalist."*

As Wilkinson says,

Because of the changes which came about in the 19th century, there arose a new type of Protestantism and a new version of the Protestant Bible. This new kind of Protestantism was hostile to the fundamental doctrines of the Reformation. Previous to this there had been only two types of Bibles in the world, the Protestant and the Catholic. Now Protestants were asked to choose between the true Protestant Bible and one which reproduced readings rejected by the Reformers.

7.   A Lone Voice

Hills says,

Since 1881, many, perhaps most, orthodox Christian scholars have agreed with Westcott and Hort that textual criticism is a strictly neutral science that must be applied in the same way to any document whatever, including the Bible. Yet there have been some orthodox theologians who have dissented from this neutral point of view. One of those was Abraham Kuyper (1894), who pointed out that the publication of the Textus Receptus was, *"no accident,"* affirming that the Textus Receptus, *"as a foundation from which to begin critical operations."* Another was Francis Pieper (1924), who emphasized that fact that *"in the Bible which is in our hands we have the Word of Christ which is to be taught by and in the Church until the last day."*

It was John W. Burgon (1813-1888), however, who most effectively combated the neutralism of naturalistic Bible study. This famous scholar spent most of his adult life at Oxford, as Fellow of Oriel College and then as vicar of St. Mary's (the University Church) and Gresham Professor of Divinity. During his last twelve years he was Dean of Chichester. In theology he was a high-church Anglican but opposed to the ritualism into which even in his day the high-church movement had begun to decline. Throughout his career he was steadfast in his defense of the Scriptures as the infallible Word of God and strove with all his power to arrest the modernistic currents which during his lifetime had begun to flow within the Church of England. Because of his learned defense of the Traditional New Testament text he has been held up to ridicule in most of the handbooks on New Testament textual criticism, but his arguments have never been refuted.

John William Burgon (1813-1888)

Although he lived one hundred years ago, Dean Burgon has the message which we need today. Since his books have now become difficult to acquire, they should all be reprinted and made available to new generations of believing Bible students. His published works on textual criticism include: *The last Twelve Verses of Mark* (1871), *The Revision Revised* (1883), and *The Traditional Text of the Holy Gospels* and *The Causes of the Corruption of the Traditional Text*, two volumes which were published in 1896, after Burgon's death.

One hundred years ago, Burgon said, *"If you and I believe that the original writings of the Scriptures were verbally inspired by God, then of necessity they must have been providentially preserved through the ages."* Since the Garden of Eden that has been the primary issue. *"Yea hath God said?"* Are you certain that you now have at every point the full and complete Word of God?

A seed that is allowed to corrupt and mildew in the granary will not do much good out in the fields. Today there is an unprecedented printing and distribution of Christian literature, but in comparison with past days, it seems to have so little effect *"out in the fields."* The reason is not hard to find--the sowers are using a corrupted seed. (I got this last thought from a Pastor in Lebanon, Ohio, who from the base of his local church prints millions of good Gospel tracts.)

Thankfully since Burgon's day, many more have entered the battle for the purity and distribution of God's Holy Word. And though our numbers are not great, we can take heart in the fact that the position taken is the historical one. For eighteen hundred years the non-Catholic and Protestant believers stood for the Received Text.

Once to every man and nation
Comes the moment to decide

In the strife of truth with falsehood
For the good or evil side.

Some great cause, God's Messiah
Offering each the bloom or blight

And the choice goes by forever
Twixt that darkness and the light.

Though the cause of evil prosper
Yet 'tis truth alone is strong

Truth forever on the scaffold
Wrong forever on the throne.

Yet that scaffold sways the future
And behind the dim unknown

Standeth God within the shadows
Keeping watch above His own.

"For ever, O LORD, thy Word is settled in heaven."
(Psalm 119:89)

Index of Words and Phrases
By Pastor D. A. Waite, Th.D., Ph.D.
President of the Dean Burgon Society

245, 250, 252, 253
260, 267, 278
King James Version . . 26, 32,
49, 61, 63, 103, 127,
160, 178, 199
223-226, 244, 260, 276
Kirsopp Lake 53, 75, 121
199, 264
Kittel's Hebrew Bible 11
Koine 14, 20
Kuenen 256
Kurt Aland 49, 63, 110
Kurtz 256
L 11, 40, 52, 72
73, 120, 147, 151, 251
Lachmann 52, 178, 258
259, 267, 268, 270
Lachmann, Tischendorf, and
Tregelles . . 258, 259, 268
Lagrange 264
Lake, K. 53, 75, 77, 82, 83
121, 182, 199, 203, 264
*Last Twelve Verses of
Mark* 89, 181, 280
Latin . . . . . v, 9, 20, 24-28, 66
67, 69, 93, 94, 108
111, 117, 118, 120, 127
130, 131, 133, 135-153
156, 157, 160, 163, 172
174 176, 178, 183-186,
190-194, 198, 201-209
212, 215, 216, 221, 222,
224-226, 228-230, 233,
238, 240, 259, 263, 269
Latin Church . . . 144, 202, 205
209, 230
Latin Fathers 24
Latin Vulgate   9, 20, 26, 66, 93
127, 133, 143,
145, 149-151, 156, 172, 176
183-185, 190, 201-204
206, 209, 216, 259

Latin Vulgate readings . . 201,
202, 204
Latin Vulgate Readings in the
Received Text 201
Latin-speaking Church . . 201,
202, 206
Laudianus 11, 120, 137
Law . . . 3-6, 13, 14, 17, 21, 22
29, 31, 71, 131, 175
176, 217, 237, 278
Law of Moses 5, 22
lectern Bible 234
lectionaries 64, 161, 205
Leningrad 11, 103, 105
letter of Aristeas 17
liberal camp 49
liberalism in theology 275
librarians 8
library shelves 83
Libyan Desert 103
Life of Moses 16
Lightfoot 180, 265, 268
271, 272, 276
Living Bible 15
Lone Voice 279
Lucian 17, 76, 78, 155
Luther . . . 9, 96, 141, 144, 194
195, 198, 210, 211
213, 214, 216, 219, 220
228, 229, 240, 250, 251
Luther's German Version . 199
Luther's version in 1522 . . 227
Lutheran in German 229
Luther's German Bible . . . 210
LXX   14-21, 23, 30, 32, 36, 38
M. Burrows (1948) 42
Maccabaeus 42
Maimonides 10
Main Surviving Manuscripts 10
mainly Fenton John Anthony
Hort 260
Man Erasmus 193

Manasseh 6, 29
Manuscripts of the Old
    Latin 137
Marcion 89, 129
Marlowe 245
Martin 9, 30, 216, 227
Mary . 156, 157, 237, 250, 265
masculine gender 208
Masoretes 9, 10, 244
Masoretic . 8, 9, 13, 15, 23, 30
    32, 37, 40, 42-45, 244
Masoretic Hebrew 45
Masoretic Hebrew text 45
Mass 75, 120, 156, 192
    206, 251, 253, 254
    259, 266, 267
Matthew 57, 58, 68, 70, 71, 92
    103-105, 116, 118, 120
    122, 137, 157, 207
    232, 239,250
Matthew Parker 239
Matthew's Bible 232, 233
Matthew's Bible: 1537 . . . 232
Maurice 256
McClure 250
Mel Trotter 251
Melanchthon 193, 210
Merril Unger 27
Mesopotamia . 32, 34, 36, 165
Messiah 16, 34, 42, 281
Messianic prophecy . . . 15, 16
methurgeman 33
methurgeman (the
    translator) 33
Metzger, Bruce . 49, 64, 66, 67
    72, 89, 204
middle ages 12, 124, 193, 228
Middle English . 174, 185, 186
Miles Coverdale 230
Miles Smith 247
Miller . . . . v, 88, 90-92, 94
    97, 153, 156, 158, 159, 181,

189, 193, 210, 251
Miller's Church History . . . 91,
    131, 186
Milligan 258
Milton 249
minuscule . . . 64, 75, 110, 123
    124, 126
minuscules 64, 124, 125
Mishna 9
misprints 200
Modern English 174
modern verse divisions . . . 226
modernists 55
Mohler 256
Monarchians 208
monasteries . . 75, 83, 216, 217
Monastery of St.
    Catherine . . 64, 112, 157
Monothelites 159
Moody 251
Moore 9, 214
Moorman . . . . 1, iii, iv
morning star of the
    reformation 149
morphology 42
Mosaic authorship 4
Moses 3-5, 7, 10, 16, 22
    31, 189, 274, 275
Moses ben Asher 10
Moulton 258, 268-270
Mount Ebal 30, 31
Mount Gerizim 29-31
Mount Sinai 64, 66, 157
Mr. D. A. Waite, Jr. iv
Muhammad 164
Muhammad (570-632 164
N.E.B 225
N.T. manuscripts v
Nablus 29, 31, 32
Napoleon 178, 255, 256
Nash 40
Natal 274, 275

Scripture Index

By Pastor D. A. Waite, Th.D., Ph.D.
President of the Dean Burgon Society

Order Blank (p. 1)

Name:_____

Address:_____

City & State:_____ **Zip:**_____

*Credit Card #:*_____ *Expires:*_____

[ ] Send *Fundamentalist Distortions on Bible Versions* by
    DAW ($6 +$3 S&H) A perfect bound book, 80 pages long

[ ] Send *Burgon's Warnings on Revision* by DAW ($7+$3
    S&H) A perfect bound book, 120 pages in length.

[ ] Send *The Case for the King James Bible* by DAW ($7
    +S&H) A perfect bound book, 112 pages in length.

[ ] Send *Foes of the King James Bible Refuted* by DAW ($9
    +$4 S&H) A perfect bound book, 164 pages in length.

[ ] Send *The Revision Revised* by Dean Burgon ($25 + $4)
    A hardback book, 640 pages in length.

[ ] Send *The Last 12 Verses of Mark* by Dean Burgon ($15+$4)
    A perfect bound paperback book 400 pages in length.

[ ] Send *The Traditional Text* hardback by Burgon ($16 + $4)
    A hardback book, 384 pages in length.

[ ] Send *Summary of Traditional Text* by Dr. Waite ($3 + $2)

[ ] Send *Summary of Causes of Corruption*, DAW ($3+2 S&H)

[ ] Send *Causes of Corruption* hardback by Burgon ($15 + $4)
    A hardback book, 360 pages in length.

[ ] Send *Inspiration and Interpretation*, Dean Burgon ($25+$4)

[ ]Send *Contemporary Eng. Version Exposed*, DAW ($3+$2)

Send or Call Orders to:
THE DEAN BURGON SOCIETY
Box 354, Collingswood, NJ 08108
Phone: 609-854-4452; FAX:--2464; Orders: 1-800 JOHN 10:9

Order Blank (p. 2)

Name:_____

Address:_____

City & State:_____Zip:_____

Credit Card#:_____**Expires:**_____

Other Materials on the KJB & T.R.

[ ] Send *Westcott & Hort's Greek Text & Theory Refuted by Burgon's Revision Revised--Summarized* by Dr. D. A. Waite ($4.00 + $3 S&H)

[ ] Send *Defending the King James Bible* by Dr.Waite $12+$4 A hardback book, indexed with study questions.

[ ] Send *Guide to Textual Criticism* by Edward Miller ($7 + $4)

[ ] Send *Westcott's Denial of Resurrection*, Dr. Waite ($4+$3)

[ ] Send *Four Reasons for Defending KJB* by DAW ($2+$3)

[ ] Send *Vindicating Mark 16:9-20* by Dr. Waite ($3 + $3)

[ ] Send *Dean Burgon's Confidence in KJB* by DAW ($3+$3)

[ ] Send *Readability of A.V. (KJB)* by D. A. Waite, Jr. ($5 +$3)

[ ] Send *NIV Inclusive Language Exposed* by DAW ($4+$3)

[ ] Send *23 Hours of KJB Seminar* (4 videos) by DAW ($50.00)

[ ] Send *Defined King James Bible* lg.prt. leather ($40+S&H)

[ ] Send the "DBS Articles of Faith & Organization" (N.C.)
[ ] Send Brochure #1: "1000 Titles Defending KJB/TR"(N.C.)
Send or Call Orders to:
THE DEAN BURGON SOCIETY
Box 354, Collingswood, NJ 08108
Phone: 609-854-4452; FAX:--2464; Orders: 1-800 JOHN 10:9
E-Mail Orders: BFT@BibleForToday.org; Credit Cards OK

Order Blank (p. 3)

Name:_____

Address:_____

City & State:_____Zip:_____

Credit Card#:_____**Expires:**_____

More Materials on the KJB &T.R.

[ ] Send *Heresies of Westcott & Hort* by Dr. Waite ($4+$3)

[ ] Send *Scrtvener's Greek New Testament Underlying the King James Bible*, hardback, $14+$4 S&H

[ ] Send *Why Not the King James Bible?--An Answer to James White's KJVO Book* by Dr. K. D. DiVietro, $9+$4 S&H

[ ] Send *Forever Settled--Bible Documents & History Survey* by Dr. Jack Moorman, $20+$4 S&H; hardback, 320 pages

[ ] Send *Early Church Fathers & the A.V.--A Demonstration* by Dr. Jack Moorman, $6 + $4 S&H.

[ ] Send *When the KJB Departs from the So-Called "Majority Text"* by Dr. Jack Moorman, $16 + $4 S&H

[ ] Send *Missing in Modern Bibles--Nestle-Aland & NIV Errors* by Dr. Jack Moorman, $8 + $4 S&H

[ ] Send *The Doctrinal Heart of the Bible--Removed from Modern Versions* by Dr. Jack Moorman, VCR, $15 +$4 S&H

[ ] Send *Modern Bibles--The Dark Secret* by Dr. Jack Moorman, $3 + $2 S&H

[ ] Send *Early Manuscripts and the A.V.--A Closer Look*, by Dr. Jack Moorman, $15 + $4 S&H

Send or Call Orders to:
THE DEAN BURGON SOCIETY
Box 354, Collingswood, NJ 08108
Phone: 609-854-4452; FAX:--2464; Orders: 1-800 JOHN 10:9
E-Mail Orders: BFT@BibleForToday.org; Credit Cards OK

DBS1428